Cognitive and Constructive Psychotherapies

**Michael J. Mahoney, PhD,** is Professor of Phychology at the University of North Texas. He received his Ph.D. degree from Stanford University in 1972. The author of 15 books and numerous scientific articles, Dr. Mahoney helped pioneer the "cognitive revolution" in psychology and is a continuing contributor to the growing interface between the cognitive and clinical sciences. Honored as a Fellow by both the American Psychological Association and the American Association for the Advancement of Science, he was chosen to be a Master Lecturer on Psychotherapy Process in 1981 and a G. Stanley Hall Lecturer in 1988. Dr. Mahoney has received several professional awards, including a 1984 Fulbright Award, the Faculty Scholar Medal from Pennsylvania State University, and a 1985 Citation Classic from Science Citation Index in recognition of the influence of his 1974 book, *Cognition and Behavior Modification.*

Dr. Mahoney has served on the Editorial Boards of 12 scientific journals and has worked with the U. S. Olympic Committee since 1978 in the area of sport psychology. His research interests include basic processes in psychological development and psychotherapy, theoretical and philosophical issues, psychology of science, and health and sport psychology. His 1991 book, *Human Change Processes: The Scientific Bases of Psychotherapy,* integrates the research literatures from several disciplines as they bear on the conceptualization and facilitation of psychological change.

Cognitive *and* Constructive Psychotherapies
Theory, Research, and Practice

Michael J. Mahoney, PhD

Editor

Donald Meichenbaum •◆ Aaron T. Beck •◆ Clive J. Robins •◆ Adele M. Hayes •◆ Albert Ellis •◆ David A. F. Haaga •◆ Gerald C. Davison •◆ Vittorio F. Guidano •◆ Michael J. Mahoney •◆ H. Martin Miller •◆ Giampiero Arciero •◆ Kenneth W. Sewell •◆ Óscar F. Gonçalves •◆ Robert A. Neimeyer

— Contributors

SPRINGER PUBLISHING COMPANY

American Psychological Association
750 First Street, NE
Washington, DC 20002

Springer Publishing Company, Inc.
536 Broadway
New York, NY 10012-3955

Cover design by Tom Yabut
Production Editor: Joyce Noulas

95 96 97 98 99/5 4 3 2 1

Library of Congress Cataloging-in-Publication Data
Cognitive and constructive psychotherapies: theory, research, and
  practice/Michael J. Mahoney, editor
      p.   cm.
  Collection of articles previously published in the *Journal of
Consulting and Clinical Psychology*, 1993.
  Includes bibliographical references and index.
  ISBN 0-8261-8610-6
  1. Cognitive therapy.   2. Personal construct therapy.   3. Rational
emotive psychotherapy.   4. Constructivism (Psychology)
I. Mahoney, Michael J.   II. *Journal of consulting and clinical
psychology*.
      [DNLM: 1. Psychoanalytic Theory—collected works.   2. Cognitive
Therapy—collected works.   3. Psychotherapy, Rational-Emotive—
collected works.   4. Personal Construct Theory—collected works.
WM 460 C6762   1994]
RC489.C63C6234   1994
616.89'14—dc20
DNLM/DLC
for Library of Congress   94-31937
                                                                CIP

Printed in the United States of America

To
Luis Joyce-Moniz

a dear and dialectical companion
in my life's ongoing narrative

Contents

Contributors

Giampiero Arciero, M.D.
Centro di Psicoterapia Cognitiva
Rome, ITALY, 00129

Aaron T. Beck, M.D.
Center for Cognitive Therapy
Philadelphia, PA 19104

Gerald C. Davison, Ph.D.
Department of Psychology
University of Southern California
Los Angeles, CA 90089

Albert Ellis, Ph.D.
Institute for Rational–Emotive
Therapy
New York, NY 10021

Óscar F. Gonçalves, Ph.D.
Universidade do Minho
PORTUGAL

Vittorio F. Guidano, M.D.
Centro di Psicoterapia Cognitiva
Rome, ITALY 00129

David A. F. Haaga, Ph.D.
Department of Psychology
The American University
Washington, DC 20016

Adele M. Hayes, Ph.D.
Department of Psychology
University of Miami
Coral Gables, FL 33124

Donald Meichenbaum, Ph.D.
Department of Psychology
University of Waterloo
Waterloo, Ontario, CANADA
N2L3G1

H. Martin Miller, Ph.D.
Psychology Services
Anoka Metro-Regional
Treatment Center
Anoka, MN 55303

Robert A. Neimeyer, Ph.D.
Department of Psychology
University of Memphis
Memphis, TN 38152

Clive J. Robins, Ph.D.
Department of Psychiatry
Duke University Medical Center
Durham, NC 27710

Kenneth W. Sewell, Ph.D.
Department of Psychology
University of North Texas
Denton, TX 76203

Preface

Psychotherapy is changing. In today's world, such a statement seems to require little explanation. We live in an age of change. Indeed, most of us are so busy coping with the challenges of modern life that we seldom pause to reflect upon the pace and pervasiveness of change in our lives. Consider one striking illustration: the average person of the last century was born, lived a lifespan of perhaps 60 years, and died—all within a radius of about 8 miles. In today's world, 8 miles seems like a short distance to most commuters. Moreover, the average citizen of the 21st century is expected to not only travel more extensively than any of his or her historical predecessors, but also to interact with more of his fellow planetary citizens than can yet be appreciated. Taking into account the exponential growth of communication technologies, it is not unreasonable to think that our descendants will interact with more people in one day than our ancestors had met in an entire lifetime. The rate of change in today's world—and the complexities of personal identity and social participation within that world—are unprecedented in human history.

The profession of psychotherapy is also changing in unprecedented fashion. In the first half of this century there were relatively few approaches to mental health practice. As we draw near the close of the century, there are several hundred distinguishable psychotherapies. Along with these differentiations, however, there have also been signs of integration. Psychotherapists from traditionally rival schools of thought have entered into productive dialogues about their similarities as well as their differences. Ideological battles over whose is the best or only correct approach to life counseling have begun to give way to genuine collaborations and refinements in our understanding as well as our services. It is a time of remarkable development.

The present volume is devoted to recent developments in what have come to be called the cognitive and constructive psychotherapies. Although the conceptual and practical roots of these therapies can be traced into the last century (and, at other levels, into classical philosophy), their recognition and expansion as ideological systems is a phenomenon of only the last 40 years. The cognitive revolution—which originated sometime around 1955—was more than a return to an earlier idea, however. Sparked by developments in several disciplines, what began to spread through the worlds of science (and not just psychology) 40 years ago has yet to reach anything resembling a zenith.

When I was a graduate student in 1969, I was enrolled in a seminar surveying the current states of development of different specializations in psychology. Each student was required to write a term paper on an approved topic in contemporary psychology. I submitted a proposal and outline for a paper titled "An Information Processing Analysis of Behavior Modification." To my dismay, my proposal was rejected on the grounds that there was not sufficient information to "support" any such attempted analysis. I wrote a term paper on some other forgotten topic, but I did not abandon my fascination with the original direction. Five years later I published a volume called *Cognition and Behavior Modification*. Now, another 20 years hence, the expanse of information on the relation between cognition and psychotherapy is well beyond the capacity of any single individual to comprehend, let alone report. Cognitive sciences and clinical services are now recognized as necessary partners in the further development of each.

In 1991 Dr. Larry E. Beutler invited me to guest edit a special section of the *Journal of Consulting and Clinical Psychology* on the topic of 'recent developments in the cognitive and constructivist psychotherapies.' It was a welcome opportunity to collaborate with other workers in the field on a series of reviews and reflections about the past, present, and future of these approaches. The present volume represents a creative emergence from that project. Seven of its chapters originally appeared as articles in that special journal section. The other five are original contributions, never having appeared elsewhere.

Part I opens with my personal reflections on theoretical developments in the cognitive and constructive psychotherapies (Chapter 1). Six major themes are discussed: (1) the differentiation of rationalist and constructivist theories of knowing, (2) the relatively recent acknowledgment of social, biological, and embodiment processes in therapy, (3) the increasingly important role granted to unconscious processes, (4) the growing interest in self-organizing processes in lifespan personality development, (5) the recent shift toward acknowledgments of emotionality and uses of experiential techniques in therapy, and (6) the involvement of cognitive and constructivist therapists in the psychotherapy integration movement.

Chapter 2 is a retrospective and prospective analysis of cognitive behavior modification by Donald Meichenbaum. He explores three major metaphors that have been offered to explain the role of cognition in behavior change: 1) conditioning, 2) information processing, and 3) narrative construction. Meichenbaum concludes with a review of important theoretical and practical implications of the narrative metaphor for further developments in the field.

Part II is devoted to cognitive therapy. Aaron T. Beck begins with his reflections on the origins of this approach, its developmental trajectory, and its maturation as a system of psychotherapy (Chapter 3). He cites an impressive amount and range of data documenting the clinical and practical relevance of applied cognitive therapy. These clinical applications of cognitive therapy and its mechanisms of change are critically examined by Clive J. Robins and Adele M. Hayes (Chapter 4). These authors note that recent developments in cognitive therapy have included (1) a distinction between "core" and "peripheral" schemata, (2) an appreciation of the role of defensive processes in the avoidance of schema-related material, (3) a greater emphasis on exploration of the therapeutic relationship and interpersonal relationships in general, (4) a greater emphasis on the role of affective arousal for the elicitation and modification of cognitive schemata, and (5) a greater emphasis on exploration of developmental experiences that may have been significant in the development of maladaptive schemata.

Part III is devoted to rational–emotive therapy (RET). Albert Ellis begins by admittedly "doing the impossible: in a few pages reflecting on the development of RET, commenting on what it is today, and suggesting some future directions" (Chapter 5). He describes the early RET of 1955 as "highly cognitive, largely positivist, and very active–directive." Ellis notes that he was pushed toward more constructivist and affective directions by later developments in the field, and the differentiates between what he terms general and "preferential" RET. In Chapter 6 David A. F. Haaga and Gerald C. Davidson scrutinize the conceptual and empirical foundations of RET. They note that meta-analytic reviews offer support for the general utility of RET while more qualitative reviews question the internal and external validity of much of the published research. Haaga and Davison conclude that, in the future, more progress may be forthcoming by examining the specific therapeutic tactics of RET in particular circumstances rather than by attempting to study its merits as an overall treatment package.

Part IV is devoted to the constructive psychotherapies. Vittorio F. Guidano begins by offering a constructivist outline of human knowing processes (Chapter 7). From a constructive perspective, knowledge is viewed as an evolutionary process in which active and predominantly tacit self-organizing processes operate pervasively. Guidano proposes that John Bowlby's attachment theory offers an integrative paradigm for understanding and facilitating the dynamic, re-organizational development of self-knowledge. These same themes are emphasized and elaborated by myself, H. Martin Miller, and Giampiero Arciero (Chapter 8). Three basic features of constructivist perspectives are noted: an emphasis on proactive processes in knowing, an acknowledgment of nuclear systemic structure (with "deep" structures constraining the content and form of "surface" structure particulars), and the pervasive role of self-organizing processes in the maintenance and development of the system. In a discussion of storage metaphors for memory and mental representation, it is argued that constructivist approaches offer more promising alternatives than traditional information processing models.

Kenneth W. Sewell then summarizes the main contentions of George Kelly's theory of personal constructs and discusses Kelly's theoretical views concerning the distinction between cognition and affect (Chapter 9). Drawing on research showing differences in the construct systems of adults with and without diagnoses of affective disorder, Sewell extrapolates practical implications. In Chapter 10 Óscar F. Gonçalves elaborates a narrative model of human knowing processes and offers an outline of what he calls cognitive narrative psychotherapy. Case materials are used to illustrate five stages in such therapy: (1) the recall of personal life narratives, (2) objectifying processes, (3) subjectifying processes, (4) the metaphorizing of narratives, and (5) the projecting of narratives. Part IV concludes with Robert A. Neimeyer's appraisal of constructivist psychotherapies (Chapter 11). He reviews emerging trends in psychotherapy research that are compatible with constructivist approaches and concludes that the latter represent a sophistication, diversification, and extension of both theory and technique in psychotherapy. Chapter 12 concludes the volume with my personal reflections on the contexts and challenges associated with cognitive and constructive psychotherapies.

Acknowledgments

Needless to say, a project like this one is truly a collaborative effort. I extend my sincere appreciation to each of the authors for their individual and collective contributions. Together they have raised important questions about recent developments in the field, and their chapters reflect conscientious and self-examing reflection on the practical relevance of cognitive and constructive perspectives. Such questions are the lifeblood of all human inquiry, and such inquiry lies at the very heart of all psychological science and all psychotherapeutic services. I am also grateful to Bill Tucker and Bob Kowkabany of Springer for their invaluable assistance in all phases of this project.

I

Introduction

1

Theoretical Developments in the Cognitive Psychotherapies

Michael J. Mahoney

Written histories are always and necessarily interpretive. Thus, those interested in tracing the development of cognitive psychotherapies are wise to consult the multiple historiographies that have been rendered (Arnkoff & Glass, 1992; Dobson, 1988; Mahoney & Arnkoff, 1978; Vallis, Howes, & Miller, 1991). Allowing for some interpretive license, it seems clear that their heritage can be readily traced to classical philosophers. Some of the parallels between ancient and contemporary practices are, indeed, noteworthy:

> The Pythagoreans, the Platonists, the Aristotelians, the Stoics, and the Epicureans were not just adherents of "philosophical systems" but members of organized "schools," also called "sects," that imposed on them a specific method of training and a way of life.... The Pythagoreans, a community bound by strict discipline and obedience to the "master," followed severe dietary restrictions, exercises in self-control ... exercises in memory recall, and memorizing for recitation.... The Platonists searched together for truth, which was expected to emerge in conversations between teacher and disciples. The Aristotelian school was a kind of research institute of encyclopedic scope. The element of psychic training was stressed among the Stoics and the Epicureans. The Stoics learned the control of emotions and practiced written and verbal exercises in concentration and meditation. (Ellenberger, 1970, pp. 41–42)

The Stoics and the Epicureans were very successful at spreading the word, and their influence on early clinical methods was enormous. A central teaching of Galen, for instance, was the mastery of one's passions. After first curbing one's most extreme emotional impulses, the "second step was to find a mentor, a wise and older counselor who would point out your defects and dispense advice; Galen stresses the paramount importance of, and difficulty in finding, such a man" (Ellenberger, 1970, p. 43). Contemporary addenda would be "or woman" and "indeed."

In the centuries that followed, developments in philosophy and religion continued to be reflected in prevailing expressions of clinical practice. Descartes's revival of rationalism and formalization of dualism contributed to the intellectual enlightenment that was to pit mind against body and reason against feeling. Because of its emphasis on experiments and experience, the empiricism championed by Bacon, Hobbes, and Locke offered a partial antidote to the doctrine of rational supremacy. Later, the constructivism of Vico and the idealism of Kant lent encouragement to more active and participatory conceptions of mind. For the most part, however, these were developments that were circumscribed in their practical effects. The first widely applied philosophy of relatively recent times was the "mind cure movement" that swept through parts of Europe and North America in the late 18th and early 19th centuries. Sometimes called the "psychology of healthy mindedness," this movement emphasized the importance of positive thinking and integrated practical exercises with the tenets of Christianity. It became (and remains) very popular, a fact acknowledged by William James (1902). Although the merits of positive thinking have been heralded most visibly by Dale Carnegie and Norman Vincent Peale in this century, they were neither the first nor the only proponents of that approach (Table 1.1). A casual stroll through the self-improvement section of any contemporary bookstore testifies to the fact that the mind cure movement is neither past nor moribund.

Although there is continuing warrant for the association of positive and healthy-minded thinking with cognitive psychotherapies (Kendall, 1992), current views of the latter tend to classify them as secular applications of the cognitive sciences. The cognitive sciences, in turn, are said to have made their appearance sometime between 1955 and 1965, and the cognitive revolution in psychology was not acknowledged until the 1970s. In this respect, it is noteworthy that the major cognitive psychotherapies emerged either before or simultaneous with cognitive psychology. For example, although George Kelly denied being a cognitivist, his *The Psychology of Personal Constructs* (1955) was to become an inspiration to many cognitive therapists. Likewise, Albert Ellis's (1962, 1992) rational-emotive therapy preceded the major developments in cognitive psychology, and Aaron T. Beck's (1963, 1991) cogni-

TABLE 1.1. **Selected Events and Individuals in the Positive Thinking Movement, 1860–1960**

Date	Event
1860s	Phineas P. Quimby achieved fame as a "mental healer"; *The Quimby Manuscripts* were published in 1921.
1869	Warren Evans, a patient of Quimby's, published *The Mental Cure* and contributed to "the Boston Craze" of metaphysics and mind cure in the 1870s.
1875	Mary Baker Eddy published *Science and Health* and founded the Christian Science movement.
1889	The Unity School of Christianity was inspired by Eddy's Christian Science.
1892	Annie Payson Call published *The Power of Repose.*
1892	The International Divine Science Association was formed.
1893	Henry Wood: *Ideal Suggestion Through Mental Photography.*
1898	Ralph Waldo Trine: *In Tune With the Infinite.*
1905	Paul Dubois: *The Psychic Treatment of Nervous Disorders.*
1906	The New Thought Alliance was formed in the tradition of Quimby's "applied therapeutic religion."
1907	Frank Haddock: *Power of Will.*
1910	Orestes S. Marden: *The Miracle of Right Thinking.*
1922	Emile Coue: *Self-Mastery Through Conscious Auto-Suggestion.*
1936	Henry Link: *The Return to Religion.*
1936	Dale Carnegie: *How to Win Friends and Influence People.*
1943	Harry Emerson Fosdick's *On Being a Real Person* pioneered modern pastoral counseling.
1946	Joshua Loth Liebman: *Peace of Mind.*
1948	Claude Bristol: *The Magic of Believing.*
1952	Norman Vincent Peale: *The Power of Positive Thinking.*
1956	Smiley Blanton: *Love or Perish.*
1960	Maxwell Maltz: *Psycho-Cybernetics.*

Note: Meyer (1965) was a primary source for much of this information.

tive therapy was already apparent in his early work on depression. Thus, clinical applications of a cognitive perspective generally predated the formal theory and research associated with cognitive psychology.

In 1980, there were five or six basic types of cognitive psychotherapy: Kelly's personal construct approach, Ellis's rational-emotive therapy, Beck's cognitive therapy, the problem-solving approaches, and a loosely grouped set of "coping skills" techniques associated with "cognitive behavior modification." The sixth possibility was Viktor Frankl's (1959) logotherapy, which focuses on the centrality of meaning in personal adaptation but is often classified as an existential or humanistic approach. By 1990, there were more than 20 different varieties of cognitive psychotherapy, and there had been significant changes in at least some of the original forms (Haaga & Davison, 1991).

In many respects, the conceptual developments within the cognitive psychotherapies have raced ahead of much of the research in the area. These conceptual developments, in turn, appear to have emerged from the practical experiences of service providers, a phenomenon that has often been repeated in the history of psychotherapy (Freedheim, 1992; Lazarus & Davison, 1971). By way of preview, I suggest that the major conceptual developments in the cognitive psychotherapies over the past three decades have been (a) the differentiation of rationalist and constructivist approaches to cognition; (b) the recognition of social, biological, and embodiment issues; (c) the reappraisal of unconscious processes; (d) an increasing focus on self- and social systems; (e) the reappraisal of emotional and experiential processes; and (f) the contribution of the cognitive psychotherapies to the psychotherapy integration movement.

RATIONALIST AND CONSTRUCTIVIST DIFFERENCES

There has been significant evolution within the cognitive revolution that swept through psychology in the 1970s. Depending on whose ac-count and terminology one uses, there have been at least three—and some say four—major conceptual strides in cognitive science since 1955 (Baars, 1986; Gardner, 1985; Mahoney, 1991; Varela, 1986). The first such stride involved the information-processing movement, sometimes also called the cybernetics movement because of its introduction of teleological (goal-directed) feedback loops to the infrastructure of early computers. As Jerome Bruner (1990) noted in his reflections on this first phase of the cognitive revolution, it quickly became sidetracked by computer technology and the simulation of artificial intelligence. Although there were prescient counterexamples (e.g., Miller, Galanter, & Pribram, 1960), early cognitive psychology became preoccupied with information (storage, retrieval, and processing) rather than with the processes of meaning making that are more central to contemporary cognitive science. The information-processing era began in the mid-1950s and peaked sometime around 1970.

Overlapping with the information-processing era was the connec-tionist movement, a development that emerged in the 1970s and 1980s with the construction of super computers. (Although there are parallels with E. L. Thorndike's turn-of-the century "connectionism," the new connectionism is considerably more sophisticated and mediational in its models.) The three defining features of modern connectionism are its reliance on "distributed parallel processing" (Rumelhart & McClelland, 1986), its attempts to simulate neuronal networks in operation (Sejnowski, Koch, & Churchland, 1988), and its concession that some aspects of biological information processing may be subsymbolic and therefore difficult (if not impossible) to program in explicit algorithms (Smolensky, 1988). Distributed parallel processing (as compared with condensed linear processing) afforded substantial increases in computational powers relative to early computers. The shift from modeling the nervous system after computers to modeling computer programs after nervous systems has spawned the hybrid field known as computational neuroscience. Finally, the suggestion of subsymbolic processes reflected an acknowledgment of a perplexing "fuzziness" in learning and knowing. Critics of connectionism have noted that it remains mired in a fundamentally computational model of knowing, and that it tends to perpetuate reification ("inner copy") models of mental representation (Fodor & Pylyshyn, 1988; Mahoney, 1991; Schneider, 1987).

The third phase in the cognitive revolution began to emerge at about the same time as modern connectionism and is commonly known as constructivism or constructive metatheory. It reflects a substantial legacy in the history of ideas and psychobiology (Bruner, 1990; Hayek, 1952; Mahoney, 1988a). Fundamental to constructivism is an emphasis on the active—indeed, proactive (and hence anticipatory)—nature of all knowing. In contrast to the relatively passive models of mind and brain proposed by information-processing perspectives, constructivism proposes intrinsic self-organizing activity as fundamental to all knowledge processes. Thus, the mind/brain is no longer viewed as a repository ("memory bank") of representations so much as an organic system of self-referencing activities. To the cybernetic notion of feedback (environmentally based information) is added the notion of "feedforward" (organismically generated form). In the tradition of Sir Charles Sherrington's (1906) idea of *The Integrative Action of the Nervous System,* Weimer (1977) and others have compared the motoric aspects of constructivism with the predominantly sensorial emphases of its cybernetic counterparts. Among other things, constructive perspectives emphasize the operation of tacit (unconscious) ordering processes, the complexity of human experience, and the merits of a developmental, process-focused approach to knowing.

A proposed fourth contender for a distinct era or approach to cognitive science is hermeneutics. The term comes from the Greek *hermeneutikos* (meaning "interpretation"), and the field was pioneered by Biblical scholars specializing in the translation and analysis of sacred texts. Following a complex series of 20th-century developments in linguistics, semiotics, and both literary and philosophical criticism, hermeneutics has become a secularized expression of the realization that all interactions between texts and readers are constrained and construed by unique individual, sociocultural, and historical influences (Madison, 1988; Messer, Sass, & Woolfolk, 1988; Palmer, 1969; Wachterhauser, 1986). Just as the constructivists have projected the mind of the knower onto the forms of the known (and the dynamics of the knowing process itself), the hermeneuts have come to contend that the reader is in the text (and vice versa). The parallels between constructivism and hermeneutics are considerable, which may be why some observers are reluctant to separate them as distinct approaches to knowing.

Constructive approaches to psychotherapy are increasingly common (e.g., Feixas & Villegas, 1990; Gonçalves, 1989; Guidano, 1987, 1991; Guidano & Liotti, 1983; Kelly, 1955; Mahoney, 1988b, 1991, 1995; Maturana & Varela, 1987; Miro, 1989, Neimeyer, 1993; Neimeyer & Mahoney, 1995; Reda, 1986), although they have only recently been so labeled. Their differentiation from traditional cognitive psychotherapies has, in fact, created the first major conceptual debate in the field. The debate centers on whether a meaningful contrast can be drawn between rationalist and constructivist cognitive therapies (Mahoney & Lyddon, 1988). Rationalist thought is said to be characterized by three related assumptions (a) that irrationality is the primary source of neurotic psychopathology, (b) that explicit beliefs and logical reasoning can easily overpower and guide emotions and behavioral actions, and (c) that the core process in effective psychotherapy is the substitution of rational for irrational thinking patterns. The rational-emotive therapy of Albert Ellis (1962) and his followers is said to be exemplary of this perspective, although Ellis (1988, 1993) denies that his system is rationalistic. Constructive metatheory, on the other hand, (a) adopts a more proactive (vs. reactive and representational) view of cognition and the organism, (b) emphasizes tacit (unconscious) core ordering processes, and (c) promotes a complex systems model in which thought, feeling, and behavior are interdependent expressions of a life span developmental unfolding of interactions between self and (primarily social) systems. Needless to say, the constructive approach is more complex and abstract than is the rationalist. Its expression has been truly international in scope, however, and it appears to be rapidly expanding. This apparent growth in popularity may also be partially attributed to the fact that some of those writers portrayed as archetypal rationalists—most notably Albert Ellis—have vigorously denied any rationalist leanings and laid strong claim to constructivist views.

As illustrated by some of the chapters in this volume, the meanings of *constructive* and the features that differentiate and cohere the cognitive psychotherapies remain sources of controversy for some of their representatives. More important than its ability to reliably differentiate camps of adherents, however, is the potential contribution that the rationalist–constructivist contrast may offer to emerging theory and research relating the cognitive sciences and clinical services (Mahoney, 1991).

SOCIAL, BIOLOGICAL, AND EMBODIMENT ISSUES

A second major conceptual development within the cognitive psychotherapies has been the increasing importance attributed to biological and social factors in the etiology, maintenance, and treatment of psychological disorders. This is not to imply that these influences were totally denied in earlier versions, but only to note the relative balance of power. Whereas Beck's early cognitive therapy for depression clearly acknowledged the role of genetic factors in some forms of that disorder, for example, more recent presentations of cognitive therapy have given decidedly more attention to ethological influences. Beck has also pioneered research into the factors contributing to individual differences in coping styles. Under conditions of stress or during the experience of distress, autonomous individuals appear to be isolative and self-reliant, whereas "sociotropic" individuals more often seek out friends and social support systems (Beck, Emery, & Greenberg, 1985). Likewise, Ellis's rational–emotive therapy now posits an inherited tendency toward irrational beliefs that may biologically predispose individuals toward developing common patterns of dysfunction (Ellis, 1976).

The significance of these factors and the dynamic boundary between biological and social influences are perhaps most apparent in some of the constructivist approaches. Maturana and Varela (1987), for example, are both biologists, yet their current work in constructivist theory is focused on love and identity, respectively (Maturana, 1989; Varela, Thompson, & Rosch, 1991), and their work has been influential in family and systems therapies. Still other constructivists (Guidano, Liotti, Mahoney, & Reda) have embraced the significance of John Bowlby's (1988) attachment theory for understanding developmental psychopathology and the essence of effective therapy. Psychobiological inquiries into early and later emotional attachments have documented the powerful role of endogenous opiates (e.g., endorphins) in the "making and breaking of affectional bonds" (Schore, 1994). Finally, constructivists studying emotionality (see later discussion) have emphasized the significance of social realities in this domain (e.g., Safran & Segal, 1990). Almost without exception, cognitive psychotherapists now acknowledge the importance of the therapeutic relationship in effective therapy and the fact that clients' private worlds are most formatively developed and revised, for better and for worse, in the context of strong affective relationships.

A related development in the cognitive therapies has been the recent attention given to issues of "embodiment" (i.e., the bodily basis for and means of experiencing; Guidano, 1987; Mahoney, in press). This attention has been particularly apparent among the constructivists, who draw on the literatures of epistemology, ethology, hermeneutics, and phenomenology to document the pervasive role of (primarily tacit) bodily experiences in psychological disorders and personality development. Although they include issues of body image and physical health, the emerging works in this area emphasize a fundamental, dynamic, and lifelong connection between mediate(d) and immediate experience. Mind–body dualism is therein challenged, and the bodily origin of "higher mental" activities is elaborated (Johnson, 1987; Varela et al., 1991). These developments overlap significantly with the trend among cognitive psychotherapists to grant greater respect to emotionality and to encourage experiential exercises (see later discussion).

UNCONSCIOUS PROCESSES

One of the more surprising theoretical developments in cognitive psychotherapy has been the relatively recent acknowledgment of the important and extensive role played by unconscious processes in human experience. The surprising aspect of this development derives from the fact that many cognitive therapists have been critical of psychoanalytic theory and, until recently, virtually all discussions of unconscious processes were psychodynamic in tone. Several pioneering cognitive therapists had, of course, been originally trained in the psychoanalytic tradition (e.g., Beck, Ellis, & Goldfried). For the most part, however, they had rejected that tradition, and, along with their more behaviorally weaned peers, they had strongly challenged the merits of psychoanalytic theory and therapy. By 1990, however, the distance between some forms of cognitive psychotherapy and psychodynamic therapy had narrowed substantially. Although not entirely responsible for this apparent rapprochement, the sometimes-reluctant acknowledgment of unconscious processes by cognitive adherents has played an important role in reducing that distance.

It is important to note that not all cognitive psychotherapists are comfortable with the above-mentioned rapprochement and, more important from a theoretical perspective, that cognitive renditions of the unconscious have been distinctly different from those rendered by

Sigmund Freud. In some cognitive approaches, there is only limited and somewhat begrudging acknowledgment of the operation of processes outside of conscious awareness. "Automatic thoughts" are an example of such processes; they have become so habitual, it is alleged, that they are functionally automatic and occur without the individual's awareness. By working backward from their emotional and behavioral effects, however, such thoughts can usually be made explicit and amenable to modification. An intermediate level of acknowledgment of unconscious activity is illustrated in approaches that emphasize cognitive schemata, which are abstract organizational processes. Finally, the greatest importance attributed to unconscious processes by cognitive adherents is generally associated with some of the constructivists, who view fundamentally tacit processes as central to all epistemic (knowing) activity.

The terminology and degrees of acknowledgment may vary, but the fact remains that cognitive adherents no longer consider it viable to maintain that all (or even most) important cognition is conscious and communicable. Indeed, some constructivists have elevated tacit processes to the level of a cardinal tenet. These unconscious processes of "self-organization" and "core ordering" are distinguished from psychoanalytic concepts, and distinctions are drawn between Freud's id-to-ego notion of psychotherapy process and what some contemporary cognitivists consider a dynamic and lifelong dance between tacit and explicit experience (Guidano, 1991; Mahoney, 1991). Nevertheless, the admission of unconscious processes onto center stage in cognitive theory and research reflects a major conceptual development (Bowers & Meichenbaum, 1984). Nor is it entirely coincidental, perhaps, that many of the modern advocates of psychotherapy integration have hailed from cognitive and psychodynamic origins (see later discussion).

SELF AND SYSTEMS DYNAMICS

The cognitive revolutions helped bring experimental psychology back inside the organism, and what researchers found there was much more than they had been seeking. It has been said that the single most important (re)discovery of 20th-century psychology may well be that of the self, and cognitive therapists have joined the rest of the field in expanding their models and methods to include this elusively core dimension of human experience. In 1990 (Vol. 14, No. 2), *Cognitive Therapy and Research* devoted a special issue to "Selfhood Processes and Emotional Disorders," and in 1992 (Vol. 6, No. 1) the *Journal of Cognitive Psychotherapy* published a special issue on personality disorders. Other illustrations of cognitivists' interest in self-system issues are not difficult to find (e.g., Hammen, 1988; Hartman & Blankstein, 1986; Hermans, Kempen, & van Loon, 1992; Segal, 1988). What is most noteworthy about the cognitive (re)discovery of the self, however, is its practical effect of having moved the focus back to factors outside the organism and, more accurately, dynamically between the organism and its milieu, particularly to social support systems, family and developmental history, cultural contexts, and, ultimately the therapeutic relationship. Whereas early cognitive therapies were relatively more introspective, individual-istic, ahistorical, and inattentive to the emotional relationship between counselor and client, the opposite of each of these is more characteris-tic of contemporary cognitive psychotherapies.

An apt illustration of this development is offered in Guidano's (1987, 1991) discussions of the epistemological issues involved in lifespan identity development. Guidano addressed the centrality of self-system issues to all forms of psychotherapy (cognitive and otherwise). At the same time, his writings discussed the complex dynamics of the experi-ence of self in major categories of psychological disorders (anxiety, depression, eating, and obsessive-compulsive). Also noteworthy is Gergen's (1991) constructivist portrayal of the "saturated" postmodern self and the exacerbation of identity crises by technological achieve-ments. With an increasing focus on self-schemata and "possible selves" (Markus & Nurius, 1986), it is apparent that contemporary cognitive psychotherapies no longer focus only on specific maladaptive beliefs or even molar processes of dysfunctional cognition. (Dis)continuities of organization and phenomenological identity cannot be denied or avoided by the practitioner who views psychotherapy as applied exer-cises in ontology (theories of reality and existence) and epistemology (theories of knowing and, inherently, the knower). The "complexities of the self," as Guidano calls them, are now central concerns of the cognitive therapist.

One of the fascinating conceptual results of this interest in the self is the current reappraisal of resistance in psychotherapy. Acknowledging that resistance to change is a professional reality, some cognitive thera-pists have moved beyond self-handicapping interpretations of this fact to more self-protective ones (Liotti, 1987; Mahoney, 1991). That is, they have begun to view core ordering processes as inherently protective of the individual's sense of personal coherence, resulting in varying de-grees and expressions of reluctance or resistance to changing patterns with which they identify. Such conjectures also suggest a balance of continuity-maintaining (or familiarity-maintaining) processes with their change-producing alternatives. Among other things, these formulations depathologize resistance and acknowledge the complexity and difficulty of core personality change.

EMOTIONALITY AND EXPERIENTIAL EMPHASES

Although not proposed as a defining feature of constructivist metatheory, the roles allotted to emotional processes in rationalist and constructivist perspectives appear to be very different. Traditionally, rationalist–cognitive therapists have viewed emotions as sources (or expressions) of problems that could be "corrected" or otherwise manipulated through the mediation of conscious reason. Constructivists, on the other hand, have challenged the validity of the distinction between cognition and emotion. They have argued, moreover, that even in an artificially conceived contest between these two dimensions, the emotional side would prove more powerful than the rational. Finally, the constructivists contend that affective processes are neither the culprits nor the causes of psychological dysfunction. They are, rather, dynamic expressions of the same (dis)organization processes that characterize the development of self-systems (Greenberg & Safran, 1987; Guidano, 1987, 1991; Mahoney, 1991, 1995).

With their reappraisal of the role of emotions in adaptation and development, cognitive psychotherapists have moved significantly in the direction of the experiential aspects of psychotherapy. Rather than simply reason their way from feeling bad to feeling good, an increasing number of clients in cognitive treatment are being encouraged to actively experience, explore, and express a much broader range and more complex mixture of affect. In the process, they are also more likely to be offered exercises and techniques that have been traditionally associated with experiential therapies. In this respect, it is interesting to note that cognitivists and behaviorists alike—and certainly the popular hybrids termed cognitive–behavioral—have found themselves on the common ground of phenomenology (immediate, lived experience). The powerful role of strong and personally meaningful emotions is now widely acknowledged by these practitioners. Although they may offer different interpretations and explanations, cognitive and behavioral therapists have reached an agreement that in vivo activity is an important element in effective psychotherapy. Under appropriate guidance, pacing, and processing, such activity has become fundamental to their respective efforts to serve as mental health professionals. Noteworthy here is the fact that the cognitivists and behaviorists who have found themselves in agreement on this point are also discovering that the terrain of affectively lived experience has long been a haunt of their psychodynamic counterparts. The "corrective emotional experiences" afforded by well-coordinated psychoanalysis turn out to be strikingly similar to those reported to be important in behavioral, cognitive, and humanistic approaches (Stolorow & Atwood, 1992).

PSYCHOTHERAPY INTEGRATION

The sixth and final theoretical development in the cognitive and constructive psychotherapies can be summarized by saying that they have assumed a major role in the contemporary movement known as psychotherapy integration. Indeed, several writers have argued that cognitive perspectives are the most promising sources of language, theory, and research methods for exploring the possibility of rapprochement among traditionally rival systems of psychotherapy (Alford & Norcross, 1991; Beck, 1991; Goldfried, 1982, 1991; Horowitz, 1991).

It is beyond the scope of this chapter to discuss the origins and developmental trajectory of the relatively recent resurgence in the popularity of eclecticism and the growing interest in the possible convergence or integration of diverse forms of psychotherapy. These phenomena are current events in the concluding years of 20th-century psychology; and they show every sign of being formative elements in its second century of development (Norcross & Goldfried, 1992). The Society for the Exploration of Psychotherapy Integration was founded in 1983, and the *Journal of Psychotherapy Integration* began publication in 1991. Both are now truly international in scope. More pertinent to the present discussion is the fact that these expressions of the integration movement have been clearly influenced by representatives of cognitive and constructive psychotherapy. Whether their contributions have been or will be more important than those of participants from other theoretical traditions is a matter of conjecture and interpretation of course, and it is not likely to be simply resolved by future historiographies of psychotherapy. What is important to note is that cognitive and constructive psychotherapists have entered productive dialogues with their behavioral, humanistic, and psychodynamic colleagues. This represents a major step beyond the sibling rivalries that characterized psychotherapy at midcentury.

Of equal significance to the contribution of cognitive and constructive therapists to psychotherapy integration is the undeniable impact that the integration movement has had on these psychotherapies. As this chapter has outlined, the contacts of cognitive psychotherapists with the concepts and practices of other approaches have been extensive and appear, if anything, to still be increasing. Although less generous interpretations are clearly possible, it seems that this diversification and dialectical activity reflect positively on both the cognitive and constructive psychotherapies and the perspectives with which they have developed such dialogues.

CONCLUDING REMARKS

Although they reflect the legacy of traditions ranging from classical philosophy to Christian Science, the cognitive and constructive psychotherapies are fundamentally a recent phenomenon. In the short span of less than four decades, they have emerged, multiplied, differentiated, and developed. I have suggested that the major theoretical developments in the cognitive psychotherapies have clustered around six basic themes; whether these developments are positive or progressive cannot be determined without first presuming to know what such developments "should" be or, in historical retroflection, what they "should have been." It is, however, very clear that the cognitive and constructive psychotherapies represent one of the most active clusters of theoretical development, research activity, and clinical innovations in this last decade of the century. Their involvement in and encouragement of open exchanges with other disciplines and traditions are also a commendable feature of these approaches. Finally, these psychotherapies have encouraged a commitment to self-examination and self-awareness that admirably reflects the centrality of exploration and inquiry in the continuing coalition of psychological science and clinical service.

REFERENCES

Alford, B. A., & Norcross, J. C. (1991). Cognitive therapy as integrative therapy. *Journal of Psychotherapy Integration, 1,* 175–190.

Arnkoff, D. B., & Glass, C. R. (1992). Cognitive therapy and psychotherapy integration. In D. K. Freedheim (Ed.), *The history of psychotherapy* (pp. 657–694). Washington, DC: American Psychological Association.

Baars, B. J. (Ed.). (1986). *The cognitive revolution in psychology.* New York: Guilford Press.

Beck, A. T. (1963). Thinking and depression: 1. Idiosyncratic content and cognitive distortion. *Archives of General Psychiatry, 9,* 324–333.

Beck, A. T. (1991). Cognitive therapy as the integrative therapy. *Journal of Psychotherapy Integration, 1,* 191–198.

Beck, A. T., Emery, G., & Greenberg, R. L. (1985). *Anxiety disorders and phobias: A cognitive perspective.* New York: Basic Books.

Bowers, K. S., & Meichenbaum, D. (Eds.). (1984). *The unconscious reconsidered.* New York: Wiley.

Bowlby, J. (1988). *A secure base.* New York: Basic Books.

Bruner, J. S. (1990). *Acts of meaning.* Cambridge. MA: Harvard University Press.

Dobson, K. S. (Ed.). (1988). *Handbook of cognitive-behavioral therapies.* New York: Guilford Press.

Ellenberger, H. F. (1970). *The discovery of the unconscious.* New York: Basic Books.

Ellis, A. (1962). *Reason and emotion in psychotherapy.* New York: Lyle Stuart.

Ellis, A. (1976). The biological basis of human irrationality. *Journal of Individual Psychology, 32,* 145–168.

Ellis, A. (1988). Are there "rationalist" and "constructivist" camps of the cognitive therapies? A response to Michael Mahoney. *Cognitive Behaviorist 10*(2), 13–17.

Ellis, A. (1992). My early experiences in developing the practice of psychotherapy. *Professional Psychology: Research and Practice, 23,* 7–10.

Ellis, A. (1993). Reflections on rational–emotive therapy. *Journal of Consulting and Clinical Psychology, 61,* 199–201.

Feixas, G., & Villegas, M. (1990). *Constructivismo y psicoterapia* [Constructivism and psychotherapy]. Barcelona, Spain: Promociones y Publicaciones Universitarias, S.A.

Fodor, J. A., & Pylyshyn, Z. W. (1988). Connectionism and cognitive architecture: A critical analysis. *Cognition, 28,* 3–71.

Frankl, V. E. (1959). *Man's search for meaning: An introduction to logotherapy.* New York: Washington Square Press.

Freedheim, D. K. (Ed.). (1992). *History of psychotherapy: A century of change.* Washington, DC: American Psychological Association.

Gardner, H. (1985). *The mind's new science: A history of the cognitive revolution.* New York: Basic Books.

Gergen, K. J. (1991). *The saturated self: Dilemmas of identity in contemporary life.* New York: Basic Books.

Goldfried, M. R. (1982). *Converging themes in psychotherapy.* New York: Springer.

Goldfried, M. R. (1991). Research issues in psychotherapy integration. *Journal of Psychotherapy Integration, 1,* 5–25.

Gonçalves, O. F. (Ed.). (1989). *Advances in the cognitive therapies: The constructivist–developmental approach.* Lisbon: APPORT.

Greenberg, L. S., & Safran, J. D. (1987). *Emotion in psychotherapy.* New York: Guilford Press.

Guidano, V. F. (1987). *Complexity of the self.* New York: Guilford Press.

Guidano, V. F. (1991). *The self in process: Toward a post-rationalist cognitive therapy.* New York: Guilford Press.

Guidano, V. F., & Liotti, G. (1983). *Cognitive processes and emotional disorders.* New York: Guilford Press.

Haaga, D. A., & Davison, G. C. (1991). Disappearing differences do not always reflect healthy integration: An analysis of cognitive therapy and rational-emotive therapy. *Journal of Psychotherapy Integration, 1,* 287–303.

Hammen, C. (1988). Self cognitions, stressful events, and the prediction of depression in children of depressed mothers. *Journal of Abnormal Child Psychology, 16,* 347–360.

Hartman, L. M., & Blankstein, K. R. (Eds.). (1986). *Perceptions of self in emotional disorder and psychotherapy.* New York: Wiley.

Hayek, F. A. (1952). *The sensory order.* Chicago: University of Chicago Press.

Hermans, H. J. M., Kempen, H. J. G., & van Loon, R. J. P. (1992). The dialogical self: Beyond individualism and rationalism. *American Psychologist, 47,* 23–33.

Horowitz, M. J. (1991). States, schemas, and control: General theories for psychotherapy integration. *Journal of Psychotherapy Integration, 1,* 85–102.

James, W. (1902). *The varieties of religious experience.* New York: New American Library.

Johnson, M. (1987). *The body in the mind: The bodily basis of meaning, imagination, and reason.* Chicago: University of Chicago Press.

Kelly, G. A. (1955). *The psychology of personal constructs.* New York: Norton.

Kendall, P. C. (1992). Healthy thinking. *Behavior Therapy, 23,* 1–11.

Lazarus, A. A., & Davison, G. C. (1971). Clinical innovation in research and practice. In A. E. Bergin & S. L. Garfield (Eds.), *Handbook of psychotherapy and behavior change* (pp. 196–213). New York: Wiley.

Liotti, G. (1987). The resistance to change of cognitive structures: A counter-proposal to psychoanalytic metapsychology. *Journal of Cognitive Psychotherapy, 1,* 87–104.

Madison, G. B. (1988). *The hermeneutics of postmodernity.* Bloomington: Indiana University Press.

Mahoney, M. J. (1988a). Constructive metatheory: I. Basic features and historical foundations. *International Journal of Personal Construct Psychology, 1,* 1–35.

Mahoney, M. J. (1988b). Constructive metatheory: II. Implications for psychotherapy. *International Journal of Personal Construct Psychology, 1,* 299–315.

Mahoney, M. J. (1991). *Human change processes: The scientific foundations of psychotherapy.* New York: Basic Books.

Mahoney, M. J. (1995). *Constructive psychotherapy.* New York: Guilford.

Mahoney, M. J. (in press). *The bodily self: A guide to integrating the head and body in psychotherapy.* New York: Guilford Press.

Mahoney, M. J., & Arnkoff, D. B. (1978). Cognitive and self-control therapies. In S. L. Garfield & A. E. Bergin (Eds.), *Handbook of psychotherapy and behavior change* (2nd ed., pp. 689–722). New York: Wiley.

Mahoney, M. J., & Lyddon, W. J. (1988). Recent developments in cognitive approaches to counseling and psychotherapy. *The Counseling Psychologist, 16,* 190–234.

Markus, H., & Nurius, P. (1986). Possible selves. *American Psychologist, 41,* 954–969.

Maturana, H. R. (1989, May). *Emotion and the origin of the human.* Paper presented at the International Conference at the Frontiers of Family Therapy, Brussels, Belgium.

Maturana, H. R., & Varela, F. J. (1987). *The tree of knowledge: The biological roots of human understanding.* Boston: Shambhala.

Messer, S. B., Sass, L. A., & Woolfolk, R. L. (Eds.). (1988). *Hermeneutics and psychological theory: Interpretive perspectives on personality, psychotherapy and psychopathology.* New Brunswick, NJ: Rutgers University Press.

Meyer, D. (1965). *The positive thinkers.* Garden City, NY: Doubleday.

Miller, G. A., Galanter, E., & Pribram, K. H. (1960). *Plans and the structure of behavior.* New York: Holt, Rinehart & Winston.

Miro, M. (1989). Knowledge and society: An evolutionary outline. In O. F. Gonçalves (Ed.), *Advances in the cognitive therapies: The constructive-developmental approach* (pp. 111–128). Lisbon, Portugal: APPORT.

Neimeyer, R. A. (1993). An appraisal of constructivist psychotherapies. *Journal of Consulting and Clinical Psychology, 61,* 221–234.

Neimeyer, R. A., & Mahoney, M. J. (Eds.). (1995). *Constructivism in psychotherapy.* Washington, D.C.: American Psychological Association.

Norcross, J. C., & Goldfried, M. R. (Eds.). (1992). *Handbook of psychotherapy integration.* New York: Basic Books.

Palmer, R. E. (1969). *Hermeneutics: Interpretation theory in Schleiermacher, Dilthey, Heidegger, and Gadamer.* Evanston, IL: Northwestern University Press.

Reda, M. A. (1986). *Sistemi cognitivi complessi e psicoterapia.* [*Complex cognitive systems and psychotherapy.*] Rome: Nuova Italia Scientifica.

Rumelhart, D. E., & McClelland, J. L. (1986). *Parallel distributed processing: Explorations in the microstructure of cognition* (2 vols.). Cambridge, MA: MIT Press.

Safran, J. D., & Segal, Z. V. (1990). *Interpersonal process in cognitive therapy.* New York: Basic Books.

Schneider, W. (1987). Connectionism: Is it a paradigm shift for psychology? *Behavior Research Methods, Instruments, and Computers, 19,* 73–83.

Schore, A. N. (1994). *Affect regulation and the origin of the self.* Hillsdale, NJ: Erlbaum.

Segal, Z. V. (1988). Appraisal of the self-schema construct in cognitive models of depression. *Psychological Bulletin, 103,* 147–162.

Sejnowski, T. J., Koch, C., & Churchland, P. S. (1988). Computational neuroscience. *Science, 241,* 1299–1306.

Sherrington, C. S. (1906). *The integrative action of the nervous system.* New Haven, CT: Yale University Press.

Smolensky, P. (1988). On the proper treatment of connectionism. *Behavioural and Brain Sciences, 11,* 1–74.

Stolorow, R. D., & Atwood, G. E. (1992). *Contexts of being: The intersubjective foundations of psychological life.* Hillsdale, NJ: The Analytic Press.

Vallis, T. M., Howes, J. L., & Miller, P. C. (Eds.). (1991). *The challenge of cognitive therapy.* New York: Plenum Press.

Varela, F. J. (1986). *The science and technology of cognition: Emergent directions.* Florence, Italy: Hopeful Monster.

Varela, F. J., Thompson, E., & Rosch, E. (1991). *The embodied mind: Cognitive science and human experience.* Cambridge, MA: MIT Press.

Wachterhauser, B. R. (Ed.). (1986). *Hermeneutics and modern philosophy.* Albany: State University of New York Press.

Weimer, W. B. (1977). A conceptual framework for cognitive psychology: Motor theories of mind. In R. Shaw & J. Bransford (Eds.), *Perceiving, acting, and knowing* (pp. 267–311). Hillsdale, NJ: Erlbaum.

2

Changing Conceptions of Cognitive Behavior Modification: Retrospect and Prospect

Donald Meichenbaum

Since its inception, cognitive behavior modification (CBM) has attempted to integrate the clinical concerns of psychodynamic and systems-oriented psychotherapists with the technology of behavior therapists. CBM has contributed to current integrative efforts in the field of psychotherapy. As in most forms of psychotherapy, CBM was the result of an evolutionary process and was part of a zeitgeist of what December (1974) called a "cognitive revolution."

Cognitive–behavioral therapies derived from a long tradition of semantic therapists ranging from Dubois to Kelly, and along the way were influenced by the social learning theories of Rotter, Bandura, Mischel, Kanfer, and others. The influential writings of Albert Ellis, Aaron Beck, and both Arnold and Richard Lazarus highlighted the role of cognitive and affective processes in psychopathology and in the behavior change process.

One major catalyst for the development of cognitive–behavioral therapy was the growing dissatisfaction with both the empirical and the theoretical bases of a strictly behavioral therapeutic approach. A number of authors, such as Breger and McGaugh (1965), Brewer (1974), McKeachie (1974), Mahoney (1974), and Meichenbaum (1977), were questioning the adequacy of learning theory explanations of both psychopathology and behavioral change. A second major catalyst was the initial results of cognitive therapists such as Aaron Beck (1970) and Albert Ellis (1962) who demonstrated the promise of their interventions.

This interest in cognitive factors in psychotherapy was often not well received by "behavioral types," who called for the exclusion of "cognitive types" from such organizations as the Association for the Advancement of Behavior Therapy. Such malcontents were supposedly diluting, if not undermining, the "purity" of behavior therapy. But Pandora's box, with all of its difficulties and challenges, had been opened as cognitive–behavioral practitioners struggled with questions as to how best to conceptualize their clients' cognitions and how to fit such cognitive processes into the complex reciprocal interrelationships with clients' feelings, behavior, and resultant consequences, as well as with physiological and social-cultural processes. The answers to these research questions have been strongly influenced by the specific conceptualizations and metaphors used to explain clients' thought processes. I will consider three of these guiding metaphors, namely, conditioning, information processing, and constructing narratives.

CONDITIONING AS A METAPHOR

Initially, cognitive-behavioral therapists proposed that an individual's cognitions could be viewed as covert behaviors, subject to the same "laws of learning" as are overt behaviors. In the tradition of Skinner and conditioning theorists, cognition was viewed as covert operants, or what Homme (1965) called "coverants," supposedly responsive to both external and internal contingencies and altered by contiguous pairings, as in the case of covert sensitization (Cautela, 1973). Clients' self-statements and images were viewed as discriminative stimuli and as conditioned responses that come to guide and control overt behavior. The focus of treatment was to "decondition" and to strengthen new connections, bolster and rehearse adaptive coping skills, and the like. The technology of behavior therapy such as modeling, mental rehearsal, and contingency manipulations was used to alter not only clients' overt behaviors, but also their thoughts and feelings.

INFORMATION PROCESSING AS A METAPHOR

A different metaphor soon began to influence the development of CBM, namely, that of the mind as a computer, with the accompanying language of information processing and social learning theory. It was proposed that clients' cognitions could be conceptualized as consisting of a number of processes, including decoding, encoding, retrieval, preattention and attention, attributional biases, and distortion mechanisms, the last in the form of cognitive errors. Moreover, these cognitive errors were viewed as being a consequence of the cognitive structures or beliefs, schemata, current concerns, and tacit assumptions that clients brought to situations. It was proposed that such beliefs were strengthened by the manner in which clients behaved. The operable terms to depict this sequence were *transactional, interactional,* and *bidirectional,* as described by Lazarus and Folkman, Bandura, Wachtel, Kiesler, and Patterson. Individuals were viewed as "architects" of their experiences, influencing the data they were creating and collecting. Rather than being passive, the information-processing perspective proposed that individuals may inadvertently, if not unwittingly and even unknowingly, behave in ways that elicited the very reactions in others (a form of data) that they could take as evidence to confirm their views of themselves and of the world.

A number of investigators (e.g., Beck, 1970, and Hollon, 1990, who studied depression; Barlow, 1988, and Clark, 1986, who studied anxiety disorders; Dodge & Coie, 1987, and Novaco, 1979, who studied aggression in children and in adults, respectively; and Marlatt & Gordon, 1985, who studied clients with addiction problems) have used an information-processing perspective to explain their clients' difficulties and to formulate an intervention plan.

From an information-processing perspective, clients are seen to be depressed because they distort reality as a result of a number of cognitive errors (e.g., dichotomous thinking, magnification, and personalization) and because they hold so-called irrational beliefs. They also hold negative views of themselves, of the past, and of the future, emitting characterological attributions of self-blame when they encounter failures and frustrations. Anxious clients who have panic attacks are seen as misinterpreting bodily cues and viewing them as personal threats given their preoccupation with physical well-being and the need to maintain a sense of personal control. Such misinterpretations or appraisals lead to "catastrophic" anxiety-engendering ideation with accompanying physiological arousal, as a vicious self-perpetuating cycle is established and maintained. Those clients who have problems with anger and who are aggressive, especially if that aggressive behavior is reactive as opposed to instrumental in nature, have been found to hold hostile attributional styles: to interpret ambiguous interpersonal cues as provocations, retrieving from memory other aggressive events; and to fail to generate and implement socially acceptable alternatives. Moreover, aggressive clients, both children and adults, behave in ways that elicit the coercive and reciprocal reactions that confirm their aggressive outlooks. Thus, their expectations and self-statements become self-fulfilling prophecies.

Cognitive–behavioral therapists have developed intervention programs that are designed to help clients become aware of these processes and teach them how to notice, catch, monitor, and interrupt the cognitive–affective–behavioral chains and to produce more adaptive incompatible coping responses. Moreover, cognitive-behavioral therapists help clients to identify high-risk situations that they are likely to encounter and to consider ways to prepare, handle, and deal with failures if they should occur (namely, a form of relapse prevention). When positive results occur, clients are encouraged to make self-attributions for the changes that they have been able to bring about. Often, clients will require specific skills training, and treatment frequently involves significant others (spouse, family members, teachers, and peers) to increase the likelihood of generalization and maintenance.

CONSTRUCTIVE NARRATIVE AS A METAPHOR

The notion that clients are architects and constructors of their environments has given rise to a third metaphor that is guiding the present development of cognitive–behavioral therapies. The constructivist perspective is founded on the idea that humans actively construct their personal realities and create their own representational models of the world. This constructivist perspective finds root in the philosophical writings of Immanuel Kant, Ernst Cassirer, and Nelson Goodman and in the psychological writings of Willhelm Wundt, Alfred Adler, George Kelly, Jean Piaget, Viktor Frankl, and Jerome Frank. More recently, the constructivist perspective has been advocated by Epstein and Erskine (1983), Mahoney and Lyddon (1988), McCann and Perlman (1990), Neimeyer and Feixas (1990), Meichenbaum (1990), and White and Epston (1990). Common to each of these proponents is the tenet that the human mind is a product of constructive symbolic activity, and that reality is a product of personal meanings that individuals create. It is not as if there is one reality and clients distort that reality, thus contributing to their problems; rather, there are multiple realities, and the task for the therapist is to help clients become aware of how they create these realities and of the consequences of such constructions. Bruner (1990), writing from a narrative psychology perspective, described how individuals make meaning or construct stories to explain their symptoms and situations. For instance, clients may use metaphors to describe their emotional experience. One client recently reported that she "always stuffed her feelings down" and then she would explode; another patient described "how he built walls between himself and others." The therapist helped these clients to appreciate the nature and impact of using such metaphors. What is the impact, what is the emotional toll, what is the price they pay for behaving in accord with such a metaphor of "stuffing feelings" and "building walls"? At this point, the therapist explored collaboratively and experientially the "price" they paid. "If this is not the way they would like things to be, then what could they do?" It is not a big step for clients to suggest that perhaps they should "not stuff feelings" and "not build walls." The therapist then says, "Not stuff feelings, not build walls, that is interesting. What did you have in mind?" In this manner the therapist enlists the client as a collaborator in engaging in what Shafer (1981) called "narrative repair".

The metaphor of a constructive narrative to explain clients' problems has a number of important theoretical and practical implications for the further development of CBM.

1.   The therapist is viewed as a co-constructivist helping clients to alter their stories, as Spence (1984) proposed. The therapist must first listen empathically and reflectively to the initial story line of the patient and then collaboratively help the client to transform his or her story. A nurturant, compassionate, nonjudgmental set of conditions is required for distressed clients to tell their story at their own pace. A number of clinical techniques, including reflective listening, Socratic dialogue, sensitive probes, imagery reconstruction of stressful experiences, and client self-monitoring, are used to help clients relate what happened and why. Thus, the role of relationship variables is critical, as is the role of affect in the therapeutic process.

2.   The therapist helps clients to cognitively reframe stressful events and to "normalize" their reactions. From this perspective, it is not the symptoms of depression, anxiety, and anger per se that interfere with functioning; rather, what clients say to themselves and others about these reactions, the stories they construct, are important to the adaptive process. The therapist not only helps to validate clients' reactions but indicates that such symptoms are normal. In fact, their emotional distress is viewed as a normal spontaneous reconstructive and natural rehabilitative adaptive process. This reconceptualization process is an attempt to formulate a "healing theory" of what happened and why (see Meichenbaum & Fitzpatrick, in press, for a fuller discussion). The therapist also helps clients relate examples of their strengths, resources, and coping abilities to convey "the rest of the story" (to use a popular metaphor). The therapist avoids holding a pathology bias, instead

looking for and building on those exceptional occasions when clients coped effectively.

3. From a narrative perspective, the therapist not only helps clients to break down global stressors into behaviorally prescriptive events so they can use problem-solving and emotionally palliative coping techniques, but also helps them build new assumptive worlds and new ways to view themselves and the world (Meichenbaum, in press).

The cognitive therapist helps clients to construct narratives that fit their particular present circumstances, that are coherent, and that are adequate in capturing and explaining their difficulties. As Shafer (1981) indicated, therapy allows clients to retell their tale "in a way that allows them to understand the origins, meanings and significance of present difficulties, and moreover, to do so in a way that makes change conceivable and attainable" (p. 38). What matters most about this story telling or narrative construction is not its "historical truthfulness," as Spence (1984) observed, but its "narrative truthfulness."

4. One of the implications of adapting the constructive narrative metaphor is that it suggests that one look at therapeutic interventions in a different fashion. Perhaps, one can even find therapeutic suggestions from the way that teachers teach narrative writing. It also suggests different types of dependent measures that individuals can use (e.g., indicators of narrative transformations) .

The field of CBM has come a long way since its inception. The story continues to unfold and to change as new metaphors are adopted and new narratives constructed.

REFERENCES

Barlow, D. (1988). *Anxiety and its disorders: The nature and treatment of anxiety and panic.* New York: Guilford Press.

Beck, A. (1970). Cognitive therapy: Nature and relation to behavior therapy. *Behavior Therapy, 1,* 184–200.

Breger, L., & McGaugh, J. (1965). Critique and reformulation of "learning theory": Approaches to psychotherapy and neurosis. *Psychological Bulletin, 63,* 338–358.

Brewer, W. (1974). There is no convincing evidence for operant or classical conditioning in adult humans. In W. Weimer & D. Palermo (Eds.), *Cognition and the symbolic processes* (Vol. 1, pp. 1–42). Hillsdale, NJ: Erlbaum.

Bruner, J. (1990). *Acts of meaning.* Cambridge, MA: Harvard University Press.

Cautela, J. (1973). Covert processes and behavior modification. *Journal of Nervous and Mental Disease, 157,* 27–35.

Clark, D. M. (1986). A cognitive approach to panic. *Behaviour Research and Therapy, 24,* 461–470.

Dember, W. (1974). Motivation and the cognitive revolution. *American Psychologist, 29,* 161–168.

Dodge, K. A., & Coie, J. D. (1987). Social information-processing factors in reactive and proactive aggression in children's peer groups. *Journal of Personality and Social Psychology, 53,* 1146–1158.

Ellis, A. (1962). *Reason and emotion in psychotherapy.* New York: Lyle Stuart.

Epstein, S., & Erskine, N. (1983). The development of personal theories of reality. In D. Magnusson & V. Allen (Eds.), *Human development: An interactional perspective* (pp. 133–147). San Diego, CA: Academic Press.

Hollon, S. D. (1990). Cognitive therapy and pharmacotherapy for depression. *Psychiatric Annals, 20,* 249–258.

Homme, L. (1965). Perspectives in psychology: Control of coverants, the operants of the mind. *Psychological Record, 15,* 501–511.

Mahoney, M. (1974). *Cognition and behavior modification.* Cambridge, MA: Ballinger.

Mahoney, M. J., & Lyddon, W. J. (1988). Recent developments in cognitive approaches to counseling and psychotherapy. *The Counseling Psychologist, 16,* 190–234.

Marlatt, G. A., & Gordon, J. R. (1985). *Relapse prevention: Maintenance strategies in the treatment of addictive behaviors.* New York: Guilford Press.

McCann, I. L., & Periman, L. A. (1990). *Psychological trauma and the adult survivor.* New York: Brunner/Mazel.

McKeachie, W. (1974). The decline and fall of the laws of learning. *Educational Researcher, 3,* 7–11.

Meichenbaum, D. (1977). *Cognitive behavior modification: An integrative approach.* New York: Plerium Press.

Meichenbaum, D. (1990). Evolution of cognitive behavior therapy: Origins, tenets and clinical examples. In J. Zeig (Ed.), *The evolution of psychotherapy: II* (pp. 96–115). New York: Brunner/Mazel.

Meichenbaum, D. (in press). Stress inoculation training: A twenty year update. In R. L. Woolfolk & P. M. Lehrer (Eds.), *Principles and practices of stress management.* New York: Guilford Press.

Meichenbaum, D., & Fitzpatrick, D. (in press). A constructivist narrative perspective of stress and coping: Stress inoculation applications. In L. Goldberger & S. Breznitz (Eds.), *Handbook of stress.* New York: Free Press.

Neimeyer, R., & Feixas, G. (1990). Constructivist contributions to psychotherapy integration. *Journal of Integrative and Eclectic Psychotherapy, 9,* 4–20.

Novaco, R. (1979). The cognitive regulation of anger and stress. In P. C. Kendall & S. D. Hollon (Eds.), *Cognitive behavioral interventions: Theory, research and procedures* (pp. 84–101). San Diego, CA: Academic Press.

Shafer, R. (1981). Narration in the psychoanalytic dialogue. In W. J. Mitchell (Ed.), *On narrative* (pp. 212–253). Chicago: University of Chicago Press.

Spence, D. (1984). *Narrative truth and historical truth: Meaning and interpretation in psychoanalysis.* New York: Norton.

White, M., & Epton, D. (1990). *Narrative means to therapeutic ends.* New York: Norton.

II
Cognitive Therapy

3

Cognitive Therapy: Past, Present, and Future

Aaron T. Beck

Can a fledgling psychotherapy challenge the giants in the field—psycho-analysis and behavior therapy? (Beck, 1976, p. 333)

In the 16 years since I raised that question, substantial information has accumulated to address it. To make a judgment, I proposed a set of standards for evaluating a system of psychotherapy. A condensed ver-sion is as follows: (a) there should be empirical evidence to support the principles underlying the therapy, which should articulate with the techniques; and (b) the efficacy of the treatment should have empirical support (Beck, 1976, p. 308). In retrospect, I added that the system should the include "a tenable theory of personality and of the process of change" (Beck, 1991a, p. 192). Although there have been many defini-tions of cognitive therapy, I have been most satisfied with the notion that cognitive therapy is best viewed as the application of the cognitive model of a particular disorder with the use of a variety of techniques designed to modify the dysfunctional beliefs and faulty information processing characteristic of each disorder. The theory of personality and psychopathology has been described in a number of publications (e.g., see Beck & Weishaar, 1989). In this review, I will focus primarily on the reports regarding the efficacy of cognitive therapy in various disorders.

LOOKING BACK

Reflecting on the accumulated knowledge in 1990, I suggested that the crucial standards relevant to the application of cognitive therapy to the field of psychotherapy had largely been supported (Beck, 1991b). Also, there was growing support for the cognitive theory of personality and psychopathology. Literature reviews by Ernst (1985) and by Haaga, Dyck, and Ernst (1991), for example, indicated strong support for the "negativity hypothesis" of the cognitive model of depression. Other aspects of the cognitive model of depression received weaker support. The cognitive models of anxiety and of panic disorders have also received support from diverse sources, as has the cognitive model of suicide (Beck, 1986, 1987; Beck, Brown, Berchick, Stewart, & Steer, 1990).

A crucial question of special interest to the practitioner and consumer is "Does it work?" Past and current findings show significant empirical support for the applications of cognitive therapy to a variety of frequently occurring disorders, with a broad range of populations, and in a variety of settings (i.e., inpatient and outpatient) and formats (individual, couples, family, and group).

Depression

End-of-Treatment Analysis. Most of the outcome studies of cognitive therapy have been concerned with unipolar depression. Dobson (1989) conducted a meta-analysis of 27 separate studies involving 34 comparisons of cognitive therapy with either some other form of treatment or a wait-list control. His analysis showed that cognitive therapy was significantly superior to other treatments, including behavior therapy, psychodynamic therapy, nondirective therapy, and other psychotherapies; as expected, cognitive therapy was superior to no treatment. Cognitive therapy was found to be superior to pharmacotherapy as well; this comparison also included the results of the National Institute of Mental Health (NIMH) collaborative study of the treatment of depression (Elkin et al., 1989). Although the results at the end of treatment of this trial did not show a robust effect of cognitive therapy in comparison with the other groups, cognitive therapy appeared to have a more durable effect after treatment was concluded (see later discussion).

Follow-Up Analysis. Of importance is the fact that cognitive therapy has generally been found to be significantly more effective than pharmacotherapy on 1-year and 2-year follow-up. As summarized by Hollon and Najavits (1988), the relapse rate for cognitive therapy was approximately 30%, as compared with a relapse rate in excess of 60%

for the pharmacotherapy group. A 2-year follow-up by Blackburn, Eunson, and Bishop (1986) also demonstrated the superiority of cognitive therapy over pharmacotherapy. A more recent study by Shea et al. (1992) of patients in the NIMH collaborative study showed that at 6- and 18 month follow-up, cognitive therapy was nonsignificantly superior to pharmacotherapy and interpersonal psychotherapy and placebo with clinical management on 9 of 11 comparisons. Of particular interest was that cognitive therapy patients had a higher rate of "clinical recovery" as measured by end of treatment improvement that persisted for 8 weeks.

Generalized Anxiety Disorder

Cognitive therapy has also been found to be effective in the treatment of generalized anxiety disorder. An uncontrolled study by Sanderson and Beck (1990) showed a substantial and significant reduction in anxiety and depression in a sample of 32 patients treated with cognitive therapy for an average of 10 weeks of treatment. Patients with personality disorders in addition to generalized anxiety disorder also improved significantly, but the treatment was longer than for those without a personality disorder.

Anxiety management training (Blowers, Cobb, & Mathews, 1987) and cognitive–behavioral techniques (Durham & Turvey, 1987) have been used with promising results. These studies, however, were compromised by methodological inadequacies, in particular the use of nonstudy concomitant medication, that could have misleadingly distorted the nature of the presenting problem.

Borkovec and Mathews (1988) conducted one of the few studies to rule out the use of nonstudy concurrent medication. They found no difference in the efficacy of nondirective therapy, coping desensitization, and cognitive therapy in the treatment of generalized anxiety disorder and panic disorder.

Three studies compared the efficacy of cognitive–behavioral therapy with pharmacological alternatives in the management of generalized anxiety disorder. Lindsay, Gamsu, McLaughlin, Hood, and Elspie (1984) reported superiority for cognitive–behavioral therapy and anxiety management training as compared with lorazepam and a waiting-list control group at 3-month follow-up. Power, Jerrom, Simpson, Mitchell, and Swanson (1989) reported superiority of cognitive–behavioral therapy when compared with diazepam or placebo at the end of the study period and at 12-month follow-up.

Power et al. (1990) reported the results of a study of a controlled comparison of 101 patients meeting criteria of the *Diagnostic and Statis-*

tical Manual of Mental Disorders (3rd ed.; American Psychiatric Association, 1980) for generalized anxiety disorder who were randomly allocated to cognitive–behavioral therapy, diazepam, placebo, cognitive–behavioral therapy plus diazepam, or cognitive–behavioral therapy plus placebo, and treated over 10 weeks. Outcome measures at the end of treatment and at 6-month follow-up revealed the superiority of all cognitive–behavioral therapy treatments, especially cognitive–behavioral therapy alone and cognitive–behavioral therapy plus diazepam.

Butler, Fennell, Robson, and Gelder (1991) reported a controlled clinical trial of 57 patients meeting criteria for generalized anxiety disorder and fulfilling an additional severity criterion. Individual treatment of 12 sessions duration showed a clear advantage for cognitive–behavioral therapy over behavior therapy and a waiting-list control. There was no attrition from the cognitive–behavioral therapy group, although patients were lost from the behavior therapy. In summary, controlled trials support the efficacy of cognitive therapy for generalized anxiety disorder.

Panic Disorder

Cognitive therapy has been particularly effective in the treatment of panic disorder. An uncontrolled study conducted by Sokol, Beck, Greenberg, Wright, and Berchick (1989) at the Center for Cognitive Therapy in Philadelphia showed a complete cessation of panic attacks in all of the patients involved in the study. These gains were maintained at 1-year follow-up. A subsequent study at the same clinic compared cognitive therapy with supportive therapy (Beck, Sokol, Clark, Berchick, & Wright, in press). At the end of 8 weeks, there was significant improvement in the cognitive therapy treatment but not in the supportive treatment; the difference between the groups was statistically significant. The supportive group was then crossed over to 12 weeks of cognitive therapy. At the end of 12 weeks of cognitive therapy, both the original cognitive therapy group and the crossover group had a minimum number of panic attacks. These results held for 1 year.

Clark (1991) reported statistically significant superiority of cognitive therapy over behavior therapy, imipramine, and placebo control at the end of treatment, and this superiority persisted until the end of 1-year follow-up.

Another index of the effectiveness of cognitive therapy is the reduction of antipanic medication. Newman, Beck, Beck, Tran, and Brown (1990) reported the results of cognitive therapy with two groups of patients: those who were receiving medication when they entered into the study and those who were not. The "medicated" group and the nonmedicated group showed substantial improvement. In addition, there was a 90% reduction of antipanic medication in the medicated group without any rebound effect or relapse. This study showed that applying the standard principles of cognitive therapy to the withdrawal symptoms enabled the patient to tolerate them without experiencing a recurrence of panic attacks.

Eating Disorders

Eating disorders appear to be responsive to cognitive therapy. Fairburn et al. (1991) reported that cognitive–behavioral therapy with bulimia patients was more effective than both interpersonal psychotherapy and a simplified behavioral version of cognitive–behavioral therapy. Agras et al. (1992) found that a combination of maintenance imipramine and cognitive–behavioral therapy produced better long-term results than imipramine alone, cognitive therapy alone, or placebo.

LOOKING AHEAD

One of the interesting developments in the application of cognitive therapy has been the formulation of a specific cognitive model for each of the "new" disorders. A central theme of the applications has been, first, the general framework of cognitive theory, namely, that there is a bias in information processing that produces dysfunctional behavior, excessive distress, or both. Second, specific beliefs incorporated into relatively stable structures—schemata—lead to these difficulties (the concept of cognitive specificity). Even when more traditional therapy formats (e.g., couples therapy or family therapy) have been retained, cognitive therapists have explored and evaluated dysfunctional beliefs and interpretations. The addition of the cognitive dimension has facilitated a more powerful approach (Beck, 1 991b).

Drug abuse patients have a series of "need" beliefs such as "I can't stand my boredom (anxiety, depression, etc.) without a fix" and permission beliefs such as "It's okay to have a smoke this one time." Addiction is viewed as based on a cluster of beliefs of this nature (Beck, Wright, Newman, & Liese, in press). An outcome study of cognitive therapy for cocaine addiction is currently under way at the University of Pennsylvania.

Studies of *bipolar disorder* are currently under way at the University of Texas in Dallas with a treatment manual (Basco & Rush, 1991). A similar study with rapid cycling bipolar affective disorder is being conducted at the University of Pennsylvania with a treatment manual authored by Newman and Beck (1992). The focus is on beliefs that undermine medication compliance (e.g., "The medication destroys my creativity, makes me a dull person, etc.") and on manic beliefs (e.g., "I have exceptional powers and should use them"), as well as on the basic depressotypic beliefs (Weissman & Beck, 1978).

Depression in patients who have tested positive for *human immunodeficiency virus* (HIV) is the subject of an outcome trial at Cornell Medical School involving the use of a treatment manual developed by Fishman (1990). A typical belief is "I am a social outcast (helpless, worthless, unlovable) because I have a dirty disease."

Outcome studies for cognitive therapy of *avoidant personality disorder* and *obsessive-compulsive disorder* are in progress at the University of Pennsylvania. The treatment manual (Beck, Freeman, & Associates, 1990) lists 140 beliefs covering all of the various personality disorders. A typical avoidant belief is "I must avoid sticking my neck out (taking chances, confrontations, experiencing distress, etc.)." Obsessive-compulsive beliefs include "I must follow a foolproof system or there will be chaos."

Studies of *sex offenders* are being conducted at the University of Oklahoma and elsewhere (Cole, 1989). A typical belief of an incest offender is "Sex with my daughter will be good for our relationship and will help her to mature."

Posttraumatic stress disorders are the subject of many studies, particularly in the United Kingdom. The work on rape victims by D. M. Clark (personal communication, December 7, 1991) at Oxford, for example, goes beyond standard revivification of traumatic episodes and focuses on the victims' specific beliefs, such as "This (rape incident) proves that I am just an object" or "I am worthless because I felt some pleasure."

Cognitive therapy is being applied in an interesting way to *multiple personalities* by Fine (in press). Cognitive techniques are used to elicit and restructure the basic beliefs of each of the "personalities" as they surface. An example is "If I kill Dora (another personality), I will be free." Strategies are used to demonstrate the unity of the entire person and the distinctiveness of the beliefs. By restructuring the separate sets of beliefs, the therapist attempts to facilitate the reintegration of the personality.

Hypochondriasis has been targeted as a disorder amenable to cognitive therapy (Warwick, 1991; Warwick & Salkovskis, 1989). Typical beliefs are "The sensations I feel must be due to a serious illness" and "Even though the doctors haven't found any pathology so far, I must have another examination." Preliminary findings indicate a notable improvement with cognitive therapy when compared with a control group not receiving any psychological intervention.

Obsessive-compulsive disorder has been studied extensively by Salkovskis (1989), who proceeded beyond the standard behavioral approach and focused on cognitions and beliefs aroused by the obsessive thoughts; for example, "I must be crazy to have thoughts like this" or "It will be my fault if I don't do something about the (presumed) danger." Outcome studies are currently evaluating this approach.

Approaches to marital problems are being investigated by Epstein (University of Maryland) and Beck (University of Pennsylvania). Texts relevant to couples therapy (Epstein & Baucom, 1988) and self-help for couples (Beck, 1988) depict the typical dysfunctional beliefs, such as "If we can't talk about our problems, our marriage is in trouble" (mostly wives) and "If we have to talk about our problems, our marriage is in trouble" (mostly husbands).

Cognitive *family therapy* has been formulated recently and focuses on the conflicting beliefs of family members. Examples of such beliefs are "A child needs continuous love and care" (mother); "A child needs discipline" (father); and "I need to be left alone" (child). Such conflicting beliefs lead to accusations of "indulging the child" (by the father) and "being too harsh" (by the mother) and to the wish, on the part of the child, to run away. This formulation has been expanded by Wright and Beck (in press).

Cognitive *group therapy* has been used extensively (Freeman, 1983). Among the many therapeutic techniques are the elucidation of the basic beliefs of individual group members and their testing and evaluation by the rest of the group. Some beliefs relevant to the group that emerge are "I appear like a fool in a group" and "I am basically undesirable."

Schizophrenic delusions and hallucinations have been studied extensively by Hole, Rush, and Beck (1979) and Kingdon and Turkington (1991). In addition to working with the patients to list their distorted conclusions, the therapists address basic beliefs, such as "If I hear voices, it means somebody is trying to control my mind" and "Being mentally ill means I am helpless (worthless, undesirable)."

The literature on schizophrenia suggests that the prognosis in terms of recurrence or rehospitalization for schizophrenics is worse for patients in families who show high levels of expressed emotions (mostly negative emotions) toward the patients.

Although the causal link has not as yet been established, further work needs to be done in terms of exploring the family's cognitions, their relationship to expressed emotions and to prognosis, and the interactions of the familial cognitions with those of the patients. There is also some evidence that higher levels of family blame of the patient are associated with higher levels of expressed emotion (Halford, 1991). Future analyses should examine how this affects the patients, particularly in terms of their beliefs about their inadequacy and social isolation, their hopelessness, and their self-criticism (Halford, 1991).

If meaningful relationships are established, then the particular cognitions of the family and of the schizophrenic member can become a focus for cognitive interventions, in cognitive family therapy as well as in individual cognitive therapy.

Cognitive therapy has been used in a number of other clinical conditions: a detailed treatment summary has been presented in *Cognitive Therapy in Clinical Practice* (Scott, Williams, & Beck 1989). Of particular interest is the application of cognitive therapy to the mentally handicapped and cancer patients (Scott, 1989).

A monograph on cognitive therapy with *cancer patients* that served as a basis for a treatment trial has been produced by Moorey and Greer (1989). A preliminary study indicated that patients in a cognitive group therapy modality showed a greater reduction of dysphoria symptoms than did a control group. Long-term follow-up examining the effects on survival is now being carried out.

Many of the other new areas in which there has been preliminary support for the application of cognitive therapy have been reported in the *Comprehensive Casebook of Cognitive Therapy*, cited by Freeman and Dattilio (in press). Although these reports do not in themselves establish the efficacy of cognitive therapy for these conditions, they can help the clinician in formulating and adapting strategies for cases involving these problems. They can also provide an impetus for controlled outcome studies. It should be noted that much of the controlled research in the past was stimulated by case reports. Chapters detailing treatment in these promising applications address the following disorders and problems: performance anxiety, posttraumatic stress disorder, stress in general, adjustment disorder, dysthymia, obesity, schizotypal personality disorder, poststroke depression, multiple personality disorder, and chronic pain. There are also chapters on the application of cognitive therapy to children, adolescents, and elderly patients.

A summary of the most recent applications of cognitive therapies to a variety of disorders and problems described in papers and posters at the World Congress of Cognitive Therapy in Toronto in June 1992 illustrates the breadth of the principles of cognitive therapy and, I hope, will serve as a stimulus for systematic research: chronic pain, criminal offenders, social phobia, chronic headaches, chronic tic disorders, HIV-related distress, alcoholism, morbid jealousy, irritable bowel syndrome, insomnia, schizophrenic disorder, guilt and shame, nicotine addiction, chest pain, organic brain damage, shoplifting, generalized tic disorder, and sexual problems.

It may be obvious to spectators in the therapeutic arena that cognitive therapy has co-opted (or been co-opted by) a large sector of the behavior therapy approaches to psychopathology. What may not be so readily discerned are many concepts derived initially from psychoanalysis (e.g., the emphasis on identifying the [conscious] meanings of pathogenic events) and the conceptualization of separate modes of cognitive processing (the reflective rational vs. the automatic nonrational), corresponding, in part, to Freudian notions of primary and secondary processing. Considerable research using strategies from cognitive psychology has supported the theoretical foundations of cognitive therapy. The very broad application of the theory and strategies bolsters the claim of cognitive therapy as a robust system of psychotherapy.

REFERENCES

Agras, W. S., Rottister, E. M., Arnow, B., Schneider, J. H., Telch, C. S., Raeburn, S. D., Bruce B., Perl, M., & Koran, L. M. (1992). Pharmacologic and cognitive-behavioral treatment for bulimia nervosa: A controlled comparison. *American Journal of Psychiatry, 149,* 82–87

American Psychiatric Association. (1980). *Diagnostic and statistical manual of mental disorders* (3rd ed.). Washington, DC: Author.

Basco, M. R., & Rush, A. J. (1991). *A psychosocial treatment package for bipolar I disorder.* Unpublished manuscript, Mental Health Clinical Research Center and Department of Psychiatry, University of Texas Southwestern Medical Center, Dallas.

Beck, A. T. (1976). *Cognitive therapy and the emotional disorders.* New York: International Universities Press.

Beck, A. T. (1986). Theoretical perspectives on clinical anxiety. In A. H. Tuma & J. D. Maser (Eds.), Anxiety and the anxiety disorders (pp. 183–196). Hillsdale, NJ: Erlbaum.

Beck, A. T. (1987). Cognitive approaches to panic disorder: Theory and therapy. In S. Rachman & J. Maser (Eds.), *Panic: Psychological perspectives* (pp. 91–109). Hillsdale, NJ: Erlbaum.

Beck, A. T. (1988). *Love is never enough.* New York: Harper & Row.

Beck, A. T. (1991a). Cognitive therapy as *the* integrative therapy: A reply to Alford and Norcross [Commentary]. *Journal of Psychotherapy Integration, 1,* 191–198.

Beck, A. T. (1991b). Cognitive therapy: A 30-year retrospective. *American Psychologist, 46,* 368–375.

Beck. A. T., Brown, G., Berchick, R. J., Stewart, B., & Steer, R. A. (1990). Relationship between hopelessness and ultimate suicide: A replication with psychiatric outpatients. *American Journal of Psychiatry, 147,*190–195,

Beck, A. T., Freeman, A., & Associates. (1990). *Cognitive therapy of personality disorders.* New York: Guilford Press.

Beck, A. T., Sokol, L., Clark, D. A., Berchick, R. J., & Wright, F. D. (in press). Focused cognitive therapy of panic disorder: A crossover design and one year follow-up. *American Journal of Psychiatry.*

Beck, A. T., & Weishaar., M. E. (1989). Cognitive therapy. In D. Wedding & R. Corsini (Eds.), *Current psychotherapies* (4th ed.). Ithaca, IL: Peacock.

Beck, A. T., Wright, F. D., Newman, C. F., & Liese, B. S. (In press). *Cognitive therapy of drug abuse.* New York: Guilford Press.

Blackburn, I. M., Eunson, K. M., & Bishop, S. (1986). A two-year naturalistic follow-up of depressed patients treated with cognitive therapy, pharmacotherapy, and a combination of both. *Journal of Affective Disorders.,10,* 67–75.

Blowers, C., Cobb, J., & Mathews, A. (1987). Generalized anxiety: A controlled treatment study. *Behaviour Research and Therapy, 25,* 493–502.

Borkovec, T. D., & Mathews, A. M. (1988). Treatment of nonphobic anxiety: A comparison of nondirective, cognitive, and coping desensitization therapy. *Journal of Consulting and Clinical Psychology, 56,* 877–884.

Butler, G., Fennell, M., Robson, P., & Gelder, H. (1991). Comparison of behavior therapy and cognitive behavior therapy in the treatment of generalized anxiety disorder. *Journal of Consulting and Clinical Psychology, 59,* 167–175.

Clark, D. M. (1991, September). *Cognitive therapy for panic disorder.* Paper presented at the National Institutes of Health Consensus Development Conference on the Treatment of Panic Disorder, Bethesda, MD.

Cole, A. (1989). Offenders. In J. Scott, J. M. G. Williams, & A. T. Beck (Eds.), *Cognitive therapy in clinical practice* (pp. 183–205). London: Routledge & Kegan Paul.

Dobson, K. (1989). A meta-analysis of the efficacy of cognitive therapy for depression. *Journal of Consulting and Clinical Psychology, 57,* 414–419.

Durham, R. C., & Turvey, A. A. (1987). Cognitive therapy vs. behavior therapy in the treatment of chronic anxiety. *Behaviour Research and Therapy, 25,* 229–234.

Elkin, I., Shea, M. T., Watkins, J. T., Imber, S. D., Sotsky, S. M., Collins, I. F., Glass, D. R., Pilkonis, P. A., Leber, W. R., Docherty, J. P., Fiester, S. J., & Parloff, M. B. (1989). NIMH treatment of depression collaborative research program: General effectiveness of treatments. *Archives of General Psychiatry, 46,* 971–982.

Epstein, N., & Baucom, D. (1988). Cognitive–behavioral marital therapy. New York: Brunner/Mazel.

Ernst, D. (1985). *Beck's cognitive theory of depression: A status report.* Unpublished manuscript, University of Pennsylvania, Philadelphia.

Fairburn, C. G., Jones, R., Peveler, R. C., Carr, S. J., Solomon, R. A., O'Connor, M . E., Burton, J., & Hope, R. A. (1991). Three psychological treatments for bulimia nervosa. *Archives of General Psychiatry, 48,* 463–469.

Fine, C. G. (in press). The treatment of multiple personality disorder. In A.

Freeman & F. M. Dattilio (Eds.), *Comprehensive casebook of cognitive therapy.* New York: Plenum Press.

Fishman, B. (1990). *Stress prevention training after HIV antibody testing: A training manual.* Unpublished manuscript, Cornell Medical School, Ithaca, NY.

Freeman, A. (Ed.). (1983). *Cognitive therapy with couples and groups.* New York: Plenum Press.

Freeman, A., & Dattilio, F. M. (in press). *Comprehensive casebook of cognitive therapy.* New York: Plenum Press.

Haaga, D. A. F., Dyck, M. J., & Ernst, D. (1991). Empirical status of cognitive theory of depression. *Psychological Bulletin, 110,* 215–236.

Halford, W. K. (1991). Beyond expressed emotion: Behavioral assessment of family interaction associated with the course of schizophrenia. *Behavioral Assessment, 13,* 99–123.

Hole, R. W., Rush, A. J., & Beck, A. T. (1979). A cognitive investigation of schizophrenic delusions. *Psychiatry, 42,* 312–319.

Hollon, S. D., & Najavits, L. (1988). Review of empirical studies on cognitive therapy. In A. J. Frances & R. E. Sales (Eds.), *American Psychiatric Press review of psychiatry* (Vol. 7, pp. 643–666). Washington, DC: American Psychiatric Press.

Kingdon, D. G., & Turkington, D. (1991). The use of cognitive behavior therapy with a normalizing rationale in schizophrenia: Preliminary report. *Journal of Nervous and Mental Disease, 179,* 207–211.

Lindsay, W. R., Gamsu, T. V., McLaughlin, E., Hood, E. M., & Elspie, C. A. (1984). A controlled trial of treatments of generalized anxiety. *British Journal of Clinical Psychology, 26,* 3–16.

Moorey, S., & Greer, S. (1989). *Psychological therapy for patients with cancer: A new approach.* Oxford, England: Heinemann Medical Books.

Newman, C. F., Beck, J. S., Beck, A. T., Tran, G. Q., & Brown, G. K. (1990, November). *Efficacy of cognitive therapy for panic disorder in medicated and nonmedicated populations.* Poster presented at the conference of the Association for the Advancement of Behavior Therapy, San Francisco.

Newman, C. F., & Beck, A. T. (1992). *Cognitive therapy for panic depressive disorder.* Unpublished manuscript, University of Pennsylvania, Philadelphia.

Power, K. G., Jerrom, D. W. A., Simpson, R. J., Mitchell, M. J., & Swanson, V. (1989). A controlled comparison of cognitive behaviour therapy, diazepam and placebo in the management of generalized anxiety. *Behavioural Psychotherapy, 17,* 1–14.

Power, K. G., Simpson, R. J., Swanson, V., Wallace, L. A., Feistner, A. T. C., & Sharp, D. (1990). A controlled comparison of cognitive behavior therapy, diazepam, and placebo, alone and in combination, for the treatment of generalized anxiety disorder. *Journal of Anxiety Disorders, 4,* 267–292.

Salkovskis, P. M. (1989). Obsessions and compulsions. In J. Scott, J. M. G. Williams, & A. T. Beck (Eds.), *Cognitive therapy in clinical practice* (pp. 50–77). London: Routledge & Kegan Paul.

Sanderson, W. C., & Beck, A. T. (1990). Syndrome comorbidity in patients with major depression or dysthymia: Prevalence and temporal relationships. *American Journal of Psychiatry, 147,* 1025–1028.

Scott, J. (1989). Cancer patients. In J. Scott, J. M. G. Williams, & A. T.: Beck (Eds.), *Cognitive therapy in clinical practice* (pp. 103–126). London: Routledge & Kegan Paul.

Scott, J., Williams, J. M. G., & Beck, A. T. (Eds.). (1989). *Cognitive therapy in clinical practice.* London: Routledge & Kegan Paul.

Shea, M. T., Elkin, I., Imber, S. D., Sotsky, S. M., Watkins, J. T., Collins, J. F., Pilkonis, P. A., Leber, W. R., Krupnick, J., Dolan, R. T., & Parloff, M. B. (1992). Course of depressive symptoms over follow-up: Findings from the National Institute of Mental Health treatment of depression collaborative research program. *Archives of General Psychiatry, 49,* 782–787.

Sokol, L., Beck, A. T., Greenberg, R. L., Wright, F. D., & Berchick, R. J. (1989). Cognitive therapy of panic disorder: A nonpharmacological alternative. *Journal of Nervous and Mental Disease, 177,* 711–716.

Warwick, H. M. C. (1991, July). *A controlled trial of cognitive therapy for hypochondriasis.* Paper presented at the 20th Annual Conference of the British Association of Behavioural Psychotherapy, Oxford, England.

Warwick, H. M. C., & Salkovskis, P. M. (1989). Hypochondriasis. In J. Scott, J. M. G. Williams, & A. T. Beck (Eds.), *Cognitive therapy in clinical practice* (pp. 78–102). London: Routledge & Kegan Paul.

Weissman, A., & Beck, A. T. (1978, November). *Development and validation of the dysfunctional attitude scale.* Paper presented at the annual convention of the Association for Advancement of Behavior Therapy, Chicago.

Wright, J. H., & Beck, A. T. (in press). Family cognitive therapy with inpatients: Part 2. In J. H. Wright, M. E. Thase, & A. T. Beck (Eds.), *The cognitive milieu: Inpatient applications of cognitive therapy.* New York: Guilford Press.

4

An Appraisal of Cognitive Therapy

Clive J. Robins and Adele M. Hayes

Because other chapters in this volume deal with therapy approaches that broadly could be termed cognitive, we have limited our appraisal to that form of cognitive therapy (CT) developed by Aaron T. Beck and his colleagues and to recent developments that have a fairly direct historical lineage to this approach. We focus on the theory and practice of CT; the evidence regarding cognitive models of psychopathology is reviewed elsewhere (Haaga, Dyck, & Ernst, 1991; Robins & Hayes, in press), and the outcome literatures on CT are evaluated in other articles in this section.

DEVELOPMENT OF COGNITIVE THERAPY

In an attempt to verify aspects of psychoanalytic theory, Beck initially investigated the thoughts and dreams of depressed individuals, looking for signs of repressed hostility. Instead, he discovered a prominent theme of defeat and a pervasive negative bias. He then began to develop a theory centered on the premise that the symptoms of depression could be conceived of as a direct result of this negative cognitive bias. In the first detailed exposition of this model, Beck (1967) differentiated among three levels of cognition that may play a role in depression and its treatment: *automatic thoughts, schemata* or underlying assumptions, and *cognitive distortions.*

Cognitve Model of Psychopathology

Automatic thoughts can be considered a surface level of cognition that can be brought into awareness fairly readily by the patient and clinician. Depressed people typically have negative thoughts about themselves, their world, and their future (the depressive triad) that embody themes of worthlessness, guilt, incompetence, defeat, deprivation, loneliness, and hopelessness. Other disorders are characterized by different distinctive thoughts. For example, patients with anxiety disorders frequently experience thoughts concerning perceived danger. These types of thoughts (or images) are referred to as "automatic" because they typically arise spontaneously, frequently are very fleeting, and may even go unrecognized unless the patient is directed to deliberately monitor them. These automatic thoughts, which reflect the individual's appraisal of a situation rather than the actual objective situation, lead directly to the patient's emotional and behavioral responses. These responses will be maladaptive to the extent that the appraisals are distorted or exaggerated, which will occur when they arise from the operation of dysfunctional schemata.

Schemata can be considered internal models of aspects of the self and the world that individuals use to perceive, code, and recall information. They develop over the course of numerous particular experiences and are adaptive insofar as they facilitate more efficient information processing. They enable new information to be linked to old information so that it can be recognized and recalled more readily and appropriate action can be taken as needed. As studies in experimental cognitive psychology and social cognition have shown, however, this efficiency automatically involves a bias toward encoding and retrieving schema-consistent information, at the expense of counterschematic information (Goldfried & Robins, 1983). The assimilation of new information to a schema occurs much more easily than accommodation of a schema to new information. Cognitive theories of psychopathology hold that individuals with emotional disorders have particular schemata that bias them toward perceiving situations in terms of loss, danger, or other types of threats to the self. Schemata organized around these themes may be universal because of their adaptational value: however, for some individuals, they are more strongly developed because of their own particular developmental experiences. Although these schemata may be relatively dormant at most times, they can become activated by the occurrence of certain stressful life events or negative mood states. Once activated, these schemata may dominate an individual's perception of new situations, thus maintaining the emotional state.

Cognitive distortions are the links between dysfunctional schemata and automatic thoughts. When new information or memories are cognitively processed, the information often is distorted or biased to fit a relevant schema. The result of this biased appraisal may then become accessible to consciousness in the form of automatic thoughts or images. Beck (1967, 1976) has described a number of specific types of distortions that tend to be present in the thoughts of individuals with emotional disorders. In *dichotomous thinking,* only one or both of two extreme alternatives are considered. In *overgeneralizing,* a single instance is taken as representative of a broader class of situations or characteristics. In *selective abstraction,* some aspects of a situation, typically negative, are attended to or remembered, at the expense of other, more positive aspects. In *mind reading,* the attitudes or future actions of others are assumed without evidence. In *personalizing,* it is assumed that an action is directed toward, or occurs because of, oneself, rather than some other aspect of the situation. In *should statements,* absolute imperatives are expressed regarding the individual's or others' behavior. In *catastrophizing,* extreme negative outcomes are anticipated without substantial evidence. In *minimizing,* the reverse of catastrophizing, the significance of positive outcomes is downplayed. Although these types of cognitive distortion can be conceptually separated, any given thought may reflect more than one type of distortion.

The cognitive model recognizes that mood influences cognition, as well as the reverse, and that cognitions also influence behavior in ways that may generate stressful situations about which individuals, in turn, will have upsetting cognitions. Thus, cognition plays just one role in an interwoven, dynamic sequence of influences. However, the model emphasizes the influence of cognition on mood and behavior, and interventions primarily aim to change patients' cognitive processes.

Cognitive Approach to Psychotherapy

Initially, a primary goal of CT is to provide symptomatic relief by helping patients to become aware of and challenge their negative automatic thoughts and imagery. It is believed that for change to be enduring, there also has to be a focus, particularly later in therapy, on restructuring the dysfunctional attitudes and belief systems that are responsible for the automatic thoughts (Beck, Rush, Shaw, & Emery, 1979).

The nature of the therapeutic relationship in CT is somewhat different than in many other therapies. Beck (1967) has referred to CT as a process of "collaborative empiricism," whereby the therapist and patient work together to establish goals, to set an agenda for each therapy session, and to systematically gather and examine evidence for or against the patient's beliefs, in a manner analogous to the scientific method of hypothesis testing. Hypothesis testing is facilitated by the use of Socratic questioning by the therapist, rather than by direct challenging of the patient's thoughts and beliefs. The patient is helped to make guided discoveries and to design behavioral experiments to test the validity of his or her automatic thoughts and assumptions. The cognitive therapist may also act in a more directive manner as an educator and skills trainer.

Although cognitive therapists typically use a variety of behavioral methods, including activity scheduling, graded task assignments, behavior rehearsal, problem solving, and relaxation training, these are viewed primarily as methods to help patients test and modify their beliefs about themselves. CT has also developed its own relatively unique therapeutic methods. Patients are asked fairly early in the course of therapy to begin to monitor their negative thoughts in a systematic manner and to attend to the links among situations, thoughts, and feelings. Through Socratic questioning, the therapist helps the patient to examine these thoughts and to generate other alternatives. A number of cognitive techniques for challenging such thoughts have been described (e.g., Beck et al., 1979; Burns, 1980; Freeman, Pretzer, Fleming, & Simon, 1990), including helping the patient to label the distortion, examining evidence for and against an assumption, challenging absolute statements by using scaling, evaluating the probabilities of outcomes, and examining other possible explanations or attributions for events. Changes in these thoughts then lead to changes in feelings and behavior. Through the process of observing themes across automatic thoughts, the therapist and patient gradually develop some hypotheses regarding possible underlying schemata. Underlying schemata also can be discovered by the vertical exploration or "downward arrow" technique (Burns, 1980), in which the consequences of a particular thought are repeatedly drawn out. In this way, the focus can shift from thoughts about particular situations to more general concerns. Once such dysfunctional schemata have been identified, patients can be encouraged to test their validity and to monitor their ongoing reactions to determine when a particular schema may be operating.

As Goldfried and Robins (1983) have pointed out, changes in views of the self often lag behind behavior changes. They suggested that it is helpful for therapists to explain to patients the resistance of schemata to change, and they provided several guidelines to assist in the modification of schemata. In addition to encouraging new behaviors so as to provide potential disconfirmatory evidence, the therapist can help patients to update their self-schemata by (a) helping them to compare their present and past functioning as treatment progresses, rather than comparing their present functioning with some ideal or how others behave; (b) adding an objective vantage point to their subjective outlook, through the use of therapist feedback and reflection, self-monitoring, and arranging for social feedback from others; and (c) helping them to retrieve from memory success experiences in disconfirming schemata (a helpful aid is to keep logs of successes).

APPLICATIONS OF COGNITIVE THERAPY

CT has been one of the most widely researched psychotherapies, particularly CT for depression. Because our focus is on the theory and practice of CT, we do not attempt to review the outcome literature here; rather, we note the variety of conditions to which CT has been applied and make some general conclusions about its effectiveness for different disorders.

CT was developed initially for the treatment of depression, and most of the earlier studies focused on depressed outpatients (Craighead, Evans, & Robins, 1992). Dobson's (1989) meta-analysis of 28 studies of the treatment of depression found that CT outperformed pharmacotherapy, behavior therapy, and other psychotherapies. However, Hollon, Shelton, and Loosen (1991) have noted that these studies often contained no placebo control group and that the pharmacotherapy in many studies may have been inadequate. A more cautious interpretation of the data may be that CT is approximately equivalent to pharmacotherapy in the treatment of an acute episode. There is some promising evidence that CT may help prevent relapse into depressive episodes, although this evidence is based on only a handful of studies (Blackburn, Eunson, & Bishop, 1986; Evans et al., 1992; Simons, Murphy, Levine, & Wetzel, 1986). The few studies have examined whether combining CT with pharmacotherapy enhances the effectiveness of either have shown evidence of an additive effect (Hollon et al., 1991). Although CT may be less effective with more severely depressed patients (Elkin et al., 1989; Thase, Bowler, & Harden, 1991), several recent studies suggest that it can be effective even with this population (Bowers, 1990; Norman, Keitner, Bishop, & Dow, 1989; Thase, Bowler, & Harden, 1991). In an uncontrolled trial, Thase et al. (1991) reported strong and significant reductions in depressive symptoms among unmedicated, endogenously depressed inpatients.

Since its initial development, CT has been applied to a variety of other disorders, including anger management, anxiety disorders, personality disorders, psychophysiological disorders, marital discord, eating disorders, addictive disorders, various childhood difficulties (see reviews by Beckham & Watkins, 1989; Hollon & Najavits, 1988; and several chapters in this volume). However, in most cases treatment has combined cognitive and behavioral methods, and there is, as yet, little empirical demonstration of the utility of CT as such with these disorders. One exciting new area of application of CT is in panic disorder Recent studies have found that approximately 90% of panic disorder patients are panic-free after 3 months of such treatment (Barlow, Craske, Cerny, & Klosko, 1989; Clark, Salkovskis, Hackmann, & Gelder, 1991; Sokol, Beck, Greenberg, Wright, & Berchick, 1989). Although these treatments combine several components, cognitive restructuring has a major role and has been demonstrated to be as effective as exposure therapy in a dismantling study (Margraf & Schneider, 1991). Furthermore, there is some initial evidence that changes in cognitions regarding the consequences of panic-related bodily sensations may be a primary mechanism of change in CT, exposure, and psychopharmacological treatment of panic (Clark et al., 1991).

There has been much recent interest in, and literature describing CT for personality disorders (Beck, Freeman, & Associates. 1990; Young, 1990). Because personality disorders can be viewed as reflecting deeply ingrained and pervasive maladaptive schemata, CT seems a particularly appropriate treatment. Given the well-known intractability of these disorders, the methods of CT have been somewhat modified for treating them, along lines that we discuss later in this chapter. However, there is, as yet, no empirical evidence regarding the effectiveness of CT for personality disorders. Because of such factors as the longer treatment and the less focused target symptoms of personality disorders, outcome research on their treatment is likely more difficult than for Axis I disorders. Nevertheless, it remains an extremely important direction for future research.

HOW DOES COGNITIVE THERAPY WORK?

The process of effective therapy can be understood from two perspectives: the components of the treatment package that are associated with improvement, and changes in the patient over the course of therapy. Process research in CT is a relatively new endeavor; thus, few studies have been conducted, and the majority of them have examined CT for depression. We next review what is known from these studies about how CT works.

Components of Cognitive Therapy Associated with Change

According to Beck (Beck et al., 1979), the effects of CT result from interventions designed to identify, reality-test, and correct distorted conceptualizations and the dysfunctional schemata that underlie them. Several studies support this assertion.

DeRubeis and Feeley (1990) identified two types of CT techniques in a factor analysis of the Collaborative Study Psychotherapy Rating Scale (CSPRS; Hollon et al., 1988): Concrete and Abstract Methods. The concrete methods focus on teaching hypothesis-testing skills by having patients examine specific beliefs, conduct direct tests of these beliefs, and practice hypothesis-testing skills in specific between-session exercises. The abstract methods involve explorations of the deeper meaning of patients' thoughts (underlying assumptions) and discussions about the nature of the therapy sessions. The use of concrete methods by therapists predicted subsequent change in depressed mood, but use of the abstract components did not.

The contributions of several of the specific concrete techniques to symptom reduction have been examined separately. Several studies have found that when therapists teach patients to test their beliefs and restructure their negative thoughts, rather than just to gather information on their negative thinking, patients show more change in automatic negative thoughts and depression at the end of a session (Persons & Burns, 1985; Teasdale & Fennell, 1982) and more improvement in depressive symptoms at the end of treatment (Hayes, Castonguay, & Goldfried, 1992; Jarrett & Nelson, 1987).

In addition to hypothesis testing during therapy sessions, CT emphasizes the between-session application of these skills by the patient. In support of this emphasis, less depression at the end of treatment has been associated with the assignment (Hayes et al., 1992) and completion (Persons, Burns, & Perloff, 1988) of more between-session exercises, and there is some evidence that this effect is not due simply to differences in motivation or willingness to use active coping strategies (Burns & Nolen-Hoeksema, 1991). Future studies could track the relationship between the use of these skills and cognitive change and symptom status over the follow-up period.

Overall, the few studies available support teaching hypothesis-testing skills and between-session practice of these skills as possible active ingredients of CT, although further research is clearly warranted. Cognitive therapists appear to be targeting cognitive change, but it remains to be determined whether their interventions are inducing changes in the depressogenic schemata (accommodation), deactivating them and activating nondepressive schemata, or teaching the patient mood-correcting, compensatory skills to use to cope with depressive thoughts (Barber & DeRubeis, 1989; Evans & Hollon, 1988).

When examining the importance of components thought to be specific to CT, it is important to consider their contribution relative to the more general components of therapy, such as warmth, rapport, support, and empathy. Evidence thus far suggests that the cognitive therapy-specific interventions for depression are associated with symptom reduction beyond the effects due to the more general therapy factors for depression (Burns & Nolen-Hoeksema, 1992; DeRubeis & Feeley, 1990; Evans et al., 1992: Hayes et al., 1992). Similarly, CT for anxiety disorders consistently performs better than support alone, suggesting that it has specific effects beyond general therapy factors (Beck, Sokol, Clark, Berchick, & Wright, 1991; Heimberg & Barlow, 1991). It is likely that most therapists consistently provide a facilitative interpersonal environment as the base upon which the active ingredients of therapy can work.

Changes in the Patient

If indeed CT has its effects by teaching patients hypothesis-testing skills, some have reasoned that patients receiving CT should show more change on cognitive measures than those receiving noncognitive interventions (e.g., Barber & DeRubeis, 1989; Beckham & Watkins, 1989; Whisman, Miller, Norman, & Keitner, 1991). The findings are mixed; for the most part, however, the data suggest that CT does not produce specific effects in the treatment of depression (Barber & DeRubeis, 1989; Beckham & Watkins, 1989) or panic (Clark et al., 1991; Margraf & Schneider, 1991). In some of the studies that found specific effects of CT on cognition (e.g., Blackburn & Bishop, 1983; Rush, Beck, Kovacs, Weissenburger, & Hollon, 1982), these effects could be accounted for simply by the greater effect of CT than pharmacotherapy on symptom reduction.

In four studies, pharmacotherapy was as effective as CT, and there was some evidence for specific effects of CT. Imber et al. (1990) reported that patients who received CT in the National Institute of Mental Health (NIMH) Treatment of Depression Collaborative Research Program (Elkin et al., 1989) had lower posttreatment scores on the Need for Social Approval factor of the Dysfunctional Attitudes Scale (DAS; Weissman & Beck, 1978) than did patients who received interpersonal therapy or imipramine with supportive clinical management. However, the groups did not differ on the other DAS factors or the total DAS. DeRubeis et al. (1990) analyzed the Hollon et al. (1992) outcome study and found that change from pretreatment to midtreatment on the Attributional Style Questionnaire (ASQ; Seligman, Abramson, Semmel, & von Baeyer, 1979), the DAS, and the Hopelessness Scale (HS; Beck, Weissman, Lester, & Trexler, 1974) predicted subsequent change in depression from midtreatment to posttreatment in the CT patients, but not in the pharmacotherapy patients. In a study of treatments for social phobia, Mattick, Peters, and Clark (1989) found that patients who received cognitive restructuring, either alone or in combination with exposure, showed significant changes in measures of phobic avoidance, negative self-evaluation, and irrational beliefs. Those treated with exposure alone improved only on measures of avoidance. Whisman et al. (1991) noted that studies that compare cognitive change at the end of treatment may not find differences between groups because differences may not emerge until after treatment is terminated. To examine this possibility, these authors compared two groups of depressed inpatients at posttreatment and 6 and 12 months after treatment. The patients who received CT plus pharmacotherapy and milieu management reported less hopelessness and fewer cognitive biases at posttreatment and at 6- and 12-month follow-up, as well as fewer dysfunctional attitudes at the 6-month follow-up assessment, than did patients who did not receive the CT component. However, although the treatment groups differed on the cognitive measures, they did not differ in depression severity at any of the assessment periods.

Researchers have attempted to demonstrate the specific effects of CT, yet Beck (1985) himself asserted that change in the cognitive structuring of experience is a common pathway through which various systems of psychotherapy and perhaps even pharmacotherapy produce therapeutic results. In line with this, there is preliminary evidence that CT, exposure therapy, and pharmacotherapy produce changes in patients' catastrophic interpretations of bodily sensations and that these cognitive changes may mediate the clinical effectiveness of all three treatments (Clark et al., 1991). As Clark et al. noted, however, the cognitive changes in each of the groups may appear similar at posttreatment, but may be the result of different processes and may differ in their stability after treatment is terminated. The changes in catastrophizing in the medication group are not likely to be sustained after medication is withdrawn because the reduction in catastrophizing is probably due to the medication simply reducing the panic-related sensations. Changes induced by exposure and CT probably are more likely to be sustained because they do provide challenges to the individual's original interpretations. These differences may well be responsible for the lower relapse rates following CT and exposure versus pharmacotherapy in the treatment of panic (Clark et al., 1991) and social phobia (Heimberg & Barlow, 1991; Mattick et al., 1989). Future research on the nature and stability of the cognitive changes in various treatments may be more fruitful than the search for specific effects on global measures of cognition .

LIMITATIONS OF COGNITIVE THERAPY

Although numerous studies have demonstrated that CT is an effective treatment approach for depression and anxiety disorders, it has become clear that some patients do not respond adequately and that some do not respond at all. It is, therefore, important to identify the non-responders and possible ways in which CT might be adapted to be more effective with them. One way to do this is to describe the characteristics of those who do not respond.

Initial severity of depression and level of cognitive dysfunction, which tend to be associated, are both related to poorer outcome of CT (Norman, Miller, & Dow, 1988; Rude & Rehm, 1991; Sotsky et al., 1991). Norman et al. (1988) estimated that approximately 50% of depressives have high levels of cognitive dysfunction and that these patients are more severely depressed at intake, are more hopeless, and have more automatic thoughts, less social support, and poorer social adjustment. They not only have more negative thoughts during the acute episode, but also after the remission of their symptoms.

Another factor related to poorer outcome in CT for depression may be severe interpersonal disturbance, including chronic marital discord, which is characteristic of approximately 50% of depressed individuals. Marital discord (Barnett & Gotlib, 1988; Beach, Sandeen, & O'Leary, 1990; Coyne, 1990) and family dysfunction (Keitner, Ryan, Miller, & Norman, 1992) have been well documented as variables influencing the course of depression. There is also substantial support for the relationship between high levels of critical communication in the families of depressives and higher rates of relapse (Hooley & Teasdale 1989). The interpersonal disturbance that often characterizes the depressed individual's life may account for the effectiveness of interpersonal therapy (Elkin et al., 1989) and behavioral marital therapy when the couple is also discordant (Jacobson, Dobson, Fruzzetti, Schmaling, & Salusky, 1991; O'Leary & Beach, 1990). These data highlight the need for cognitive therapists to attend to the very real interpersonal difficulties of many patients, not just to the ways in which they misconstrue situations. The importance of addressing the patient's interpersonal context has also been emphasized in the treatment of anxiety disorders (e.g., Barlow, 1988). In response to these data on the importance of interpersonal factors in the course of psychiatric disorders, CT has begun to expand into this realm with cognitive–behavioral marital therapy (e.g., Baucom & Epstein, 1990; Dattilio & Padesky, 1990).

Coexisting personality disorders have also been found in many studies to be related to a poorer response to treatment for depression and a less favorable prognosis for long-term outcome (Frank, Kupfer, Jacob, & Jarrett, 1987). In the NIMH collaborative treatment of depression study, patients with definite or probable personality disorders (74%) had a significantly worse response to all of the treatments and had worse posttreatment social functioning than did those without personality disorders (Shea et al., 1990). Barlow (1988) has also highlighted the need to address Axis II disorders that often co-occur with the anxiety disorders. Young (1990) has noted that the following assumptions of short-term CT often do not apply to patients with personality disorders: (a) Patients have ready access to their feelings (some personality-disordered patients have difficulty in expressing and even accessing their feelings); (b) patients have ready access to their thoughts and images; (c) patients have readily identifiable target problems; (d) patients are motivated to do homework assignments; (e) patients can relatively quickly develop a collaborative relationship with the therapist; (f) work on the therapist-patient relationship does not need to be a major focus of treatment; and (g) cognitions, feelings, and behaviors can be changed through empirical analysis, logical discourse, experimentation, and graduating practice. These techniques help many patients with personality disorders to achieve some intellectual insight, but not "emotional insight" or behavior change.

Another way to begin to describe nonresponders is to examine what therapists do in sessions with these patients. Vallis and Shaw (1987) identified a subgroup of "difficult" depressed patients by describing those with whom cognitive therapists "strayed" from the procedures of the CT protocol. Patients rated as more difficult by observational raters had more depression at intake, lower activity levels, less willingness for self-exploration and a negative attitude toward the therapist. These severely depressed patients may have been less able or willing to participate in CT because they were overwhelmed by the somatic symptoms of depression, negative thinking, and perhaps more negative interpersonal circumstances.

Hayes et al. (1992) identified the aspects of patient functioning that cognitive therapists targeted in sessions of patients who had more depression at intake, posttreatment, and over a 2-year follow-up period. With the more severely depressed patients, cognitive therapists focused more on behavioral activation and less on teaching hypothesis testing. Thus, if hypothesis-testing skills are indeed important in the change process, the more severely depressed patients received less of this component. Worse functioning at the end of treatment and over the follow-up period was associated with more of a focus on patients' maladaptive interpersonal patterns, their mates, and the assessment and identification of their negative thinking. More of a therapist focus on issues related to maintaining the collaborative structure of CT was associated with less improvement at the end of treatment but did not relate to status at follow-up. An emphasis on another interpersonal variable, the effect of other people on the patient, was related to worse functioning at follow-up. Although one cannot determine the causal direction of patient and therapist behaviors, these data suggest that, compared with responders, nonresponders may have more negative thoughts to assess, may have more interpersonal difficulties, and may need more work to maintain the therapeutic relationship. This description is strikingly similar to our earlier characterizations of the high cognitive dysfunction subgroup (Norman et al., 1988) and of the difficult patient (Vallis & Shaw, 1987), and it is consistent with poorer outcomes associated with severity, interpersonal problems, and personality disorders. In the next section, we review the ways in which CT has expanded from the original approach (Beck et al., 1979) to address the issues associated with a poorer response to CT.

RECENT DEVELOPMENTS IN COGNITIVE THERAPY

A number of authors have discussed how CT can be modified and refined to address the clinical challenges of patients who do not respond adequately to standard CT and to address the cogent theoretical criticisms of Mahoney (1980), Arnkoff (1980), Coyne and Gotlib (1983), and others. Although some of these developments have involved borrowing theoretical concepts or techniques from other therapeutic approaches, they can best be viewed as an evolution in the sophistication of the CT model itself rather than a new form of psychotherapy, because they retain a conceptual framework that emphasizes the role of dysfunctional schemata. Indeed, many of these developments involve an increased emphasis on, or refinement of, certain aspects of CT originally described in Beck's earlier writings but not emphasized then. At the same time, researchers and scholars in other theoretical approaches have also begun to look to cognitive psychology and CT as a language for redescribing or developing psychodynamic and other approaches (e.g., Ryle, 1985; Weston, 1988).

The developments that have occurred in CT include (a) a distinction between "core" and more "peripheral" schemata, (b) an appreciation for the role of defensive processes in the avoidance of schema-related material, (c) a greater emphasis on exploration of the therapeutic relationship and on the patient's interpersonal relationships in general, (d) a greater emphasis on the role of affective arousal for the elicitation and modification of schemata, and (e) a greater emphasis on exploration of developmental experiences that may have been significant in the development of maladaptive schemata. Although the utility of these modifications or emphases has not yet been demonstrated empirically, we discuss them here in some depth because they are likely to play increasingly important roles in the practice of CT and in future research.

Core Versus Peripheral Schemata

A number of authors have suggested that schemata may be organized hierarchically, some being more peripheral and others more centrally related to one's basic sense of identity (Guidano & Liotti, 1983; Kelly, 1955; Mahoney, 1982; Meichenbaum & Gilmore, 1984). As Young (1990) has described them, core beliefs tend to be unconditional rather than conditional. For example, whereas a relatively peripheral belief might be "If someone rejects me, then I am less of a person," a more basic core belief might be "I am unlovable" or "I am bad." Such beliefs tend to be much more resistant to change and tend to be self-perpetuating.

Safran, Vallis, Segal, and Shaw (1986) have identified several guidelines for assessing core cognitive processes. First, core schemata tend to be reflected in self-referent cognitions. The use of the vertical exploration or downward arrow technique described earlier can be used to move from cognitions about a situation to the more core cognitions about the self. Second, core schemata will tend to be manifested across a broad range of situations, so that the therapist can look for cross-situational consistencies. Third, there are common themes that occur across different patients, in particular themes involving lovability (sociotropy) and competence (autonomy). Fourth, in addition to the "content markers" just mentioned, therapists can be alert for "process markers" (i.e., how patients report their experience). Core schemata tend to generate a high level of affect when they are activated. Finally, Safran and his colleagues have suggested that the therapist can develop hypotheses about the patient's core schemata from therapeutic strategies that have been ineffective, difficulties in the therapeutic relationship, and resistance by the patient, which may all indicate having tapped into a core schema. In developing hypotheses about core schemata, it is important for the therapist not always to challenge dysfunctional cognitions. At times, it is more important initially to encourage patients to elaborate on their negative thoughts, particularly through imagery, to gain better access to their core beliefs (Safran & Segal, 1990).

As just noted, there are common themes in patients' core schemata. Beck (1983) has suggested that depressions and other emotional disorders may be differentiated according to the degree to which the individual's core concerns are primarily in the area of interpersonal relations (sociotropy) or autonomous achievement (autonomy), respectively. Evidence has begun to accrue that supports the hypotheses (Beck, 1983) that (a) depression may be related to the congruent interactions of sociotropy with the occurrence of negative interpersonal events, and autonomy with negative autonomous achievement events, and not to noncongruent interactions (e.g., Hammen, Ellicott, Gitlin, & Jamison, 1989; Robins, 1990; Robins, Hayes, Block, Kramer, & Villena, 1993; Segal, Shaw, Vella, & Katz, 1992), and (b) each of these personality dimensions may be related to different clinical presentations of depression (Robins & Luten, 1991; Robins et al., 1993). Although these preliminary data are encouraging regarding the utility of sociotropy and autonomy in understanding depression, so far there has been almost no research linking these characteristics to treatment. Peselow, Robins, Sanfilipo, Block, and Fieve (1992) reported that autonomy strongly predicted a positive response to antidepressant drug treatment and predicted a poor response to placebo, whereas sociotropy was associated with a poor response to antidepressant drugs. An important extension of this work would be to examine sociotropy and autonomy as predictors of response to CT and whether they interact with the presence versus absence of an emphasis on the therapeutic relationship within the context of CT. Highly sociotropic individuals may prefer and benefit more from a more interpersonal focus within CT, whereas highly autonomous individuals may prefer and differentially benefit from a more task-oriented approach.

Defensive Processes

Several cognitive theorists have suggested that awareness or expression of core dysfunctional beliefs generates anxiety, from which individuals may protect themselves by developing sets of beliefs that seem to run counter to the content of the core schema. For example, a patient who has a core schema of worthlessness may have developed a protective set of schemata concerning his or her strengths and aptitudes and may present in a grandiose, narcissistic manner. Young (1990) has referred to the activation of these protective schemata as "schema compensation," and Safran and Segal (1990) have similarly discussed "security operations." Young also discussed another defensive process, schema avoidance, in which the schema is avoided cognitively by repression of memories, denial, or depersonalization; emotionally by numbing, dissociation, or minimizing of painful experiences; or behaviorally by avoidance of situations likely to trigger the core schema. Rather than challenging these processes, which is likely to be highly threatening to the patient, these authors have recommended that the therapist generate hypotheses about the beliefs and associated affects that are being avoided and gradually help the patient become more aware of them.

Cognitive–Interpersonal Cycles and the Therapeutic Relationship

The most important schemata that need to be worked with in psychotherapy frequently are interpersonal schemata, internal working models of relationships that are developed over the course of years of specific relationship events but are particularly influenced by early relationships. Many patients' current difficulties reflect the operation of dysfunctional interpersonal schemata. Safran (1990; Safran & Segal, 1990) has been particularly influential in arguing that such schemata tend to persist not only because of selective inattention to potentially disconfirmatory interpersonal evidence, but largely because they influence the person's behavior such that it actually meets with the very interpersonal consequences that support the schema. For example, an individual who has a strong schema regarding unlovability may tend to be clinging and demanding of reassurance about being loved, which may, in time, drive others away, thus providing evidence that actually supports the schema of unlovability. This concept of cognitive–interpersonal cycles has also been described by authors from interpersonal and psychodynamic traditions (e.g., Leary, 1957; Ryle, 1985; Wachtel, 1977), and it helps to bridge the gap between cognitive theory and accounts that emphasize environmental determinants of emotional problems (e.g., Coyne & Gotlib, 1983). In this view, depression and other emotional disturbances may indeed result in large part from situational determinants, but these cannot be separated from the role that the individual's cognitive processes may play, not only in interpreting the situations but also in generating many of them. This points to the importance for therapy of helping patients to examine and modify their maladaptive cognitive–interpersonal cycles. In addition, the negative reality of many patients' interpersonal worlds often requires direct interventions, through such methods as social skills training, marital therapy, and problem solving.

In addition to exploration of the patient's relationships outside of therapy, the therapeutic relationship itself can provide important opportunities for understanding and modifying interpersonal schemata and behavior. Cognitive therapists have recently drawn greater attention to these opportunities (e.g., Jacobson, 1989; Liotti, 1991; Persons, 1989; Safran & Segal, 1990). Because it is frequently the complementary interpersonal behavior of others that maintains the maladaptive schema of the patient, Safran and Segal (1990) recommended that therapists pay particular attention to their own feelings and action tendencies with regard to the patient, which are likely to reflect the "pull" from the patient (cf. Ryle's [1985] concept of reciprocal role procedures). The tasks of the therapist are then to find a way to "unhook" himself or herself from this interaction so as not to perpetuate the cycle, to "metacommunicate" with the patient about his or her own feelings and action tendencies, and then to help the patient explore the thoughts and feelings he or she experienced during the interaction. One particular type of juncture in the therapeutic relationship that is particularly useful for such exploration, according to Safran and Segal (1990), is what they referred to as an alliance rupture, in which there is some evidence that patients are having negative feelings about the therapeutic relationship or the therapy or in which they hesitate to follow the therapist's suggestions. Safran and Segal advocated focusing much attention on understanding and healing such alliance ruptures, not only to "get on with" the other tasks of therapy, but primarily because healing such ruptures can itself be particularly therapeutic insofar as it disconfirms the patient's cognitive–interpersonal schemata.

Liotti (1991) and others have suggested that the therapeutic relationship often can be viewed helpfully in terms of attachment theory (Bowlby, 1977), according to which all humans have an innate need, beginning in infancy to attach themselves to significant adults. Patterns of attachment behavior are influenced by the responses of those significant adults to the infant and form the basis of the interpersonal schemata that influence the individual's relationships later in life. Developmental research on responses to separation has identified three types of insecure attachment. *Avoidant attachment,* in which the infant tends to avoid the caregiver after a temporary separation, tends to occur when the caregiver is rejecting or neglecting. *Anxious attachment,* in which the infant requires an excessive amount of time to become soothed after a separation, is often seen when the caregiver is intrusive and overcontrolling. *Disorganized or disoriented attachment,* in which the infant seems dazed after separation or alternates between proximity seeking and avoidance, tends to occur in infants whose parents are frightened or frightening, confused or confusing. They may expect to be comforted by their children. According to Liotti (1991), these attachment behavior patterns will be activated, particularly in relationships in which the person feels vulnerable and asks for help from a caregiver, such as in a therapeutic relationship. The patient may also expect the therapist to act in ways similar to the early caregiver. It is important for the therapist to understand these behavior patterns and expectations when they occur, and to help the patient understand them, rather than generating greater resistance by confronting the patient's maladaptive behavior. Without such understanding, it may be difficult indeed, with patients with a history of insecure attachments, to develop the collaborative relationship necessary for CT.

The Role of Affect

Several theorists have suggested that it is when particular thoughts and attitudes are tested in the context of appropriate affective arousal that fundamental change can occur. Beck (1976) himself made this point many years ago, but it has been developed more fully by others. Persons and Miranda (1991) suggested that dysfunctional beliefs are particularly likely to be accessible early in treatment when the patient is most distressed, so this phase of therapy can be critical for the eliciting of core dysfunctional beliefs, even if they may not be addressed until later in the therapy. Several authors have suggested methods for accessing and changing dysfunctional beliefs in the context of affective arousal, including the use of such techniques as shame-attacking exercises, having patients conduct imaginary dialogues with their parents or with different sides of themselves, imagery regarding recent or past life events, dreams, repetition and exaggeration of key phrases, and focusing on bodily sensations that are associated with feelings experienced at the moment (Edwards, 1989; Ellis, 1974; Greenberg & Safran, 1987; Young, 1990). The role of affect in therapeutic change has been discussed more fully by Greenberg and Safran (1987, 1989), who described five ways to use affect-enhancing techniques: (a) to evoke and intensify emotion, (b) to facilitate the patient's synthesis and acknowledgment of emotional responses that were previously out of awareness, (c) to access state-dependent core beliefs, (d) to restructure the cognitive–emotional network underlying problematic responses, and (e) to modify maladaptive emotional responses.

Increased Emphasis on Developmental Issues

Although cognitive therapists focus primarily on the patient's present functioning, several therapists recently have demonstrated an increased appreciation for the utility of discussing with patients the historical roots of their maladaptive beliefs. For example, Young (1990) referred to core schemata as "early maladaptive schemas" and suggested that one way to identify them, among others, is to conduct a careful developmental history. It has been our clinical experience that simply focusing on developmental experiences is unlikely, by itself, to lead to schematic change; however, when patients understand the developmental roots of their current beliefs and behavior, they frequently are less self-blaming and may feel less hopeless about changing things that now are clearly seen to have been learned. Patients' beliefs about themselves, such as being incompetent, worthless, or unlovable, can be challenged and weakened using standard CT methods if their recollections of actual transactions with their parents and significant others can be seen instead as reflecting maladaptive expectations or behaviors of those individuals (McKay & Fanning, 1991; Young, 1990). Edwards (1990) has discussed the use of patients' imagery of their early memories to access beliefs in an emotionally charged way. Important early memories are frequently of traumatic instances of abuse, continued neglect, intrusion, or role reversal. Particularly traumatic memories may be avoided, consciously or not, and often have to be approached in a gradual manner. Although there may or may not be value simply in the expression of such memories (catharsis–habituation), they provide an important opportunity to evaluate patients' implicit assumptions about the meaning of recalled events for their sense of self-worth and relations with others. The therapist's reaction to the disclosure of such memories can itself either strongly reinforce or help to disconfirm patients' beliefs in this regard.

CONCLUSIONS

Beck's CT has been documented to be an effective treatment for a variety of clinical disorders. It has not remained a closed system, but rather a system into which theoretical concepts and techniques from other approaches have been incorporated to meet the demands of clinical work and to address theoretical and empirical challenges. Just as CT teaches patients to examine all of the available evidence, so have its proponents modified the approach with new evidence of its limitations. CT has begun to expand into the realms of interpersonal dysfunction and personality disorders and to address issues that have received a greater emphasis in other orientations, such as core schemata, defensive processes, the therapeutic relationship, affective arousal, and early experiences. In a recent article, Beck (1991) nominated CT as *the* integrative therapy because he views cognitive change as a common factor operating across effective treatments and, therefore, asserts that the cognitive model can be used as the framework for the selection of techniques from a variety of other psychotherapies.

CT grew out of astute clinical observations and systematic empirical examinations of its efficacy. Consistent with this history, much work remains to be done to subject the recent applications and developments of CT to empirical scrutiny. In addition, process research with this approach is in its infancy, and future research will need to continue to identify the active ingredients of CT, mechanisms of change in the patient, and the interaction of therapy components and patient variables. It also remains an empirical question whether CT has its effects by deactivating depressogenic schemata and activating new ones, building new adaptive schemata to compete with negative ones, restructuring old schemata, or teaching the patient compensatory skills without changing the schemata directly.

Although it is important to understand how CT works, another task for researchers is to understand why and for whom it does not work. Very few studies have described nonresponders and how CT is delivered to these patients, but this perspective, coupled with a better understanding of why CT is effective, can contribute to further expansion and refinement of this form of treatment.

REFERENCES

Arnkoff, D. B. (1980). Psychotherapy from the perspective of cognitive theory. In M. J. Mahoney (Ed.), *Psychotherapy process: Current issues and future directions* (pp. 339–361). New York: Plenum Press.

Barber. J. P., & DeRubeis, R. J. (1989). On second thought: Where the action is in cognitive therapy for depression. *Cognitive Therapy and Research, 13,* 441–457.

Barlow, D. H. (1988). *Anxiety and its disorders: The nature and treatment of anxiety and panic.* New York: Guilford Press.

Barlow, D. H., Craske, M. G., Cerny, J. A., & Klosko, J. S. (1989). Behavioral treatment of panic disorder. *Behavior Therapy, 20,* 261–282.

Barnett, P., & Gotlib, I. (1988). Psychosocial functioning and depression: Distinguishing among antecedents, concomitants, and consequences. *Psychological Bulletin, 104,* 97–126.

Baucom, D. H., & Epstein, N. (1990). *Cognitive-behavioral marital therapy.* New York: Brunner/Mazel.

Beach, S. R. H., Sandeen, E. E., & O'Leary, K. D. (1990). *Depression in marriage: A model for etiology and treatment.* New York: Guilford Press.

Beck, A. T. (1967). *Depression: Clinical, experimental, and theoretical aspects.* New York: Harper & Row.

Beck, A. T. (1976). *Cognitive therapy and the emotional disorders.* Madison, CT: International Universities Press.

Beck, A. T. (1983). Cognitive therapy of depression: New perspectives. In P. J. Clayton & J. E. Barrett (Eds.), *Treatment of depression: Old controversies and new approaches* (pp. 265–290). New York: Raven Press.

Beck, A. T. (1985). Cognitive therapy, behavior therapy, psychoanalysis, and pharmacotherapy: A cognitive continuum. In M. J. Mahoney & A. Freeman (Eds.), *Cognition and psychotherapy.* (pp. 325–347). New York: Plenum Press.

Beck, A. T. (1991). Cognitive therapy as *the* integrative therapy. *Journal of Psychotherapy Integration, 3,* 191–198.

Beck, A. T., Freeman, A., & Associates. (1990). *Cognitive therapy of personality disorders.* New York: Guilford Press.

Beck, A. T., Rush, A. J., Shaw, B. F., & Emery, G. (1979). *Cognitive therapy of depression.* New York: Guilford Press.

Beck, A. T., Sokol, L., Clark, D. A., Berchick, B., & Wright, F. (1991). *Focused cognitive therapy of panic disorder: A crossover design and one year follow-up.* Manuscript submitted for publication.

Beck, A. T., Weissman, A., Lester, D., & Trexler, L. (1974). The measurement of pessimism: The Hopelessness Scale. *Journal of Consulting and Clinical Psychology, 42,* 861–865.

Beckham, E. E., & Watkins, J. T. (1989). Process and outcome in cognitive therapy. In A. Freeman, K. Simon, L. Beutler, & H. Arkowitz (Eds.), *Comprehensive handbook of cognitive therapy.* (pp. 61–81). New York: Plenum Press.

Blackburn, I. M., & Bishop, S. (1983). Changes in cognition with pharmacotherapy and cognitive therapy. *British Journal of Psychiatry, 43,* 609–617.

Blackburn, I. M., Eunson, K. M., & Bishop, S. (1986). A two-year naturalistic follow-up of depressed patients treated with cognitive therapy, pharmacotherapy, and a combination of both. *Journal of Affective Disorders, 10,* 67–75.

Bowers, W. A. (1990). Treatment of depressed inpatients: Cognitive therapy plus medication, and medication alone. *British Journal of Psychiatry, 156,* 73–78.

Bowlby, J. (1977). The making and breaking of affectional bonds: 1. Aetiology and psychopathology in the light of the attachment theory. *British Journal of Psychiatry, 130,* 201–210.

Burns, D. D. (1980). *Feeling good: The new mood therapy.* New York: Morrow.

Burns. D. D., & Nolen-Hoeksema, S. (1991). Coping styles, homework compliance, and the effectiveness of cognitive behavioral therapy. *Journal of Consulting and Clinical Psychology, 59,* 305–311.

Burns, D. D., & Nolen-Hoeksema, S. (1992). Therapeutic empathy and recovery from depression in cognitive-behavioral therapy: A structural equation model. *Journal of Consulting and Clinical Psychology, 60,* 441–449.

Clark, D. M., Salkovskis, P. M., Hackmann, A., & Gelder, M. (1991, November). *Long-term outcome of cognitive therapy for panic disorder.* Paper presented at the meeting of the Association for Advancement of Behavior Therapy, New York.

Coyne, J. C. (1990). Interpersonal processes in depression. In G. I. Keitner (Ed.), *Depression and families: Impact and treatment* (pp. 33–53). Washington, DC: American Psychiatric Press.

Coyne, J. C., & Gotlib, I. H. (1983). The role of cognition in depression: A critical appraisal. *Psychological Bulletin, 94,* 472–505.

Craighead, W. E., Evans, D. D., & Robins, C. J. (1992). Unipolar depression. In S. M. Turner, K. S. Calhoun, & H. E. Adams (Eds.), *Handbook of clinical behavior therapy* (2nd ed., pp. 99–116). New York: Wiley

Dattilio, F. M., & Padesky, C. A. (1990). *Cognitive therapy with couples.* Sarasota, FL: Professional Resource Exchange.

DeRubeis, R. J., Evans, M. D., Hollon, S. D., Garvey, M. J., Grove, W. M., & Tuason, V. B. (1990). How does cognitive therapy work? Cognitive change and symptom change in cognitive therapy and pharmacotherapy for depression. *Journal of Consulting and Clinical Psychology, 58,* 862–869.

DeRubeis, R. J., & Feeley, M. (1990). Determinants of change in cognitive therapy for depression. *Cognitive Therapy and Research, 14,* 469–482.

Dobson, K. S. (1989). A meta-analysis of the efficacy of cognitive therapy for depression . *Journal of Consulting and Clinical Psychology, 57,* 414–419.

Edwards, D. J. A. (1989). Cognitive restructuring through guided imagery. In A. Freeman, K. Simon, L. Beutler, & H. Arkowitz (Eds.), *Comprehensive handbook of cognitive therapy* (pp. 283–297). New York: Plenum Press.

Edwards, D. J. A. (1990). Cognitive therapy and the restructuring of early memories through guided imagery. *Journal of Cognitive Psychotherapy, 4,* 33–50.

Elkin, I., Shea, T., Watkins, J. T., Imber, S. D., Sotsky, S. M., Collins, J. F., Glass, D. R., Pilkonis, P. A., Leber, V. R., Docherty, J. P., Fiester, S. J., & Parloff, M. B. (1989). National Institute of Mental Health Treatment of Depression Collaborative Research Program: General effectiveness of treatments. *Archives of General Psychiatry, 46,* 971–982.

Ellis, A. (1974). *How to stubbornly refuse to be ashamed of anything* [Cassette recording]. New York: Institute for Rational Living.

Evans, M. D., & Hollon, S. D. (1988). Patterns of personal and causal inference: Implications for the cognitive therapy of depression. In L. Alloy (Ed.), *Cognitive processes in depression* (pp. 344–377). New York: Guilford Press.

Evans, M. D., Hollon, S. D., DeRubeis, R. J., Piasecki, J., Grove, W. M., Garvey, M. J., & Tuason, V. B. (1992). Differential relapse following cognitive therapy and pharmacotherapy for depression. *Archives of General Psychiatry, 49,* 802–808.

Frank, E., Kupfer, D. J., Jacob, M., & Jarrett, D. (1987). Personality features and response to acute treatment in recurrent depression. *Journal of Personality Disorders, 1,* 14–26.

Freeman, A., Pretzer, J., Fleming, B., & Simon, K. (1990). *Clinical applications of cognitve therapy.* New York: Plenum Press.

Goldfried, M. R., & Robins, C. J. (1983). Self-schema, cognitive bias, and the processing of therapeutic experiences. In P. C. Kendall (Ed.), *Advances in cognitive-behavioral research and therapy* (Vol. 2, pp. 33–80). San Diego, CA: Academic Press.

Greenberg, L. S., & Safran, J. D. (1987). *Emotion in psychotherapy: Affect cognition, and the process of change.* New York: Guilford Press.

Greenberg, L. S., & Safran, J. D. (1989). Emotion in psychotherapy. *American Psychologist, 44,* 19–29.

Guidano, V. F., & Liotti, G. (1983). *Cognitive processes and emotional disorders.* New York: Guilford Press.

Haaga, D. A. F., Dyck, M. J., & Ernst, D. (1991). Empirical status of cognitive theory of depression. *Psychological Bulletin, 110,* 215–236.

Hammen, C., Ellicott, A., Gitlin, M., & Jamison, K. R. (1989). Sociotropy/ autonomy and vulnerability to specific life events in patients with unipolar depression and bipolar disorders. *Journal of Abnormal Psychology, 98,* 154– 160.

Hayes, A. M., Castonguay, L., & Goldfried, M. R. (1992). *The relationship between the focus of therapist interventions and treatment response in cognitive therapy for depression.* Manuscript submitted for publication.

Heimberg, R. G., & Barlow, D. H. (1991). New developments in cognitive-behavioral therapy for social phobia. *Journal of Clinical Psychiatry, 52,* 21– 30.

Hollon, S. D., DeRubeis, R. J., Evans, M. D., Wiemer, M. J., Garvey, M. J., Grove, W. M., & Tuason, V. B. (1992). Cognitive therapy and pharmacotherapy for depression: Singly and in combination. *Archives of General Psychiatry, 49,* 774–781.

Hollon, S. D., Evans, M. D., Auerback, A., DeRubeis, R. J., Elkin, I., Lowry, A., Tuason, V. B., Kriss, M., & Piasecki, J. (1988). *Development of a system for rating therapies for depression: Differentiating cognitive therapy, interpersonal therapy, and clinical management with pharmacotherapy.* Unpublished manuscript, University of Minnesota, Minneapolis.

Hollon, S. D., & Najavits, L. (1988). Review of empirical studies on cognitive therapy. In A. J. Frances & R. E. Hales (Eds.), *Review of psychiatry* (Vol. 7, pp. 643–666). Washington, DC: American Psychiatric Press.

Hollon, S. D., Shelton, R. C., & Loosen, P. T. (1991). Cognitive therapy and pharmacotherapy for depression. *Journal of Consulting and Clinical Psychology, 59,* 88–99.

Hooley, J. M., & Teasdale, J. D. (1989). Predictors of relapse in unipolar depressives: Expressed emotion, marital distress, and perceived criticism. *Journal of Abnormal Psychology, 98,* 229–235.

Imber, S. D., Pilkonis, P. A., Sotsky, S. M., Elkin, I., Watkins, J. T., Collins, J. F., Shea, M. T., Leber, W. R., & Glass, D. R. (1990). Mode-specific effects among three treatments for depression. *Journal of Consulting and Clinical Psychology, 58,* 352–359.

Jacobson, N. S. (1989). The therapist-client relationship in cognitive behavior therapy: Implications for treatment depression. *Journal of Cognitive Psychotherapy, 3,* 85–96.

Jacobson, N. S., Dobson, K., Fruzzetti, A. E., Schmaling, K. B., & Salusky, S. (1991). Marital therapy as a treatment for depression. *Journal of Consulting and Clinical Psychology, 59,* 547–557.

Jarrett, R. B., & Nelson, R. O. (1987). Mechanisms of change in cognitive therapy of depression. *Behavior Therapy, 18,* 227–241.

Keitner, G. I., Ryan, C. E., Miller, I. W., & Norman, W. H. (1992). Recovery and major depression: Factors associated with twelve-month outcome. *American Journal of Psychiatry, 149,* 93–99.

Kelly, G. A. (1955). *The psychology of personal constructs.* New York: Norton.

Leary, T. (1957). *Interpersonal diagnosis of personality.* New York: Ronald Press.

Liotti, G. (1991). Patterns of attachment and the assessment of interpersonal schemata: Understanding and changing difficult patient–therapist relationships in cognitive psychotherapy. *Journal of Cognitive Psychotherapy, 5,* 105–114.

Mahoney, M. J. (1980). Psychotherapy and the structure of personal revolutions. In M. J. Mahoney (Ed.), *Psychotherapy process: Current issues and future directions* (pp. 157–180). New York: Plenum Press.

Mahoney, M. J. (1982). Psychotherapy and human change processes. In J. H. Harvey & M. M. Parks (Eds.), *Psychotherapy research and behavior change* (pp. 73–122). Washington, DC: American Psychological Association.

Margraf, J., & Schneider, S. (1991, November). *Outcome and active ingredients of cognitive–behavioral treatments for panic disorder.* Paper presented at the meeting of the Association for Advancement of Behavior Therapy, New York.

Mattick, R. P., Peters, L., & Clark, J. C. (1989). Exposure and cognitive restructuring for social phobia: A controlled study. *Behavior Therapy, 20,* 3–23.

McKay, M., & Fanning, P. (1991). *Prisoners of belief: Expressing and changing beliefs that control your life.* Oakland, CA: New Harbinger Publications.

Meichenbaum, D., & Gilmore, B. (1984). The nature of unconscious processes: A cognitive-behavioral perspective. In K. S. Bowers & D. Meichenbaum (Eds.), *The unconscious reconsidered* (pp. 273–298). New York: Wiley.

Miller, I. W., Norman, W. H., Keitner, G. I., Bishop, S. B., & Dow, M. (1989). Cognitive–behavioral treatment of depressed inpatients. *Behavior Therapy, 20,* 25–47.

Norman, W. H., Miller, I. W., & Dow, M. G. (1988). Characteristics of depressed patients with elevated levels of dysfunctional cognitions. *Cognitive Therapy and Research, 12,* 39–52.

O'Leary, K. D., & Beach, S. R. H. (1990). Marital therapy: A viable treatment for depression and marital discord. *American Journal of Psychiatry, 147,* 183–186.

Persons, J. B. (1989). *Cognitive therapy in practice: A case formulation approach.* New York: Norton.

Persons, J. B., & Burns, D. D. (1985). Mechanisms of action of cognitive therapy: The relative contributions of technical and interpersonal interventions. *Cognitive Therapy and Research, 9,* 539–551.

Persons, J. B., Burns, D. D., & Perloff, J. M. (1988). Predictors of dropout and outcome in cognitive therapy for depression in a private practice setting. *Cognitive Therapy and Research, 12,* 557–575.

Persons, J. B., & Miranda, I. (1991). Treating dysfunctional beliefs: Implications of the mood-state hypothesis. *Journal of Cognitive Psychotherapy,* 15–25.

Peselow, E. D., Robins, C. J., Sanfilipo, M. P., Block, P., & Fieve, R. R. (1992).

Sociotropy and autonomy: Relationship to antidepressant drug treatment response and endogenous/nonendogenous dichotomy. *Journal of Abnormal Psychology, 101,* 479–486.

Robins, C. J. (1990). Congruence of personality and life events in depression. *Journal of Abnormal Psychology, 99,* 393–397.

Robins, C. J., & Hayes, A. M. (in press). The role of causal attributions in the prediction of depression. In G. Buchanan & M. E. P. Seligman (Eds.), *Explanatory style.* Hillsdale, NJ: Erlbaum.

Robins, C. J., Hayes, A. M., Block, P., Kramer, R. J., & Villena, M. (1993). *Interpersonal and achievement concerns and the depressive vulnerahility and symptom specifcity hypotheses: A prospective study.* Manuscript submitted for publication.

Robins, C. J., & Luten. A. G. (1991). Sociotropy and autonomy: Differential patterns of clinical presentation in unipolar depression. *Journal of Abnormal Psychology, 100,* 74–77

Rude, S. S., & Rehm, L. P. (1991). Response to treatments for depression: The role of initial status on targeted cognitive and behavioral skills. *Clinical Psychology Review, 11,* 493–514.

Rush, A. J., Beck, A. T., Kovacs, M., Weissenburger, J., & Hollon, S. D. (1982). Comparison of the effects of cognitive therapy and pharmacotherapy on hopelessness and self-concept. *American Journal of Psychiatry, 139,* 862–866.

Ryle, A. (1985). Cognitive theory, object relations and the self. *British Journal of Medical Psychology, 58,* 1–7.

Safran, J. D. (1990). Towards a refinement of cognitive therapy in light of interpersonal theory: 1. Theory. *Clinical Psychology Review, 10,* 87–105.

Safran, J., & Segal, Z. V. (1990). *Interpersonal process in cognitive therapy.* New York: Basic Books.

Safran, J. D., Vallis, T. M., Segal, Z. V., & Shaw, B. F. (1986). Assessment of core cognitive processes in cognitive therapy. *Cognitive Therapy and Research, 10,* 509–526.

Segal, Z. V., Shaw, B. F., Vella, D. D., & Katz, R. (1992). Cognitive and life stress predictors of relapse in remitted unipolar depressed patients: A test of the congruency hypothesis. *Journal of Abnormal Psychology, 101,* 26–36.

Seligman, M. E. P., Abramson, L. Y., Semmel, A., & von Baeyer, C. (1979). Depressive attributional style. *Journal of Abnormal Psychology, 88,* 242–247.

Shea, M. T., Pilkonis, P. A., Beckham, E., Collins, J. F., Elkin, I., Sotsky, S. M., & Docherty, J. P. (1990). Personality disorders and treatment outcome in the NIMH Treatment of Depression Collaborative Research Program. *American Journal of Psychiatry, 147,* 711–718.

Simons, A. D., Murphy, G. E., Levine, J. L., & Wetzel, R. D. (1986). Cognitive therapy and pharmacotherapy for depression: Sustained improvement over one year. *Archives of General Psychiatry, 43,* 4348.

Sokol, L., Beck, A. T., Greenberg, R. L., Wright, F. D., & Berchick, R. J. (1989). Cognitive therapy of panic disorder: A non-pharmacological alternative. *Journal of Nervous and Mental Disease, 177,* 711–716.

Sotsky, S. M., Glass, D. R., Shea, T., Pilkonis, P. A., Collins, J. F., Elkin, I., Watkins, J. T., Imber, S. D., Leber, W. R., Moyer, J., & Oliveri, M. E. (1991).

Patient predictors of response to psychotherapy and pharmacotherapy: Findings in the NlMH Treatment of Depression Collaborative Research Program. *American Journal of Psychiatry, 148,* 997–1008.

Teasdale, J. D., & Fennell, M. J. V. (1982). Immediate effects on depression of cognitive therapy interventions. *Cognitive Therapy and Research, 3,* 343–352.

Thase, M. E., Bowler, K., & Harden, T. (1991). Cognitive behavior therapy of endogenous depression: Part 2. Preliminary findings in 16 unmedicated inpatients. *Behavior Therapy, 22,* 469–478.

Vallis, T. M., & Shaw, B. F. (1987). *An investigation of patient difficulty and its relationship to therapist competence in cognitive therapy for depression.* Manuscript submitted for publication.

Wachtel, P. L. (1977). *Psychoanalysis and behavior therapy.* New York: Basic Books.

Weissman, A., & Beck, A. T. (1978, November). *Development and validation of the Dysfunctional Attitudes Scale: A preliminary investigation.* Paper presented at the annual meeting of the American Educational Research Association, Toronto.

Weston, D. (1988). Transference and information processing. *Clinical Psychology Review, 8,* 161–179.

Whisman, M. A., Miller, I. W., Norman, W. H., & Keitner, G. I. (1991). Cognitive therapy with depressed inpatients: Specific effects on dysfunctional cognitions. *Journal of Consulting and Clinical Psychology, 59,* 282–288.

Young, J. E. (1990). *Cognitive therapy for personality disorders: A schema-focused approach.* Sarasota, FL: Professional Resource Exchange.

III

Rational–Emotive Therapy

5

Reflections on Rational–Emotive Therapy

Albert Ellis

Let me, in a few pages, do the impossible: reflect on the development of rational–emotive therapy (RET), comment on what it is today, and suggest some future directions.

As the first of today's cognitive–behavioral therapies, RET in 1955 was highly cognitive, largely positivist, and very active–directive. Its ABC theory of human disturbance held that people experience undesirable activating events (A), that they have rational and irrational beliefs (B) about these stimuli, and that they create appropriate emotional and behavioral consequences (aC) with their rational beliefs (rB) or they create inappropriate and dysfunctional consequences (iC) with their irrational beliefs (rB). At first, RET largely followed the "scientific" philosophy of logical positivism that was then in vogue, favoring empirical "reality" and data seeking tied in with human observation and sensation. Holding that unrealistic and illogical self-talk about unfortunate life events, and not these events in their own right, created or "caused" emotional disturbance, it heavily espoused rational instead of irrational cognition and actively–directively disputed (D) clients' anti-empirical and overgeneralized self-statements while teaching them how to do hypothetical–deductive disputing for themselves (Ellis, 1962).

Early RET, however, had many humanistic existential, emotive–evocative, and holistically oriented theories and practices (Ellis, 1962), so it was far from being rationalist, sensationalist, or strictly positivist, as it has sometimes wrongly been accused of being.

As the years went by, the cognitive revolution in psychology progressed and psychotherapy became increasingly cognitive–behavioral. But my own work with thousands of clients, as well as my familiarity with the subsequent work of Aaron Beck, Donald Meichenbaum, and other cognitive therapists, most of whom were too empirical and not sufficiently philosophical for my taste, pushed me in more constructivist and more affective directions. During the late 1960s, moreover, I somewhat merged RET with the encounter movement, conducted many rational encounter marathons, and began to do considerable group therapy and public workshops that included live affective demonstrations of RET.

As a result of this activity, I began to differentiate general RET, which I see as synonymous with general cognitive–behavioral therapy, from preferential RET, which I see as a unique kind of cognitive therapy that partially overlaps with general cognitive–behavioral therapy but also differs from it in several significant respects. Preferential RET, which I have practiced and written about for the last 15 years, is distinctly constructivist and humanistic. Very briefly, it includes the following points:

1. RET holds that humans largely learn their goals and preferences for success and approval from their families and culture and feel appropriately frustrated and disappointed when they fail and are disapproved. But they mainly construct (because they are innately prone to do so) absolutist "musts" and demands about their desires. Hence, when they are neurotic, they do not get disturbed by obnoxious environmental influences but largely make themselves emotionally and behaviorally dysfunctional .

2. When people make irrational (self-defeating) demands on themselves, on others, and on the conditions under which they live, they also tend to construct, as derivatives of their musts, unrealistic misperceptions, inferences, and attributions that make important contributions to their disturbances. Thus, if they insist, "John absolutely must like me!" and John actually ignores them, they rashly conclude (and devoutly believe) that (a) "He hates me!" (b) "It's awful that he hates me!" (c) "I'm worthless because he hates me!" and (d) "No decent person will ever like me!"

3. To help people overcome their dysfunctional beliefs and the disturbances that accompany them, RET not only shows them their unrealistic inferences and attributions and how to dispute them but also shows them their imperative musts and demands that usually unconsciously and tacitly underlie and lead to these dysfunctional imperatives. It teaches them how to look for their necessitizing on their own, and shows them how to try to ultimately arrive at the "elegant" RET solution

to neurosis: to arrange, for the rest of their lives, that they rarely (not never) change their preferences to grandiose demands and thereby make themselves significantly less upsettable.

4. RET holds that cognitions, emotions, and behaviors are practically never pure or disparate but integrally and holistically interact with and include each other. Although it is highly philosophical, RET fully recognizes that feelings and behaviors have an important influence on beliefs, that beliefs affect feelings and behaviors, and that feelings affect beliefs and behaviors (Ellis, 1962, 1988, 1991). Thus, RET is always multimodal and uses a good number of cognitive, emotive, and behavioral methods with most clients.

5. RET theorizes that people often are biologically predisposed to strongly, passionately, and rigidly construct and hold on to their disturbance-creating musts and other irrational beliefs. Therefore, RET tries to persuade and teach clients to vigorously, powerfully, and persistently think, feel, and act against their demandingness and to return to their preferences. Consequently, it almost always uses a number of emotive–evocative techniques with individual and group therapy clients. These include unconditional acceptance of the client by the therapist, rational–emotive imagery, shame-attacking exercises, powerful coping statements, role playing, encouragement, humor, and other emotive methods (Ellis, 1988; Ellis & Dryden, 1987; Walen, DiGiuseppe, & Dryden, 1992).

6. RET theorizes that people tend to become habituated to their disturbed thoughts, feelings, and actions and easily and automatically keep repeating them, even when they "know" they bring about poor results. To change, they therefore often have to force themselves, quite uncomfortably, to push themselves to break their dysfunctional habits. But they often have a low frustration tolerance and irrationally believe that "I *shouldn't* have to do the work of changing myself and *must* find comfortable, magical ways to change." They also often have secondary disturbances of "ego-downing" about their primary disturbances, and they consciously or unconsciously insist that "I *must not* upset myself in this foolish manner! I'm a worthless idiot for doing so!" RET looks for and concentrates on uprooting their secondary as well as their primary disturbances; in doing so it uses a number of cognitive and emotive methods. But it also emphasizes behavioral homework, including reinforcements and penalties, in vivo desensitization, implosive counterphobic procedures, and response prevention. It thereby tends to be more heavily behavioral then some of the other cognitive behavioral therapies.

7. RET has always been psychoeducational and consequently uses a great deal of bibliotherapy, audiotherapy, courses, workshops, lectures,

and other teaching methods. It helps each person in a dysfunctional system (such as a crisis-creating family) to change himself or herself in spite of the system. But it also teaches people problem solving, skill training, and social change methods, so that they can modify the environment and the system in which they live.

8. RET theorizes that virtually all humans, however reared, have two opposing creative tendencies: (a) to damn and to deify themselves and others, as noted earlier, and thereby to make themselves disturbed and dysfunctional, and (b) to change and actualize themselves as healthier and less disturbed. RET tries to show them how to use their self-actualizing to reduce their self-disturbing tendencies, and thus to construct a more enjoyable life.

9. RET is opposed to rigidity, "must-urbation," one-sidedness, and stasis and strongly favors openness, alternative seeking, anti-dogma, and flexibility. It holds that science intrinsically is knowledge seeking, free of dogma, skeptical, and flexible, and that it uses empiricism and logic unrigidly to arrive at better (and still imperfect) solutions to world mysteries and to increased human happiness. This kind of scientific outlook, RET hypothesizes, is closely related to what is often called mental health.

10. Although RET holds that people are innately creative and constructive, and that whenever they needlessly upset themselves they also have the tendency and ability to think about their dysfunctional thinking, feeling, and behaving to reconstruct the self-defeating ways they have largely constructed, it also hypothesizes that once people upset themselves, their emotional reactions—especially their panic, depression, and self-hatred—are often so strong and consuming that these emotions interfere with their curative powers and sabotage some of their constructiveness. Also, as noted earlier, their disturbance about their disturbance often blocks them from changing.

Consequently, if left to their own devices in an existential encounter with their therapists, clients will receive less help and often become more disturbed than if guided and taught by a more active–directive therapist. In addition to strongly upholding an existentialist philosophy that people can fully accept themselves merely because they exist and because they choose to be self-accepting—and not because they perform well or are approved by significant others—RET goes one step further and teaches clients that they do not have to rate or measure their self, their being, or their totality at all but can choose to merely rate their acts, deeds, and performances in relation to their goals and desires. Thus, they can say *"It* is good that I succeed and am loved" or *"It* is bad when I fail and get rejected." But they had better not say "I am good for succeeding" and "I am bad for getting rejected."

Unlike Carl Rogers and other existential therapists, who believe that unconditional positive regard can be given by the therapist's modeling it and accepting clients unconditionally, RET practitioners try to give this kind of acceptance to all clients but also teach them how to give it to themselves. In this way, RET is both humanistic–existential and didactic and active–directive.

What about RET's directions for the future? These are potentially many: RET is increasingly applied to business, management, politics, economics, marriage and family, and many other fields. The one I would most like to stress, however, is education. Even if RET and cognitive–behavioral therapy stay on a good track, their future in psychotherapy may always be somewhat limited because psychotherapy itself, in its individual and group applications, has the serious limitation of being available, now and in the foreseeable future, only to limited numbers of paying clients. But RET and cognitive–behavioral therapy, unlike most of the other popular therapies, have the unique potential of being properly introduced to the general public in books, audio- and videocassettes, lectures, workshops, and other mass media presentations, and thus considerably helping vast numbers of people. They are already being, and can continue to be, widely applied in educational settings, from nursery school to graduate school and adult education settings. Therefore, the main future of RET will be, I predict, in its psychoeducational applications, and I hope this kind of usage will be of considerable help to clients who are in therapy as well as those who are in various kinds of self-help groups. Better yet, perhaps, it will help literally millions of people who never have had any form of individual or group treatment to clearly see some of the ways in which they are needlessly disturbing themselves; to work at overcoming their self-constructed emotional, cognitive, and behavioral problems; and to achieve a more self-actualized and self-fulfilled existence.

REFERENCES

Ellis, A. (1962). *Reason and emotion in psychotherapy*. Secaucus, NJ: Citadel.

Ellis, A. (1988). *How to stubbornly refuse to make yourself miserable about anything— yes, anything!* Secaucus, NJ: Lyle Stuart.

Ellis, A. (1991). The revised ABCs of rational–emotive therapy. *Journal of Rational–Emotive and Cognitive–Behavior Therapy, 9,* 139–192.

Ellis, A., & Dryden, W. (1987). *The practice of rational–emotive therapy.* New York: Springer.

Walen, S., DiGiuseppe, R., & Dryden, W. (1992). *A practitioner's guide to rational– emotive therapy.* New York: Oxford University Press.

6

An Appraisal of Rational–Emotive Therapy

David A. F. Haaga and Gerald C. Davison

Rational–emotive therapy (RET) was developed by Albert Ellis in the 1950s in response to his dissatisfaction with the effectiveness and efficiency of psychoanalysis (Ellis, 1957, 1962). RET is based on an "ABC" theory of psychopathology, the core premise of which is that activating events (A) do not directly cause emotional and behavioral consequences (C). Beliefs (B) about these events are instead the most critical causes of feelings and actions. If one adheres to rational beliefs (deemed by Ellis as those that promote survival and happiness, are likely to find empirical support in the environment, and express preferences), then difficulties and losses will lead to "appropriate" negative emotions such as sorrow, annoyance, or regret. If one holds irrational beliefs (those that are unlikely to find empirical support and reflect "musts" and demands; e.g., "I must do well and win approval, or else I rate as a rotten person" (Ellis & Bernard, 1985), then setbacks will lead to "inappropriate" negative emotions such as depression, anxiety, and extreme anger.

Rational–emotive therapists attempt to teach patients to forcefully dispute their irrational beliefs. Disputation can involve questioning the evidence for the belief or the utility of holding it, questioning catastrophic implications the patient may have drawn about her or his situation, or demonstrating that the belief is illogical (e.g., if there is no valid measuring instrument for human worth, how can a person be said to be completely worthless? [DiGiuseppe, 1991]). Sometimes the therapeutic focus is on the form rather than on the content of the belief: intervention here entails changing shoulds or musts into woulds (e.g., "It *would* be nice if Alice did not behave as she does in front of my friends—and maybe there is a way I could persuade her not to—but that does not mean she *should* not").

In-session verbal disputation, sometimes supplemented by imaginal disputation, as in systematic rational restructuring (Goldfried, Decenteceo, & Weinberg, 1974), is routinely complemented by homework assignments such as self-monitoring attempts to use disputation on one's own. Behavioral assignments tend toward in vivo rather than imaginal exposure and toward situations the patient is likely to find most difficult. Shame-attacking exercises, for instance, might call for a socially phobic patient to do something ridiculous in public to see that nothing catastrophic results.

Like other psychotherapeutic approaches, the applicability of RET is largely a function of the therapist's construction of the patient's problem (Davison, 1991). People seldom consult a therapist with clearly stated irrational beliefs (an exception perhaps being patients who have heard or read about RET and have already conceptualized their predicament in rational–emotive terms). For example, an overweight man who wishes to lose pounds might well be served by a functional analysis of his eating in terms of escape from social–evaluative anxiety that is construed as deriving from unproductive (irrational) needs to please everyone all the time.

RET has had a strong impact on the profession of psychotherapy, being in the historical forefront of the cognitive trend; Albert Ellis is regarded by clinicians as one of the most, if not the most, influential of psychotherapists (D. Smith, 1982; Warner, 1991). RET has been applied creatively to many clinical problems (Ellis & Grieger, 1986), explained to the lay public as a self-help method (Ellis & Harper, 1975), and adapted as a psychoeducational program for children (Knaus, 1974). Less clear than its professional impact is RET's scientific status, the primary subject of the remainder of this article. We shall examine progress on this front in terms of debate on three fundamental issues: (a) What is an irrational belief? (b) How can irrational beliefs be measured? and (c) What is RET, and what does research say about its effectiveness? It is commonly held that confronting criticism and opposing viewpoints is an effective means of making scientific progress (Kenrick & Funder, 1988). We shall argue that this has been true for RET theory and research with respect to our first two issues but not yet with regard to treatment research per se.

WHAT IS AN IRRATIONAL BELIEF?

Several conceptual definitions that have been offered for irrational beliefs seem problematic on close inspection. For instance, Ellis and Bernard (1986) proposed that "rational thoughts are defined in RET as those thoughts that help people live longer and happier" (p. 7), which would only render true by definition the prediction that irrational beliefs lead to dysfunction.

Alternatively, Ellis and Bernard (1986) portrayed rational beliefs as deriving from rigorous information processing, indicating that "nondisturbed individuals tend to . . . regulate their emotions and actions by . . . applying the rules of logic and the scientific method to evaluating these consequences" (p. 9). By this definition, we would have to conclude that much of the thinking of nondistressed people is irrational, because considerable research indicates that the stories people tell themselves in order to live (Didion, 1979) frequently have illusionary elements (e.g., Geer, Davison, & Gatchel, 1970; Taylor & Brown, 1988). Indeed, it is possible that, to achieve something unique or outstanding, one sometimes has to harbor beliefs that might be seen as unrealistic by those not committed to a cause (Bandura, 1986, p. 516). Ellis (1989) conceded the following:

> Some unrealistic and illogical ideas—such as the dogmatic belief that one absolutely will go to heaven and experience eternal bliss if one prays to God every day—may sometimes lead to little disturbance and to some benefits, so they easily can be tolerated. Only self-defeating shoulds and musts had better be surrendered! (p. 203)

This specification of which unrealistic views are problematic ("self-defeating" ones) tends to make the definition of irrationality more like the essentially tautological one proposed by Ellis and Bernard (1986).

Thus, it is difficult to devise a rigorous, consistent definition of irrationality in terms of scientific methods and empirical accuracy. Ultimately, RET therapists—and their patients—decide that it would be more personally useful, hence better, to think about the world in certain ways. This decision is based on what one believes is functional and not necessarily on what is strictly objective or rational (Davison & Neale, 1990). This implies that a critical aspect of RET—as indeed for all forms of psychosocial intervention (Davison, 1976, 1991)—is its ethics, because definitions that allude to notions of utility presuppose a set of values, whether implicit or explicit, concerning what constitutes a useful, worthwhile existence. Like all other therapists, but more explicitly and straightforwardly than most (Woolfolk & Sass, 1989), Ellis advocates an ethical system. To wit: Ellis assumes generally that people should lead happy and long lives and specifically that it is desirable, in attaining this aim, to "maximize their individuality, freedom, self-interest, and self-control rather than to submit to the control and direction of others" (Ellis, 1990, p. 88).

A pragmatic solution to the challenge of defining irrationality in RET has been to define irrational beliefs by examples, proceeding from lists of a dozen or so such beliefs commonly encountered in clinical practice (Ellis, 1962), to lists of several hundred specific ones, to a few general categories with many derivatives (Ellis & Bernard, 1985). Questions about the theoretical adequacy of these ostensive definitions have prompted new attempts to conceptually define irrationality. For example, Rorer (1989a, 1989b) has reformulated RET theory in terms of comprehensively critical rationalism (Bartley, 1984) and derived two categories of irrational beliefs: "(1) grandiose beliefs that the world or someone or something in it should be different than it, she, or he is, because one wants it to be, and (2) beliefs that evaluations are factual rather than definitional" (Rorer, 1989a, p. 484).

HOW CAN IRRATIONAL BELIEFS BE MEASURED?

A fundamental requirement for research on rational–emotive theory is valid measurement of irrationality. In a series of reviews (e.g., T. W. Smith, 1989) and empirical studies (e.g., Zurawski & Smith, 1987), T. W. Smith and his collaborators have argued that the most commonly used measures of irrational beliefs lack discriminant validity. Specifically, the Rational Behavior Inventory (RBI; Shorkey & Whiteman, 1977) and especially the Irrational Beliefs Test (Jones, 1968) correlate about as highly with depression and anxiety measures as with each other, suggesting that they might be measuring the broad-band disposition of negative affectivity (Watson & Clark, 1984). Confounding of measures of irrational beliefs with negative emotion measures undermines the interpretive logic of studies correlating irrational belief with distress, or relating change in such belief to change in distress, as tests of RET theory.

This issue has been addressed through the development of several recent questionnaire measures designed to maximize discriminant validity, in part by taking pains to write items that do not include emotion statements such as the RBI's "I often get excited or upset when things go wrong" (Robb & Warren, 1990, p. 304). The Belief Scale (Malouff & Schutte, 1986), for instance, was judged by independent raters to contain items reflecting only belief rather than emotional or behavioral consequences (Robb & Warren, 1990). Accordingly, it has shown some evidence of discriminant validity, correlating positively with anxiety and depression measures but more strongly with other measures of irrational beliefs (Malouff & Schutte, 1986; Malouff, Valdenegro, & Schutte, 1987).

Thus, there are grounds for optimism that critiques of assessments of irrational beliefs have had a favorable impact. Next steps in this area could include developing measures based on more refined abstract definitions of irrationality, such as Rorer's (1989a, 1989b), rather than on the early lists of examples of irrational beliefs. Also, researchers might explore the utility of measurement formats other than the standardized questionnaire, in hopes that such new methods might be more sensitive to the possibility that some irrational beliefs are tacit except in stressful situations (Davison, Feldman, & Osborn, 1984; Muran, 1991) involving the thwarting of particularly central personal goals (Ellis, 1991).

WHAT IS RET, AND WHAT DOES RESEARCH SAY ABOUT ITS EFFECTS?

RET has fared well in meta-analytic reviews of treatment outcome research. The original psychotherapy meta-analysis (M. L. Smith & Glass, 1977) cited RET as yielding the second highest (to systematic desensitization) average effect size among 10 major forms of psychotherapy. A quantitative review of 70 RET outcome studies (Lyons & Woods, 1991) found RET to exceed the effectiveness of no-treatment (average $d = 0.98$) or wait-list controls (average $d = 1.02$). Average effect sizes for comparisons of RET with behavioral ($d = 0.30$) or alternate cognitive–behavioral ($d = 0.14$) methods were also positive, albeit much lower.

Qualitative reviewers, however, have been critical of the methodological adequacy of much of the evidence on which such quantitative summaries are based (Haaga & Davison, 1989a; Kendall, 1984; Zettle & Hayes, 1980). Perhaps the clearest expression of this point of view was offered by Hollon and Beck (1986):

> RET appears to have the least clear empirical support of any of the major variants [of cognitive–behavioral therapy], although that state of affairs may derive as much from the fact that the bulk of the trials involving that approach were earlier, less rigorously conducted efforts. (p. 476)

Such negative appraisals of RET outcome research and its impact seem to us to derive from two main sources.

Insufficient Testing of Unique RET Hypotheses

First, distinctive RET hypotheses about mechanisms of change, as opposed to general comparisons of the overall effectiveness of RET and other treatments, have not been tested often (Haaga & Davison, 1989b). For example, RET is hypothesized to exceed the effectiveness of other cognitive–behavioral treatments by virtue of promoting unconditional self-acceptance and reducing "secondary problems" such as self-criticism about having problems (Boyd & Grieger, 1986). This viewpoint (which is obviously reminiscent of Carl Rogers) resonates with an increased recent emphasis in behavior therapy on acceptance (Hayes, 1987; Linehan, 1987) but has not been reflected in RET research, which has tended to use conventional self-esteem indices rather than measures of self-acceptance (Haaga & Davison, 1989a).

Inattention to Generally Applicable Method Criteria

Second, RET outcome studies have tended to fare poorly in terms of generic methodological criteria (Kazdin, 1986). The norm has been to use inexperienced therapists, conducting brief group RET for subclinical problems, with no follow-up evaluation and outcome measured largely in terms of self-reported symptoms and irrational beliefs. These limitations call into question the validity of even apparently favorable results. Some reassurance on these issues can, however, be culled from the quantitative review by Lyons and Woods (1991), who found larger effect sizes for studies with therapy patients as subjects than for studies of student subjects, as well as larger effects for studies rated as high in internal validity (e.g., using low-reactivity measures and random assignment).

Some remaining sources of concern in this respect include (a) nonreporting of the clinical significance of treatment effects (Jacobson & Revenstorf, 1988), (b) infrequent collection of follow-up data (57 of 70 studies reviewed by Lyons and Woods [1991] did not report follow-up results), and (c) inattention to attrition (61 of 70 studies did not report on attrition rates; Lyons & Woods, 1991). Taking attrition into account seems especially important in view of Ellis's advocacy of a forceful style of intervention, hypothesized by some to promote attrition (e.g., Young, in Ellis, Young, & Lockwood, 1987) and reactance on the part of patients (Goldfried & Davison, 1976).[1]

Like removing emotional content from measures of irrational beliefs, adhering to these generically relevant methodological criteria seems feasible, and some RET research already has done so. Mersch, Emmelkamp, and their colleagues (Mersch, Emmelkamp, Bogels, & van der Sleen, 1989; Mersch, Emmelkamp, & Lips, 1991), for example, compared RET with social skills training for carefully diagnosed social phobics, using self-report and observational outcome measures, 14-month follow-up assessment, extensive information on the reasons for subject dropout and on the seeking of further treatment by some subjects during the follow-up period, with a specific focus on prediction of differential response to treatments based on patient characteristics. To be sure, the substantive results might be viewed as disappointing (both treatments appeared to be helpful, neither significantly more so than the other, and treatments matched to the relative deficit of a patient—low social skill or high irrational beliefs—were no more effective than mismatched treatments), but the method appears to have been sound in many ways.

A more difficult method criterion for RET researchers to meet is achieving a clear definition and measurement of RET itself, the independent variable (Haaga, Dryden, & Dancey, 1991). Conflicting evaluations of RET's research status often turn on differing interpretations of what is included and excluded by the label *RET* (Ellis, 1989; Lazarus, 1989; Mahoney, Lyddon, & Alford, 1989). Commenting on our earlier qualitative review of RET outcome research, Ellis (1989) stated that "these RET experiments have almost always unclearly defined what RET really is and have only very partially included the main RET methods" (p. 229) and that "virtually none of the outcome studies cited by Haaga and Davison deal with ... preferential and 'real' ... RET. Aside from a few studies (such as Forsterling, 1985), it has not yet been tested" (p. 231).[2]

A survey of 41 published RET outcome studies indicated that a majority $(n = 23)$ provided no information about attempts to measure treatment adherence, the extent to which treatment conformed to the specifications of the therapy system being evaluated (Haaga et al., 1991). Moreover, most studies $(n = 38)$ did not assess the differentiability (by blind raters) of RET from comparison treatments, and all but one failed to measure the quality of RET intervention; the exception (Warren, McLellarn, & Ponzoha, 1988) used global ratings of competence by Albert Ellis on the basis of session tapes. Thus, low treatment integrity or low therapist competence might always be cited to explain away any unfavorable results with RET. Conversely, favorable results might be ascribed by skeptics to non-RET interventions inadvertently included in the RET condition.

If the only problem in this respect were insufficient attention to the need to measure treatment integrity and quality, this could be readily corrected in future research. However, there might be limits in principle to how well researchers can represent and measure RET as depicted by theorists. Ellis (1980) defined RET broadly, subsuming as its "elegant" or "specialized" (Dryden & Ellis, 1988) form the aspects researchers have typically focused on as distinctive of RET (e.g., forceful disputation of irrational beliefs) and as its "inelegant" or "general" form essentially the entirety of other cognitive–behavioral approaches. This expansiveness of definition leads to quite basic disagreements. For instance, should exposure in vivo be considered a RET intervention for anxiety disorders, or is this a different approach, to be controlled for (Lazarus, 1991) or excluded (Mersch et al., 1989) when evaluating RET? Is Beck's (1964) cognitive therapy something other than RET, as implied by the organization of this volume and by theoretical (Haaga & Davison, 1991) and empirical (DiGiuseppe, McGowan, Sutton, Simon, & Gardner, 1990) comparisons of the two, or is it a fallback RET technique to be used when specialized RET's forceful disputation fails to work?

CONCLUSION: WHICH WAY TO GO?

Previous reviews of RET have noted the difficulty of pinning down precisely what it includes and excludes as a therapeutic system, differentiating it from related approaches, and evaluating whether these differences make a difference in outcome. The high evaluation given by most researchers to standardization of treatment techniques within a condition, as well as differentiation from other systems, reflects an acceptance of what Docherty (1984) described as a "technological model" of psychotherapy. It is possible that further theoretical refinements will lead to greater consensus on what RET is and is not and how it might be applied and measured as a standardized technology. History does not support boundless optimism on this score, though. Researchers appear to be caught between the Scylla of being so vague about what was done that readers are unsure what to make of their results (Haaga et al., 1991) and the Charybdis of specifying RET in a way that its adherents view as partial and of insufficient scope (Ellis, 1989).

Perhaps it is time to consider the possibility that RET is not susceptible to traditional scientific outcome evaluation. Just as studies of "behavior therapy" (e.g., Sloane, Staples, Cristol, Yorkston, & Whipple, 1975) have given way to studies of, say, breathing retraining for panic attacks, perhaps studies of RET will be replaced by studies of specific tactics in particular circumstances (e.g., logical disputation of self-rating for depressed persons voicing global negative self-evaluations). Such studies could begin to address the theoretically and clinically interesting issue of when and for whom RET's distinctive methods are helpful.

Ellis currently advocates using specialized RET disputation techniques first, then, "if they do not seem to work too well in individual cases, I add various other therapeutic modalities" (Ellis, 1989, p. 218). Ellis has estimated that 30% of patients respond well to this initial disputation phase (Ellis et al., 1987). Research aimed at determining prognostic indicators of who these patients are, whether others would benefit more from specialized RET disputation later in treatment rather than at the beginning or from omitting philosophical disputation altogether, and so on, could be highly valuable even in the absence of professional consensus as to whether these variations speak directly to the efficacy of RET.

NOTES

1. A prior question is whether RET practitioners actually follow Ellis's lead on this point. Survey data indicate that a majority of experienced RET therapists disagree with Ellis's view that "excessive" therapist warmth reinforces unhealthy beliefs about needs for approval, and nearly one half (47%) disagreed with his contention that "forceful persuasive disputing is usually more effective than more subtle, perhaps indirect disputing" (Warren & McLellarn, 1987, p. 85).
2. Forsterling (1985) was not a treatment outcome study but instead a series of studies of students' ideas about the relations between (ir)rational beliefs and emotional reactions to success and failure.

REFERENCES

Bandura, A. (1986). *Social foundations of thoughts and action: A social cognitive theory* . Englewood Cliffs, NJ: Prentice-Hall.

Bartley, W. W. III. (1984). The retreat to commitment (2nd ed.). New York: Knopf.

Beck, A. T. (1964). Thinking and depression: 2. Theory and therapy: *Archives of General Psychiatry, 10,* 561–571.

Boyd, J., & Grieger, R. M. (1986). Self-acceptance problems. In A. Ellis & R. M. Grieger (Eds.), *Handbook of rational–emotive therapy* (Vol. 2, pp. 146–161). New York: Springer.

Davison, G. C. (1976). Homosexuality: The ethical challenge. *Journal of Consulting and Clinical Psychology, 44,* 157–162.

Davison, G. C. (1991). Constructionism and morality in therapy for homosexuality. In J. C. Gonsiorek & J. D. Weinrich (Eds.), Homosexuality: Research implications for public policy (pp. 137–148). Newbury Park, CA: Sage.

Davison, G. C., Feldman, P. M., & Osborn, C. E. (1984). Articulated thoughts, irrational beliefs, and fear of negative evaluation. *Cognitive Therapy and Research, 8,* 349–362.

Davison, G. C., & Neale, J. M. (1990). *Abnormal psychology* (5th ed.). New York: Wiley.

Didion, J. (1979). *The white album.* New York: Pocket Books.

DiGiuseppe, R. (1991). Comprehensive cognitive disputing in RET. In M. E. Bernard (Ed.), *Using rational–emotive therapy effectively: A practitioner's guide* (pp. 173–195). New York: Plenum Press.

DiGiuseppe, R., McGowan, L., Sutton Simon, K., & Gardner, F (1990). A comparative outcome study of four cognitive therapies in the treatment of social anxiety. *Journal of Rational–Emotive and Cognitive–Behavior Therapy, 8,* 129–146.

Docherty, J. P. (1984). Implications of the technological model of psychotherapy. In J. B. W. Williams & R. L. Spitzer (Eds.), *Psychotherapy research: Where are we and where should we go?* (pp. 139–147). New York: Guilford Press.

Dryden, W., & Ellis, A. (1988). Rational–emotive therapy. In K. S. Dobson (Ed.), *Handlbook of cognitive–behavioral therapies* (pp. 214–272). New York: Guilford Press.

Ellis, A. (1957). Outcome of employing three techniques of psychotherapy. *Journal of Clinical Psychology, 13,* 344–350.

Ellis, A. (1962). *Reason and emotion in psychotherapy.* New York: Lyle Stuart.

Ellis, A. (1980). Rational–emotive therapy and cognitive behavior therapy: Similarities and differences. *Cognitive Therapy and Research, 4,* 325–340.

Ellis, A. (1989). Comments on my critics. In M. E. Bernard & R. DiGiuseppe (Eds.), *Inside rational–emotive therapy: A critical appraisal of the theory and therapy of Albert Ellis* (pp. 199–233). San Diego, CA: Academic Press.

Ellis, A. (1990). Special features of rational–emotive therapy. In W. Dryden & R. DiGiuseppe (Eds.), A *primer of rational–emotive therapy* (pp. 79–93). Champaign, IL: Research Press.

Ellis, A. (1991). The revised ABC's of rational–emotive therapy (RET). *Journal of Rational–Emotive and Cognitive–Behavior Therapy, 9,* 139–177.

Ellis, A., & Bernard, M. E. (1985). What is rational–emotive therapy (RET)? In A. Ellis & M. E. Bernard (Eds), *Clinical applications of rational–emotive therapy* (pp. 1–30). New York: Plenum Press.

Ellis, A., & Bernard, M. E. (1986). What is rational-emotive therapy? In A. Ellis & R. M. Grieger (Eds), *Handbook of rational–emotive therapy* (Vol. 2, pp. 3–30). New York: Springer.

Ellis, A., & Grieger, R. M. (Eds.). (1986). *Handbook of rational–emotive therapy* (Vol. 2) New York: Springer.

Ellis, A., & Harper, R. A. (1975). *A new guide to rational living.* North Hollywood, CA: Wilshire.

Ellis, A., Young, J., & Lockwood, G. (1987). Cognitive therapy and rational–emotive therapy: A dialogue. *Journal of Cognitive Psychotherapy: An International Quarterly, 1,* 205–255.

Forsterling, F. (1985). Rational–emotive therapy and attribution theory: An investigation of the cognitive determinants of emotions. *British Journal of Cognitive Psychotherapy, 3,* 12–25.

Geer, J. H., Davison, G. C., & Gatchel, R. I. (1970). Reduction of stress in humans through nonveridical perceived control of aversive stimulation. *Journal of Personality and Social Psychology, 16,* 731–738.

Goldfried, M. R., & Davison, G. C. (1976). *Clinical behavior therapy* . New York: Holt, Rinehart & Winston.

Goldfried, M. R., Decenteceo, E. T., & Weinberg, L. (1974). Systematic rational restructuring as a self-control technique. *Behavior Therapy, 5,* 247–254.

Haaga, D. A. F., & Davison, G. C. (1989a). Outcome studies of rational–emotive therapy. In M. E. Bernard & R. DiGiuseppe (Eds.), *Inside rational–emotive therapy: A critical appraisal* (pp. 155–197). San Diego, CA: Academic Press.

Haaga, D. A. F., & Davison, G. C. (1989b). Slow progress in rational–emotive therapy outcome research: Etiology and treatment. *Cognitive Therapy and Research, 13,* 493–508.

Haaga, D. A. F., & Davison, G. C. (1991). Disappearing differences do not always reflect healthy integration: An analysis of cognitive therapy and rational–emotive therapy. *Journal of Psychotherapy Integration, 1,* 287–303.

Haaga, D. A. F., Dryden, W., & Dancey, C. P. (1991). Measurement of rational–emotive therapy in outcome studies. *Journal of Rational–Emotive and Cognitive–Behavior Therapy, 9,* 73–93.

Hayes, S. C. (1987). A contextual approach to therapeutic change. In N. Jacobson (Ed.), *Psychotherapists in clinical practice: Cognitive and behavioral perspective* (pp. 327–387). New York: Guilford Press.

Hollon. S., & Beck, A. T. (1986). Cognitive and cognitive–behavioral therapies. In S. L. Garfield & A. E. Bergin (Eds.), *Handbook of psychotherapy and behavior change* (3rd ed., pp. 443–482). New York: Wiley.

Jacobson, N. S., & Revenstorf, D. (1988). Statistics for assessing the clinical significance of psychotherapy techniques: Issues, problems, and new developments. *Behavior Assessment, 10,* 133–145.

Jones, R. (1968). *A factored measure of Ellis's irrational belief system.* Unpublished doctoral dissertation, Texas Technological College, Lubbock.

Kazdin, A. E. (1986). Comparative outcome studies of psychotherapy: Methodological issues and strategies. *Journal of Consulting and Clinical Psychology, 54,* 95–105.

Kendall, P. C. (1984). Cognitive processes and procedures in behavior therapy. In C. M. Franks, G. T. Wilson, P C. Kendall, & K. D. Brownell (Eds.), *Annual review of behavior therapy: Theory and practice* (Vol. 10, pp. 123–163). New York: Guilford Press.

Kenrick, D. T., & Funder, D. C. (1988). Profiting from controversy: Lessons from the person–situation debate. *American Psychologist, 43,* 23–34.

Knaus, W. (1974). *Rational–emotive education: A manual for elementary school teachers.* New York: Institute for Rational Living.

Lazarus, A. A. (1989). The practice of rational–emotive therapy. In M. E. Bernard & R. DiGiuseppe (Eds.), *Inside rational–emotive therapy: A critical appraisal of the theory and therapy of Albert Ellis* (pp. 95–112). San Diego, CA: Academic Press.

Lazarus, A. A. (1991). A plague on Little Hans and Little Albert. *Psychotherapy, 28,* 444–447.

Linehan, M. M. (1987). Dialectical behavior therapy: A cognitive–behavioral approach to parasuicide. *Journal of Personality Disorders, 1,* 328–333.

Lyons, L. C., & Woods, P. J. (1991). The efficacy of rational–emotive therapy: A quantitative review of the outcome research. *Clinical Psychology Review, 11,* 357–369.

Mahoney, M. J., Lyddon, W. J., & Alford, D. J. (1989). An evaluation of the rational–emotive theory of psychotherapy. In M. E. Bernard & R. DiGiuseppe (Eds.), *Inside rational–emotive therapy: A critical appraisal of the theory and therapy of Albert Ellis* (pp. 69–94). San Diego, CA: Academic Press.

Malouff, J. M., & Schutte, N. S. (1986). Development and validation of a measure of irrational belief. *Journal of Consulting and Clinical Psychology, 54,* 860–862.

Malouff, J. M., Valdenegro, J., & Schutte, N. S. (1987). Further validation of a measure of irrational belief. *Journal of Rational–Emotive Therapy, 5,* 189–193.

Mersch, P. P. A., Emmelkamp, P. M. G., Bogels, S. M., & van der Sleen, J. (1989). Social phobia: Individual response patterns and the effects of behavioral and cognitive interventions. *Behaviour Research and Therapy, 27,* 421–434.

Mersch, P. P. A., Emmelkamp, P. M. G., & Lips, C. (1991). Social phobia: Individual response patterns and the long-term effects of behavioral and cognitive interventions: A follow-up study. *Behaviour Research and Therapy, 29,* 357–362.

Muran, J. C. (1991). A reformulation of the ABC model in cognitive psychotherapies: Implications for assessment and treatment. *Clinical Psychology Review, 11,* 399–418.

Robb, H. B. III, & Warren, R. (1990). Irrational belief tests: New insights, new direction. *Journal of Cognitive Psychotherapy: An International Quarterly, 4,* 303–311.

Rorer, L. G. (1989a). Rational–emotive theory: 1. An integrated psychological and philosophical basis. *Cognitive Therapy and Research, 13,* 475–492.

Rorer, L. G. (1989b). Rational–emotive theory: 2. Explication and evaluation. *Cognitive Therapy and Research, 13,* 531–548.

Shorkey, C. T., & Whiteman, V. L. (1977). Development of the Rational Behavior Inventory: Initial validity and reliability. *Educational and Psychological Measurement, 37,* 527–534.

Sloane, R. B., Staples, F. R., Cristol, A. H., Yorkston, N. J., & Whipple, K. (1975). *Psychoanalysis versus behavior therapy.* Cambridge, MA: Harvard University Press.

Smith, D. (1982). Trends in counseling and psychotherapy. *American Psychologist, 37,* 802–809.

Smith, M. L., & Glass, G. V. (1977). Meta-analysis of psychotherapy outcome studies. *American Psychologist, 32,* 752–760.

Smith, T. W. (1989). Assessment in rational–emotive therapy: Empirical access to the ABCD model. In M. E. Bernard & R. DiGiuseppe (Eds.), *Inside* rational–emotive therapy: A critical appraisal of the theory and therapy of Albert Ellis* (pp. 135–153). San Diego. CA: Academic Press.

Taylor, S. E., & Brown, J. D., (1988). Illusion and well-being: A social psychological perspective on mental health. *Psychological Bulletin, 103,* 193–210.

Warner, R. E. (1991). A survey of theoretical orientations of Canadian clinical psychologists. *Canadian Psychology, 32,* 525–528.

Warren, R., & McLellarn, R. W. (1987). What do RET therapists think they are doing? An international survey. *Journal of Rational–Emotive Therapy, 5,* 71–91.

Warren, R., McLellarn, R., & Ponzoha, C. (1988). Rational–emotive therapy versus general cognitive–behavior therapy in the treatment of low self-esteem and related emotional disturbances. *Cognitive Therapy and Research, 12,* 21–38.

Watson, D., & Clark, L. A. (1984). Negative affectivity: The disposition to experience aversive emotional states. *Psychological Bulletin, 96,* 465–490.

Woolfolk, R. L., & Sass, L. A. (1989). Philosophical foundations of rational–emotive therapy. In M. E. Bernard & R. DiGiuseppe (Eds.), *Inside rational–emotive therapy: A critical appraisal of the theory and therapy of Albert Ellis* (pp. 9–26). San Diego, CA: Academic Press.

Zettle, R. D., & Hayes, S. C. (1980). Conceptual and empirical status of rational–emotive therapy. In M. Hersen, R. M. Eisler, & P. M. Miller (Eds.), *Progress in behavior modification* (Vol. 9, pp. 126–166). San Diego, CA: Academic Press.

Zurawski, R. M., & Smith, T. W. (1987). Assessing irrational beliefs and emotional distress: Evidence and implications of limited discriminant validity. *Journal of Counseling Psychology, 34,* 224–227.

IV

The Constructive Psychotherapies

7

A Constructivist Outline of Human Knowing Processes

Vittorio F. Guidano

The cognitive-behavioral approach, which emerged in the 1970s, can be considered a development of the traditional associationist paradigm. While allowing for the description, analysis, and modification of isolated beliefs, internal dialogues, and distortions of thought, this approach left unsolved the most basic problem for the foundation of an applied cognitive psychology, namely, the development and organization of human knowledge. The central role of an individual's acquired knowledge of self and the world in regulating his or her perception of and activity toward environmental events has become more and more evident. Data corroborating the importance of such knowledge has emanated from such basic disciplines as experimental cognitive psychology, neuropsychology, and artificial intelligence. We are also beginning to sense that the development, maintenance, and change of individual knowledge appear to reflect uniform (although not necessarily strictly coherent) processes across different cognitive domains. An individual obviously knows himself or herself and is known by others as consistent even while, at different moments, he or she is expressing different or even contradictory beliefs, opinions, emotions, and behaviors.

In the face of such problems, it seems unreasonable to continue attempts to extend the range of applicability of the associationist-behaviorist paradigm. The shift toward a new epistemological framework capable of providing a more integrative model of human cognitive processes has shown promise (Guidano, 1987, 1991; Guidano & Liotti,

1983; Mahoney, 1980, 1982, 1991; Weimer, 1982). The aim of this chapter is twofold: to outline the main theoretical implications deriving from the assumption of a nonassociationist epistemology and to explore some of the main consequences of this perspective for our understanding of the development and organization of human knowledge.

A CONSTRUCTIVIST FRAMEWORK

The elaboration of a constructivist framework stems from a set of basic assumptions grounded in the literatures of evolutionary epistemology (Campbell, 1974; Lorenz, 1973; Popper, 1972; Popper & Eccles, 1977; Radnitzky & Bartley, 1987). They can be briefly outlined as follows.

Knowledge as an Evolutionary Process

A biological conception of the origin and evolution of knowledge allows one to define it as a specific field of the natural sciences. It therefore permits one to create a specific demarcation from the fields of philosophy and metaphysics, which have been popular domains for the study of human knowledge processes. This demarcation also makes it possible to conduct research on knowledge using the same procedures employed in modern scientific methodology: an experimentally falsifiable approach testing hypotheses arising from the interaction of available, tenable theories and emerging observational data.

The concept of knowledge structures as evolutionary patterns of life processes—processes that are progressively shaped in response to challenging environmental pressures—implies that an organism's activity is the key feature of its interaction with the world (Popper, 1975). Indeed, every perspective on the mind implicitly presupposes a model of interaction between organism and environment within which the processes that mediate the interaction are defined. From an associationist perspective the organism–environment interaction views perception as the fundamental mediator, whereas a constructivist perspective considers the organism's activity itself to be its basic mediator. This does not mean that a constructivist approach denies the importance of sensory perception: The organism's activity is constantly expressed at a motor level (environmental exploration), a sensory level (constructing perceptual regularities), and a cognitive level (making and matching hypotheses). In this sense, as Piaget (1970) asserts, to know an object essentially means to act upon it.

From a constructivist perspective, knowing is conceptualized as an ongoing, evolutionary process that unfolds in a progressive elaboration of the living system's active attempts to organize its experience. As Weimer (1975) cogently put it, organisms are active and embodied "theories of their environment." According to this viewpoint, the main process of mental functioning is not what the associationists had proposed—that is, the forming and breaking up of associative ties derived from the passive acquisition of chronological (classical conditioning) or consequential (operant conditioning) contingency relationships. To the contrary, mental functioning is primarily a constructive scaffolding of experience via active (and predominantly tacit) expectations, hypotheses, and theories. Because all learning is relative to prior knowledge (Hamlyn, 1981), knowing is necessarily a time-binding, historical process.

If knowledge processes are emergent products of the ongoing interaction between the knowing subject and his or her medium, knowledge itself appears to be very far from either a mere sensory copy of reality (empiricism) or a mere unfolding of schemata already preformed in the individual (innatism). To the contrary, knowledge appears to be a progressive, hierarchical construction of models of being. The representational validity of these working models is technically and theoretically unknowable, and it is their viability that is of more central concern to the constructive epistemologist (Bowlby, 1988; Mahoney, Miller, & Arciero, *this volume*; Maturana & Varela, 1987). These working models play an essential role in directing the interaction of the individual with his or her world. Indeed, such models determine the possible patterns with which the individual can see and conceive the world (as well as the self). By thus influencing the range and form of possible experience, they constrain individual phenomenology in a way that is critically important to our understanding of psychopathology and our practice of psychotherapy.

Motor Theories of Mind

From the perspective here outlined, the mind appears as an active, constructive system capable of producing not only its output but also, to a large extent, the input it receives, including the basic sensations underlying the construction of itself. In recent years there has been a decline in the popularity of "sensory theories" that depict the mind as a mere collector of sensations. These theories, which were popular in learning theories and early information-processing models of cognition, had been based on objectivist assumptions. That is, they had assumed an inherent correspondence in which an external reality imposed its order on our nervous systems through relatively passive registration on our sensory receptors. In contrast to and in competition with these sensory theories are the "motor theories" of mind, which have become increasingly popular in the past few years (Hayek, 1952, 1978; Piaget, 1970; Popper, 1972; Weimer, 1977). According to the motoric perspective, the mind is to be considered a system of abstract rules bringing about a relational order in experience and activity (Weimer, 1982). As Hayek (1978) pointed out, the richness of the sensory world that we experience is not the starting point from which the mind derives abstractions, but, to the contrary, it is the product of a great range of abstractions the mind must perform in order to be capable of experiencing such richness of details. What was taken for granted in explaining the functioning of the human mind—that the concrete seems primary, and the abstract appears to be derived from it—now appears to be an error of our subjective experience, reflecting the complex and automatic ordering ability that the human mind has acquired in its evolutionary history (Hayek, 1952). Two essential aspects of motor theories of mind should be taken into account in any attempt to outline a model of knowing processes: (1) the centrality of unconscious processes and (2) the relation between tacit and explicit levels of knowing.

Centrality of Unconscious Processes

From a constructivist perspective, tacit processes of mental activity are deep structure ordering rules that organize ongoing experience and anticipate imminent experience. This means that abstract tacit processes operate pervasively in our experience, and yet, as the words *abstract* and *tacit* imply, their operations are well beyond our conscious awareness. This does not mean that they necessarily operate at a subconscious level, however. (The tendency to relegate tacit knowing processes to a subconscious realm is probably a legacy of the theoretical hegemony of psychoanalytic theory up to the past few decades.) Hayek (1978) has argued that these tacit ordering processes are by no means *below* our explicit (verbal) consciousness but that they would be more accurately described as functioning *above* that consciousness. In other words, they operate not at a *sub*conscious level but at a *super*conscious one, because they govern the conscious processes without appearing in them (Franks, 1974; Polanyi, 1966; Reber & Lewis, 1977; Turvey, 1974; Weimer, 1973, 1982).

Tacit and Explicit Levels of Knowing

In viewing human knowing processes from such a perspective, the distinction between deep and surface cognitive structures—that is, between tacit and explicit levels of knowing—follows automatically. Increasingly convergent evidence shows that deep and surface aspects of mental processing are the expression of a structured differentiation between two closely interconnected levels of cognitive processes (Airenti, Bara, & Colombetti, 1980, 1982; Tulving, 1972; Weimer, 1975). The tacit processes provide a necessary level of organization that functions like an "apprehensional" or anticipatory frame for orienting attentional processes and constructing the particulars of experience. The tacit level of knowing—an individual's system of deep ordering rules—is thus reflected in explicit knowledge (expectations, beliefs, emotions, behaviors, and so on). According to this model, cognition is the emergent result of an ogoing interaction between deep and surface levels of knowing—that is, between the tacit and the explicit.

The procedure by which tacit knowledge is converted into explicit knowledge and vice versa is not, however, a simple one-to-one mapping but rather a constructive, generative process (Piaget, 1970; Reber & Lewis, 1977). The search for consistency and a complementary sensitivity to contrast appear to be regulators of the whole process. That is, the tacit ordering processes appear to be biased by a tendency to recognize or shape incoming information in ways that are consistent with already available knowledge structures (a process described as assimilation by Piaget). The perception of discrepancies—unexpected anomalies in experience—can result in modifications of the tacit order (a process called accommodation by Piaget). The search for consistency seems to be inherent to the epistemic subject, whereas the development of capacities to learn from inconsistencies appears to be a more recent evolutionary development. The latter capacity was dramatically accelerated with the development of linguistic abilities, which allow their user the power of symbolic negation.

The essential characteristic of human knowledge is therefore the ongoing pursuit of order via contrast. In this way, progressively more integrative and comprehensive knowing patterns are made possible. The ability to perceive the range of discrepancies is continuously remodeled so as to further elaborate working knowledge. If constructive abilities are the hallmark of the interaction of an active mind with its environs, then consistency (the capacity for recognition) and discrepancy are the domains of exchange in which that interaction takes place (Mahoney, 1982, 1991). Thus, the relation between tacit and explicit knowledge involves an active and ongoing interdependence. Tacit knowing processes exhibit a "feed-forward" tendency, in which the demands of adaptation are anticipated from one moment to the next. Explicit knowing and surface structure activity are more immediately driven by feedback processes. An important challenge facing the knowing system is the maintenance of a balance between these processes so that discrepancies remain below a critical level relative to the coherence-dependent operations of the overall system.

ORGANIZATION OF HUMAN KNOWING PROCESSES

The foregoing discussion now permits some conjectures on human knowing processes. As I have tried to elaborate elsewhere, our understanding of those processes is central to all of our efforts in psychotherapy (Guidano, 1987, 1991). Here I shall condense my remarks and organize them around four interrelated themes: (1) human self-organizing abilities, (2) attachment theory as an integrative paradigm, (3) development as self-knowledge reorganization, and (4) knowledge evolution as a dynamic process of equilibration.

Human Self-Organizing Abilities

There is now considerable evidence documenting the important role of biological individuation in evolutionary development (Ferracin, Panichelli, Benassi, DiNallo, & Steindler, 1978; Popper & Eccles, 1977; Varela, 1979). More relevant for therapeutic concerns, however, is the fact that humans exhibit more complex and elaborated capacities for levels of individuation than are demonstrated by other life forms. These capacities are unquestionably related to "languaging" abilities, and they are of inestimable significance to the practice of psychotherapy. The sense of individual uniqueness and historical continuity is a cardinal feature of what it means to be human. Indeed, without a sense of personal identity and the stabilities that it affords, most of what we consider the "higher" mental processes would be psychologically impossible. Human experience—from the level of perception to abstraction—presupposes a level of stability and coherence. Traditional views of human nature, which were permeated with the assumptions of objectivism, associationism, and sensory theories of mind, presumed that external reality was the primary source of experiential stability. It is now increasingly apparent that the individual human knower contributes significantly to the coherence and stability that he or she experiences.

The importance of this point for our understanding of individual lives is difficult to exaggerate and impossible to capture in the words of any language. Suffice it to say that the maintenance of our own perceived personal identity becomes almost as important to us as life itself. Without the sense of self as a center of agency and experiencing, we would be incapable of most forms of everyday functioning. It is for this reason, among others, that I maintain that all psychotherapies are ultimately psychotherapies of the self and that the process of psycho-therapy can be understood adquately only if these life-span "selfhood" processes are appreciated (Guidano, 1987, 1991).

Attachment Theory: An Integrative Paradigm of Human Development

Although human beings are born with a complex inborn repertoire and a remarkable capacity to begin self-organization, the newborn is not yet a self in the psychological sense of that term. The development of a self—and hence of self-knowledge—is an active learning process stem-ming from a specific set of evolutionary constraints. "Learning to be a self" (Popper & Eccles, 1977) represents the basic process through which a human organism learns to recognize itself, progressively unifies knowledge about itself into a definite and relatively stable identity, and eventually puts its identity at the center of reality—that is, at the center of all its knowledge.

The well-known theory that human beings acquire self-knowledge through interaction with other people (Cooley, 1902; Mead, 1934) is now supported by considerable evidence from research on primates, from studies of child development, and from studies of the psycho-therapeutic process (Curtiss, Fromkin, Krashen, Rigler, & Rigler, 1974; Guidano, 1987, 1991; Hayes & Nissen, 1971; Hill, Bundy, Coallup, & McClure, 1970; Linden, 1974; Mahoney, 1991; von Senden, 1960). An infant learns to know by exploring and actively interacting with her own environment, and people are undoubtedly the most important objects in this environment (Brazelton, Koslowski, & Main, 1974; Lewis & Lee-Painter, 1974). Mainly from the qualitative aspects of their ongoing interactions with other people, children become progressively able to recognize the invariant aspects by which they can define and evaluate themselves as separate and unique persons. Of this phenomenon, known as the looking-glass effect, Popper gives the following defini-tion: "Just as we learn to see ourselves in a mirror, so the child becomes conscious of himself by seeing his reflection in the mirror of other people's consciousness of himself" (Popper & Eccles, 1977, p. 110).

A logical consequence of the looking-glass effect is the implication that interpersonal and relational domains play a crucial role in the development of self-knowledge. John Bowlby's attachment theory is a heuristic explanatory framework for organizing our current under-standing of human self-knowledge development (Ainsworth, Blehar, Waters, & Wall, 1978; Bowlby, 1969, 1973, 1980, 1988). It is a paradigm of human development that offers an inclusive and organized vision of the main factors that contribute to the structuring of self-knowledge. According to attachment theory, the sense of self and all other things that can be considered self-knowledge emerge from an interpersonal matrix.

Development as Self-Knowledge Reorganization

According to this perspective, developmental stages can be considered as a progressive series of qualitative transformations beginning with the structuring of elementary patterns of self-organization and ending with the emergence of a structured self-identity. In this steplike procedure, each emerging conception of self depends in its structuring on the level previously reached and in turn determines the possible direction in which the next can develop. Thus, each emerging self-conception is new in form (structure), not just in content (Broughton, 1981), and is the expression of the whole structural reorganization involving the reflective dimension of consciousness and paralleling the ascension to higher structural levels of knowing.

Assuming a comprehensive view, human development may thus be seen as a process characterized by a structural gap. On one side is the progressive scaffolding of experience that brings about an even more complex system of abstract rules. On the other side is the slow unfolding of cognitive abilities that makes it possible to become (partially) aware of their presence only at a later stage of intellectual development, usually no earlier than adolescence. At this point in the individual's development, the prelogical and emotional conceptions of self and the world undergo a conceptual reelaboration, becoming a conscious self-image central to subsequent self-organization. The main stages in this development of self-knowledge can be sketched as follows:

1. *Infancy and preschool years (from about 2½ to 5 years of age).* The level of cognitive growth possible at this stage allows for the elaboration of a primordial nucleus of self-knowledge. There is an organization of basic deep-structural relations that affords relatively stable patterns of self and world perception. In the process of this development, there is an inherent biasing of further self-knowledge development, which is constrained by the domains of meaning selectively constructed by the young child.

2. *Childhood (roughly corresponding to primary school age).* The cognitive development possible in this stage is comparable to that associated with Piaget's (1970) stage of concrete operations. Qualitative changes in epistemic capacities permit a more differentiated organization of experience, an organization that is characterized by its relative empha-

sis on immediate and concrete qualities. During this stage there is an emergence and elaboration of self-conceptions that result in the discovery of the self as an object (Dickstein, 1977).

3. *Adolescence and youth (from about 12 to 18 years of age).* In this third stage of development, which corresponds to Piaget's stage of formal operations, the qualitative changes in knowing allow the individual to experience the self both as an already existing agent and as something to be discovered through a process of self-reflection. In other words, adulthood begins with an epistemological understanding in which the self emerges as "a knower" endowed with a full sense of personal identity and an active role in its own continuing self-organization (Chandler, 1975; Dickstein, 1977).

Knowledge Evolution as a Dynamic Equilibration Process

The dynamic equilibrium that characterizes the temporal evolution of knowledge unfolds through feed-forward oscillative processes involving a discontinuous emergence of more and more integrated models of self and reality. This feed-forward procedure rests on the basic mechanism underlying the unfolding of knowledge processes: a discontinuous structuring of more integrated sets of invariant tacit rules as the result of the ongoing ordering of unfolding experience. As discussed earlier, the relation between tacit and explicit knowledge is controlled, step by step, by the dynamic balance of consistency and discrepancy. The search for consistency (maintenance processes) is the basic procedure for structuring and stabilizing available levels of self-identity and self-awareness, and emotional perturbations aroused by the perception of discrepancies are the main regulators eliciting a restructuring of more integrated levels of self-identity and self-awareness (change processes). That is, change processes derive from attempts to convert emergent core schemata into beliefs and thought procedures and are regulated and modeled, step by step, by maintenance processes aimed at preserving the functional continuity and the sense of oneness inherent in selfhood structures. To allow any consistent degree of modification in the concepts of self and world, the individual must gradually elaborate an alternative self-image without experiencing unmanageable interruptions in his or her structured sense of subjective continuity. Any substantial interruptions would represent a loss of the very sense of reality. Thus, maintenance and change processes, rather than opposite polarities, are to be considered as interdependent and overlapping processes that, though simultaneous, show different modalities during the temporal becoming of knowledge. Whereas maintenance processes are continuous, change processes are continuous only as challenges or possibilities but are discontinuous in their occurrence.

Indeed, it should be emphasized that the temporal evolution of knowledge is not a continuous, smooth process but rather a discontinuous, steplike one. The passage from one step to the next is, in turn, a relatively unpredictable process, both in the ways and in the timing of its occurrence. The term *oscillative*, therefore, is meant to indicate this uncertain pattern characterizing human change processes (see Mahoney, 1991, for similar uses of this term). Oscillative patterns are exhibited in the emergence of organizational changes during the evolution of any open system, as has been noted by researchers in a number of different disciplines (Jacob, 1977; Kuhn, 1962; Lakatos, 1974; Nicolis & Prigogine, 1977; Prigogine, 1978; Waddington, 1975).

CONCLUSION

I conclude this theoretical outline by mentioning some controversial points pertaining to the temporal evolution of knowledge organization. One well-known problem concerns the relation between abnormal early experiences and adult psychopathology (e.g., Rutter, 1972, 1979). Although there is increasing evidence of variability and resilience in individual responses to early trauma, it is a warranted generalization that such trauma is usually associated with psychological vulnerabilities in later development. Until recently, however, the only proposed explanations for this correlation were deterministic in flavor (psychic determinism in psychodynamic interpretations and environmental determinism in behavioristic approaches). An alternative possibility is offered by a constructivist perspective. If, as I have outlined in this chapter, early experiences influence the structuring of tacit self-knowledge, it can be seen that the vulnerabilities to psychopathology that later emerge are reflections of ongoing (and self-perpetuating) limitations in epistemic capacities. In other words, the influence of early experiences on knowledge development and organization can be conceptualized as an active, constructive process whose generative capabilities gradually unfold in stages during the emergence of later levels of knowing.

Another problem worthy of note stems from the common observation that the control function carried out by personal identity tends to increase progressively with the passing of time. During the juvenile and even the intermediate phase of life, a consistent restructuring of one's personal identity seems more possible than in late adulthood, when the possibilities of a significant identity change are generally assumed to decrease. As Luckmann (1979) points out, personal identity tends to become a historical form of life. Other authors have used such terms as "plan of life" (Popper & Eccles, 1977) or "life theme" (Csikszentmihalyi & Beattie, 1979) to describe the progressive unification that characterizes a person's knowledge and actions over the course of his or her life. In reading biographies, we often get the impression that the individual, almost without realizing it, followed a sort of guiding track or a script.

It should be evident that, from a constructivist perspective, the life theme is something progressively and dynamically constructed moment by moment, day by day, and year by year. The individual's personal "style of being" unfolds over the course of life events and the activities and meanings derived from them. The consequences of the individual's choices and actions in turn become events that, unified in individual memory, allow one to build an even more uniform and comprehensive image of self and life. A constructivist approach thus acknowledges the self-begetting inertia of earlier knowledge structures, but it also emphasizes that changes in the personal sense of self (and, hence, world) require an epistemic restructuring that is far more complex than determinist approaches have acknowledged. The parameters influencing that restructuring remain one of the most important challenges facing constructivist theorists, researchers, and therapists in the years to come.

REFERENCES

Ainsworth, M. D. S., Blehar, M. C., Waters, E., & Wall, S. (1978). *Patterns of attachment*. Hillsdale, NJ: Erlbaum.

Airenti, G., Bara, B., & Colombetti, M. (1980). Semantic network representation of conceptual and episodic knowledge. In R. Trappl (Ed.), *Advances in cybernetics and system research* (Vol. 11). Washington, DC: Hemisphere.

Airenti, G., Bara, B., & Colombetti, M. (1982). A two level model of knowledge and belief. In R. Trappl (Ed.), *Proceedings of 6th E.M.C.S.R.* Amsterdam: North Holland.

Bowlby, J. (1969). *Attachment and loss: Vol. 1. Attachment*. New York: Basic Books.

Bowlby, J. (1973). *Attachment and loss: Vol. 2. Separation: Anger and anxiety*. New York: Basic Books.

Bowlby, J. (1980). *Loss, sadness and depression*. London: Hogarth Press.

Bowlby, J. (1988). *A secure base*. New York: Basic Books.

Brazelton, T. B., Koslowski, B., & Main, M. (1974). The origins of reciprocity: The early mother–infant interaction. In M. Lewis & L. A. Rosenblum (Eds.), *The effect of the infant on its caregivers*. New York: Wiley.

Broughton, J. M. (1981). The divided self in adolescence. *Human Development, 24*, 13–32.

Campbell, D. T. (1974). Evolutionary epistemology. In P. A. Schilpp (Ed.), *The philosophy of Karl Popper*. LaSalle, IL: The Library of Living Philosophers.

Chandler, M. J. (1975). Relativism and the problem of epistemological loneliness. *Human Development, 18*, 171–180.

Cooley, C. H. (1902). *Human nature and the social order*. New York: Scribner.

Csikszentmihalyi, M., & Beattie, O. V. (1979). Life themes: A theoretical and empirical exploration of their origins and effects. *Journal of Humanistic Psychology, 19*, 45–63.

Curtiss, S., Fromkin, V., Krashen, S., Rigler, D., & Rigler, M. (1974). The linguistic development of Genie. *Language, 50*, 528–555.

Dickstein, E. (1977). Self and self-esteem: Theoretical foundations and their implications for research. *Human Development, 20*, 129–140.

Ferracin, A., Panichelli, E., Benassi, M., DiNallo, A., & Steindler, C. (1978). Self-organizing ability and living systems. *Biosystems, 10*, 307–317.

Franks, J. J. (1974). Toward understanding understanding. In W. B. Weimer & D. S. Palermo (Eds.), *Cognition and the symbolic processes*. Hillsdale, NJ: Erlbaum.

Guidano, V. F. (1987). *Complexity of the self: A developmental approach to psychopathology and therapy*. New York: Guilford.

Guidano, V. F. (1991). *The self in process: Toward a post-rationalist cognitive therapy*. New York: Guilford.

Guidano, V. F., & Liotti, G. (1983). *Cognitive processes and emotional disorders*. New York: Guilford.

Hamlyn, D. W. (1981). Cognitive systems, "folk psychology" and knowledge. *Cognition, 10*, 115–118.

Hayek, F. A. (1952). *The sensory order*. Chicago: University of Chicago Press.

Hayek, F. A. (1978). *New studies in philosophy, politics, economics and the history of ideas*. Chicago: University of Chicago Press.

Hayes, K. J., & Nissen, C. H. (1971). Higher mental functions in a home-raised chimpanzee. In A. M. Schrier & F. Stollnitz (Eds.), *Behavior of nonhuman primates*. New York: Academic Press.

Hill, S. D., Bundy, R. A., Gallup, G. G., & McClure, M. K. (1970). Responsiveness of young nursery reared chimpanzees to mirrors. *Proceedings of the Louisiana Academy of Science, 33*, 77–82.

Jacob, F. (1977). Evolution and tinkering. *Science, 196*, 1161–1166.

Kuhn, T. S. (1962). *The structure of scientific revolutions*. Chicago: University of Chicago Press.

Lakatos, I. (1974). Falsification and the methodology of scientific research programmes. In I. Lakatos & A. Musgrave (Eds.), *Criticism and the growth of knowledge*. Cambridge: Cambridge University Press.

Lewis, M., & Lee-Painter, S. (1974). An interactional approach to the mother–infant dyad. In M. Lewis & L. Rosenblum (Eds.), *The effects of the infant on its caregivers*. New York: Wiley.

Linden, E. (1974). *Apes, men and language*. New York: Penguin.

Lorenz, K. (1973). *Behind the mirror*. New York: Harcourt Brace Jovanovich.

Luckmann, T. (1979). Personal identity as an evolutionary and historical problem. In M. von Cranach, K. Foppa, W. Lepenies, & D. Ploog (Eds.), *Human ethology.* Cambridge: Cambridge University Press.

Mahoney, M. J. (1980). Psychotherapy and the structure of personal revolutions. In M. J. Mahoney (Ed.), *Psychotherapy process.* New York: Plenum.

Mahoney, M. J. (1982). Psychotherapy and human change processes. In J. H. Harvey & M. M. Parks (Eds.), *Psychotherapy research and behavior change.* Washington, DC: American Psychological Association.

Mahoney, M. J. (1991). *Human change processes.* New York: Basic Books.

Maturana, H. R., & Varela, F. J. (1987). *The tree of knowledge.* Boston: Shambala.

Mead, G. H. (1934). *Mind, self and society.* Chicago: University of Chicago Press.

Nicolis, G., & Prigogine, I. (1977). *Self-organization in nonequilibrium systems: From dissipative structures to order through fluctuations.* New York: Wiley.

Piaget, J. (1970). *L 'epistemologie genetique.* Paris: Presses Universitaires de France.

Polanyi, M. (1966). *The tacit dimension.* Garden City, NY: Doubleday.

Popper, K. R. (1972). *Objective knowledge: An evolutionary approach* (2nd ed.). Oxford: Clarendon Press.

Popper, K. R. (1975). The rationality of scientific revolutions. In R. Harre (Ed.), *Problems of scientific revolutions.* Oxford: Clarendon Press.

Popper, K. R., & Eccles, J. C. (1977). *The self and its brain.* New York: Springer International.

Prigogine, I. (1978). Time, structure, and fluctuations. *Science, 201,* 777–785.

Radnitzky, G., & Bartley, W. W. (Eds.) (1987). *Evolutionary epistemology.* LaSalle, IL: Open Court.

Reber, A. S., & Lewis, S. (1977). Implicit learning: An analysis of the form and structure of a body of tacit knowledge. *Cognition, 5,* 333–361.

Rutter, M. (1972). *Maternal deprivation reassessed.* Harmondsworth, England: Penguin Books.

Rutter, M. (1979). Maternal deprivation 1972–1978: New findings, new concepts, new approaches. *Annals of the Academy of Medicine, 8,* 312–323.

Tulving, E. (1972). Episodic and semantic memory. In E. Tulving & W. Donaldson (Eds.), *Organization of memory,* New York: Academic Press.

Turvey, M. T. (1974). Constructive theory, perceptual systems and tacit knowledge. In W. B. Weimer & D. S. Palermo (Eds.), *Cognition and the symbolic processes,* Hillsdale, NJ: Erlbaum.

Varela, F. J. (1979). *Principles of biological autonomy.* New York: North Holland.

von Senden, M. (1960). *Space and sight: The perception of space and shape in the congenitally blind before and after operation.* Glencoe, IL: Free Press.

Waddington, C. H. (1975). *The evolution of an evolutionist.* Edinburgh: Edinburgh University Press.

Weimer, W. B. (1973). Psycholinguistics and Plato's paradoxes of the *Meno. American Psychologist, 28,* 15–33.

Weimer, W. B. (1975). The psychology of inference and expectation: Some preliminary remarks. In G. Maxwell & R. M. Anderson (Eds.), *Induction, probability and confirmation* (Minnesota Studies in the Philosophy of Science, No. 6). Minneapolis: University of Minnesota Press.

Weimer, W. B. (1977). A conceptual framework for cognitive psychology: Motor theories of the mind. In R. Shaw &. J. D. Bransford (Eds.), *Perceiv-*

ing, acting, and knowing: Toward an ecological psychology. Hillsdale, NJ: Erlbaum.

Weimer, W. B. (1982). Hayek's approach to the problems of complex phenomena: An introduction to the theoretical psychology of *The Sensory Order.* In W. B. Weimer & D. S. Palermo (Eds.), *Cognition and the symbolic processes.* Hillsdale, NJ: Erlbaum.

8

Constructive Metatheory and the Nature of Mental Representation

Michael J. Mahoney, H. Martin Miller, and Giampiero Arciero

It is not unusual for observers to depict their own time as one of significant transition from the past to the future and, of course, there is always some measure of warrant for such an assertion. Nevertheless, some historical periods involve different qualities and quantities of change than do others. To be specific, it is our contention that the late 20th century is one of those periods for psychology—a period of sweeping conceptual changes and methodological developments. This contention is not ours alone, of course, and it has been rendered provocatively by a number of contemporary observers (Altman, 1987; Fiske & Schweder, 1986; Mahoney, 1991; Manicas, 1987). The number, nature, and significance of these developments are matters of interpretation, to be sure, and they are viewed quite differently by individual analysts.

The so-called cognitive revolution is a case in point. Proponents of that revolution have hailed it as a welcome and promising development (e.g., Gardner, 1985), whereas its opponents have become increasingly intolerant of its growth. The purpose of this chapter, however, is neither to defend the cognitive revolution nor to comment on the lively polemics that are still emanating from some quarters. Rather, our goal is to briefly describe an evolution within the cognitive movement that has timely significance for current debates about the nature and functions of human mentation. It will be our contention that what we term *constructive metatheory* represents a promising alternative to traditional information-processing models of cognition. Although *constructivism* has only recently begun to draw substantial attention from cognitive scientists, its historical legacy can be traced to the early works of Giambattista Vico, Immanuel Kant, and Hans Vaihinger (cf. Berlin, 1976; Pompa, 1975; Vaihinger, 1911/1924; Verene, 1981; Vico, 1725/ 1948; von Foerster, 1984; von Glaserfeld, 1984; Watzlawick, 1984). Our aim is to outline the major conceptual features of constructive meta-theory and to then briefly note its implications for modern debates about mental representation and cognitive processes.

BASIC FEATURES OF CONSTRUCTIVE METATHEORY

To begin with, it is important to remember that a *metatheory* is not a single theory or monolithic conceptual system but rather a family of theories related to one another by shared assumptions and asser-tions. It is, if you will, a "ballpark" of abstractions that allow an infinite diversity of individual theories within limits imposed by the conceptual features that define that metatheory. In this section, we briefly describe three features considered central to constructive metatheory (Mahoney, 1988)—namely, (1) the proactive nature of cognitive processes, (2) the nuclear structure of human psychological organization, and (3) the self-organizing characteristics of psychologi-cal development.

Proactive Nature of Cognitive Processes

What might well be considered the cardinal feature of constructivism is its assertion that *human knowing* is active, anticipatory, and literally "constructive" (form-giving). In contrast to the more passive portrayal of the mind and mental processes offered by nonconstructive theories, constructivism views mentation as proactive, generative, and embodied. In one sense, then, constructivism argues that humans are literal co-creators of the "realities" to which they respond. This is an assertion that can be traced at least as far back as the 18th-century writings of Giambattista Vico and Immanuel Kant, and it has been elaborated in the 19th and 20th centuries by such writers as Hans Vaihinger (1911/ 1924), Wilhelm Wundt (1912), Franz Brentano (1929/1981), Frederic Bartlett (1932), Jean Piaget (1970), and George Kelly (1955; see also Maher, 1969). Because of this proactive portrayal of mentation, constructive metatheory embraces more of a "top-down" than a "bottom-up" approach to knowing (Gardner, 1985, Guidano, 1987, 1991; Hayek, 1952; Mahoney, 1988, 1991; Weimer, 1977).

Another way of conveying this point is to note that constructive theories challenge the assertion that information is transferred from the environment to the organism in neatly packaged "bits" rendered through the sense organs. Rather, for the constructivist, "information" is literally what the etymology of that term would suggest: *in formare*, that which is formed from within (Varela, 1979). A point of technical distinction here has to do with the degree of autonomy an organism can exert in organizing its own experience. "Radical constructivists" tend toward the extreme of philosophical idealism, asserting that all experienced order is self-generated and organismically recursive. "Critical constructivists," on the other hand, acknowledge that the "external" world does, indeed, constrain an organism's constructions. For more elaborate discussions of these technicalities, see Bartley (1987), Blackmore (1979), Maturana and Varela (1980, 1987), and Weimer (1977, 1979, 1982a, 1982b).

A second technicality worth noting here is that constructivist theories challenge what has been called the tradition of *objectivism*—the assertion that humans can achieve absolute and certifiable knowledge about a singular, stable, external reality (e.g., Johnson, 1987; Lackoff, 1987). This point will be elaborated in a later section, but it bears on assumptions about the sources of knowledge and, in particular, the role of sense data and evidence in warrantable knowing. In a nutshell, constructivism asserts that the function of data (sense and scientific) in knowledge development is essentially one of selecting or winnowing enacted hypotheses. Thus, according to constructivism, data do not authoritatively "justify" or form the foundations of *valid* knowedge but instead selectively eliminate less *viable* explorations and conjectures. This distinction between validity and viability is central to the distinction between constructivist and "rationalist" cognitive therapies (Mahoney, 1988; Mahoney & Gabriel, 1987). In constructivist psychotherapy, for example, the key issue is the pragmatic utility, rather than bedrock validity, of the client's system of understanding (Mahoney, 1988, 1991, 1995). Constructivism is thus a complexly commonsensical approach.

Returning now to the proactive nature of cognitive processes, we can anticipate that the nature and meanings of "representation" will be rendered differently by rationalist and constructivist perspectives. Rationalist theories generally portray the human mind as a relatively passive organ whose primary function is to develop valid internal copies of the external world. These copies are thought to guide behavior and emotional experiences by linking stimuli with their appropriate responses through the medium of stored memories. Rationalist metatheory thus endorses what is called the *correspondence theory* of mental representation (which maintains that mental copies correspond, albeit imperfectly, to entities in the outside world). Rationalist perspectives also serve to maintain the Platonic/Cartesian dualism between mind and matter, as well as the behaviorist ("black box") dogma of input and output:

> Common to these positions is an implicit notion that cognition is to be understood "from the outside inward," that it is a matter of the structuring of sensory information by intrinsically sensory systems, and that the products of cognition must somehow be married (in a peculiar sort of shotgun wedding) to action. (Weimer, 1977, p. 270)

Recent analyses in the cognitive sciences have suggested that this input/ output, sensory/motor dualism may lie at the heart of behaviorists' and rationalists' failure to construct an adequate theory of human experience. As long as stimuli and responses, or inputs and outputs, are distinct species, the psychological theorist must somehow explain how they come to get connected and coordinated. This is, of course, a relative of the historical problem posed by the "Höffding step"—the leap from sense data to perception—which (along with the paradox of stimulus equivalence) has effectively thwarted behaviorist and associationist models of human learning (Bever, Fodor, & Garrett, 1968; Hayek, 1952; Weimer, 1977).

Rationalist metatheories of mind are fundamentally "sensory" and passive in their depiction of cognitive processes. Reflecting Locke's "tabula rasa" doctrine of learning, their portrayal of the mind is that of a repository in the head where sensations and mental copies are deposited and stored. This formulation has been aptly termed the "bucket theory of mind" by philosopher Karl Popper (1972). In contrast to this approach are the constructivist perspectives described as "motoric" by Weimer (1977) due to their emphases on the pervasive activity of all cognitive processes (sensory, perceptual, and conceptual):

> What the motor metatheory asserts is that there is no sharp separation between sensory and motor components of the nervous system which can be made on functional grounds, and that the mental or cognitive realm is intrinsically motoric, like all the nervous system. The mind is intrinsically a motor system, and the sensory order by which we are acquainted with external objects as well as ourselves . . . is a product of what are, correctly interpreted, constructive motor skills. (Weimer, 1977, p. 272)

Hayek (1952) made much the same point when he noted that "much that we believe to know about the external world is, in fact, knowledge about ourselves" (pp. 6–7).

Constructive processes are not (constructed) figments of constructivists' imaginations, however. Numerous studies in neurophysiology and motor learning have now shown that human brain activities involve powerful *feedforward mechanisms* that proactively influence patterns of perception and action (Eccles, 1977; Granit, 1977, 1982; Mahoney, 1991; Pribram, 1971: Roy, 1980; Weimer, 1977). To render an adequately balanced model of person–environment interactions and the cognitive processes involved, the familiar concept of feedback in cybernetic analyses must thus be supplemented with that of feedforward. This acknowledgment of reciprocity between domains is a cardinal feature of constructive metatheory—whether it be the reciprocity between sensation and action or that between organism and environment.

Nuclear Morphogenic Structure

A second major feature of constructive metatheory is called "nuclear morphogenic structure," which refers to the assertion that humans are organized with a central/peripheral structure such that their central (core, nuclear) processes are (a) given special "protection" from challenge (and hence change) and (b) that these central processes constrain the range of particulars that can emerge at a peripheral ("surface structure") level. *Morphogenic* means "form-generating," and *nuclear* refers to a center-based structural organization. This feature in constructivism has a direct parallel to Chomsky's distinction between *deep structure* and *surface structure* in linguistics. Deep structures are composed of abstract ordering rules that impose constraints on what may be meaningfully expressed in any particular surface-structure expression. Hayek (1978) has termed this "the primacy of the abstract," arguing that the deep/surface structure distinction applies to *all* psychological activity (not just language):

> ... the richness of the sensory world in which we live, and which defies exhaustive analysis by our mind, is not the starting point from which the mind derives abstractions, but the project of a great range of abstractions which the mind must possess in order to be capable of experiencing that richness of the particular. (p. 44)

Hayek's (1952) insightful analysis of "the sensory order" elaborates this notion of the human nervous system as a classificatory complex that projects its own continually updated order onto the ongoing flux of experience.

Among other things, this means that the structure of human experience necessarily entails abstract—and hence, tacit or unconscious—processes. Because mere mention of the term *unconscious* may evoke associations with psychoanalysis, however, it is worth noting Hayek's (1978) distinction between Freud's intended meaning and his own:

> It is generally taken for granted that in some sense conscious experience constitutes the highest level in the hierarchy of mental events, and that what is not conscious has remained sub-conscious because it has not yet risen to that level. . . . If my conception is correct . . . [we are not aware of much that happens in our mind] not because it proceeds at too low a level but because it proceeds at too high a level. It would seem more appropriate to call such processes not sub-conscious but super-conscious, because they govern the conscious processes without appearing in them. (p. 45)

Hayek's ideas about abstract ordering processes are thus very different from Freud's reification of "the unconscious" as a repository of repressed impulses. Moreover, there appears to be increasing convergence on the merits of viewing the organization and functioning of the human nervous system as heterarchical or coalitional in nature (i.e., exhibiting multiple decentralized control systems rather than a simple linear hierarchy or centralized [executive] control mechanism [cf. Bienenstock, 1985; Hilgard, 1977; Weimer, 1987).

Besides entailing the deep/surface structure distinction and the primacy of abstract (unconscious) ordering processes, the constructivist feature of morphogenic structure has both theoretical and practical implications. Constructive theorists have noted, for example, that the deep structure or nuclear core of an individual system will be less accessible and amenable to change (cf. Guidano, 1984, 1987, 1991; Guidano & Liotti, 1983; Kelly, 1955; Liotti, 1987; Mahoney, 1980, 1991). The tacit ordering rules that constrain an individual's sense of self and world, and their relationship, are thus not only viewed as difficult to access and describe but also acknowledged to be more resistant to change than are more peripheral aspects of the person. They are, indeed, the essence of *resistance* as viewed from a constructivist perspective (Mahoney, 1991, 1995). The senior author has elsewhere hypothesized that the core themes of reality, identity, power, and valence are among the most difficult to alter, with or without professional assistance.

A final point worth noting here has to do with the different meanings of "structure," particularly as it has been used by North American psychologists (which is contrasted below with its current use by some European theorists). For the former group, *structuralism* has been generally employed in reference to the tradition associated with Titchener and attempts to identify the "architecture" of mind and the structural properties of experience. In contrast, however, many contemporary European psychologists use the term *structuralism* to refer to a conceptual and literary tradition associated with deSaussure, Jakobson, Levi-Strauss, Marx, Greimas, and Barthes. Indeed, this tradition forms the reference point from which have emanated the revolutionary "poststructuralist" writings of the likes of Lacan, Foucault, and Derrida (Harland, 1987; Kurtzman, 1987; Sheridan, 1980). The difference between the two uses is thus formidable and should at least be noted.

Constructivist views of structure cover a wide range of intended meanings. Of particular importance to this discussion is the predominantly North American emphasis on *static ordering relationships,* which should be contrasted with the European tendency to view structure as *dynamic, developmental, and dialectical.* Piaget's works are a good example of the latter. In our opinion, the dynamic–developmental versions of structuralism hold more conceptual promise than do their static counterparts. Viewed from the former perspective, the "equilibrium" of an adapting system is not a fixed "set point" so much as a flowing balance.

Self-Organizing Development

The third and final dimension we shall address as a defining feature of constructivism is clearly related to the first two and relates to the self-organizing nature of development. In essence, this feature asserts that *individual human systems organize themselves so as to protect and perpetuate their integrity, and they develop via structural differentiations.* According to this tenet, each person is literally the central reference point for all of their experience and survival efforts. This point is conveyed in the opening words of Guidano's (1987) powerful analysis, *Complexity of the Self*:

> In the last decade, an evolutionary, holistic, and process-oriented perspective to living systems has directed special attention to such concepts as hierarchical organization, temporal becoming, and dynamic equilibrium. This focus has led to the conceptualization of the human knowing system as a self-referent, organized complexity whose distinctive hallmark is its self-organizing ability. . . .
> The essential feature of this perspective considers the self-organizing ability of a human knowing system as a basic evolutionary constraint that, through the maturational ascension of higher cognitive abilities, progressively structures a full sense of self-identity with inherent feelings of uniqueness and historical continuity. The availability of this stable and structured self-identity permits continuous and coherent self-perception and self-evaluation in the face of temporal becoming and mutable reality. For this reason, the maintenance of one's perceived identity becomes as important as life itself; without it the individual would be incapable of proper functioning and would lose, at the same time, the very sense of reality. (p. 3)

Constructivist theories contend that psychological realities are inherently private, that the forum of significant psychological change lies in the domain of the self, and that the "self," in turn, is a dynamic complexity originating in and modified by interpersonal relationships. There are now rich and extensive literatures in the areas of self psychology, object relations theory, and attachment theory that point to the centrality of understanding and facilitating self system development (e.g., Bowlby, 1988; Goldberg, 1985; Guidano, 1987, 1991, Harter, 1983; Hartman & Blankstein, 1986; Kegan, 1982; Leahy, 1985; Mahoney, 1991; Marsella, Devos, & Hsu, 1985; Rosenberg, 1979; Schore, 1994; Wilber, Engler, & Brown, 1986). Moreover, two areas of relevance to this topic are rarely acknowledged in the psychological literature and deserve at least brief mention here.

Self-Organization and Autopoiesis

The first such area has to do with *spontaneously self-ordering complex phenomena*. Research in this area has been gaining momentum for more than a decade and is considered by some to be at the leading edge of scientific developments. An example of early work on spontaneous self-organization is that of Manfred Eigen, the Nobel laureate who first described the autocatalytic "hypercycle" (cf. Eigen & Schuster, 1979; Jantsch, 1980). Eigen's work was at the molecular level and represented a major step in linking organic and inorganic worlds. Put simply, he showed that certain dynamic patterns of energy exchange afford the emergence of self-perpetuating structures, called hypercycles, which form the basis for higher-order life support processes in organic systems. "A hypercycle is a closed circle of transformatory or catalytic processes in which one or more participants act as autocatalysts" (Jantsch, 1980, p. 32). In other words, stability emerges out of previously random energy dynamics, and stability is maintained by recursive (self-referencing) mechanisms that contribute to their own perpetuation.

A second major contribution to this area has involved the work of Ilya Prigogine, who was awarded a 1977 Nobel Prize for his work on "dissipative structures" (Prigogine, 1980; Prigogine & Stengers, 1984). Both theoretically and experimentally, Prigogine was able to demonstrate that the Second Law of Thermodynamics does not apply to open systems. Open systems exhibit self-organizing capacities that serve to maintain and extend their dynamic equilibrium. If perturbations caused by internal or environmental challenges exceed a system's assimilation capacities, the system goes into cycles of disorganization that can contribute to deep structural reorganization (reminiscent to some degree of Piaget's concept of accommodation). Out of the disorganization emerges a structural transformation that (if it is viable) allows the system to now accommodate the perturbing challenge and to move forward in time at a higher (generally, more complex) level of self-organization.

Prigogine's work has focused on the dynamic role of disequilibrium and the self-reorganizing capacities of open systems. Research and theory in this area may therefore be seen as complementary to Eigen's work on the stabilizing energy structures in closed systems. A third development that spans both of these and addresses the life sciences is that represented by the area called *autopoiesis*. The term was coined by Maturana and Varela (1980) to refer to self-organizing systems. They place particular emphasis on the centrality of "identity" maintenance in system viability—that is, that an autopoietic system is one whose own organization (defining network of relations) is a fundamental invariant. Research and theory in autopoiesis has dovetailed with that emanating from the first two areas (Atlan, 1972; Bienenstock, Soulie, & Weisbuch, 1986; Eigen & Schuster, 1979; Jantsch, 1980, 1981; Varela, 1979; Zeleny, 1980). The relevance of self-organizing phenomena for psychotherapy are clearly worthy of consideration (cf. Brent, 1978, 1984; Dell, 1982; Keeney, 1983; Mahoney, 1991).

Evolutionary Epistemology

The second major area worth briefly noting here is that called *evolutionary epistemology*—literally, the study of evolution or development in knowing systems. Evolutionary epistemology was pioneered by Herbert Spencer and James Mark Baldwin at the turn of the century and was later elaborated in the writings of Donald Campbell (1974) and Karl Popper (1972). In the past few years there has been a veritable explosion of work in this area (cf. Butterworth, Rutkowska, & Scaife, 1985; Depew & Weber, 1985; Kauffman, 1982; Kohn, 1985; Pollard, 1984; Wuketits, 1984). Studies of the evolution of knowing suggest that the same processes apply to both individual and collective knowledge development (Callebaut & Pinxten, 1986: Radnitzky & Bartley, 1987). Bartley (1987) states this point clearly:

> Human knowledge appears to develop . . . like animal adaptation, [as] the product of blind variation and selective retention—or, to use Popper's phrase, through conjecture and refutation. Science is, on this account, *utterly unjustified and unjustifiable.* It is a shot in the dark, a bold guess going far beyond all evidence. The question of its justification is irrelevant: it is as irrelevant as any question about whether a particular mutation is justified. The issue, rather, is of the viability of the mutation—or of the new theory. This question is resolved by exposing it to the pressure of natural selection—or attempted criticism and refutation. Survival in this process

does not justify the survivor either: a species that survived for thousands of years may nonetheless become extinct. A theory that survived for generations may eventually be refuted—as was Newton's. There is no justification—ever. The process that began with unjustified variations ends in unjustified survivors. (p. 24)

This is, of course, not a reassuring conclusion to those who would like to believe that knowing and knowledge are built on ("justified" or "authorized" by) solid foundations. At the same time, however, there is an exciting convergence here between the "new look" in philosophies of knowing (namely, nonjustificational epistemologies) and the "new look" in evolutionary theories (namely, active vs. passive neo-Darwinism). Consider, for example, the following abbreviated sketches of some basic principles of knowledge development:

1. Variation is extremely important, usually expressed behaviorally in the form of (often risky) explorations into the unknown.
2. Selection processes serve to eliminate unviable variations.
3. In some primates, vicarious learning and symbolic processes allow "internal" selection processes to eliminate hypotheses rather than their owners.

Research in evolutionary epistemology underlies the importance of open exchange in knowledge growth, a point that can be applied with warrant to policy and practice in science as well as psychotherapy (Mahoney, 1985a, 1985b).

THE ELUSIVE NATURE OF MENTATION

The foregoing overview of three characteristic features of constructive metatheory can now provide a background for a brief discussion of the conceptual morass surrounding current models of psychological structure and mental functions. Due to the limits of time, space, and language, what follows must be a necessary simplification of complex and interdependent issues in the study of knowing systems. For more extended reading on this topic, we recommend in particular Guidano (1987, 1991), Hayek (1952, 1978), Johnson (1987), Lackoff (1987), Mahoney (1991), Maturana and Varela (1987), and Weimer (1977; 1982a, 1982b; 1987). It is not accidental, of course, that many of these works are decidedly constructivist in flavor, just as it is not coincidental that the inchoate but emerging "new look" in cognitive science seems to be increasingly identified with theories and research questions associated with complexity, the dynamics of reorganization ("learning") and the role of recursive ("self-referencing") processes in balancing structural stability with functional plasticity and creative generativity. With terms and concepts like these, of course, we are already on the edge of technical familiarity and perhaps obscuring some more familiar terms and issues in the study of human cognition.

Let us therefore turn to a succinct statement of the problem of representation in cognition. Shanon (1987) has recently offered the following condensation:

> Practically all of contemporary cognitive science—both natural and artificial—is conducted within the representational–computational framework. This perspective may be defined by the following three tenets:
>
> 1. Man behaves by virtue of knowledge.
> 2. Knowledge consists of mental representations, i.e., of well-defined symbols organized in well-formed semantic structures . . .
> 3. Cognitive activity consists of the manipulation of these symbols, i.e. of computations. (p. 33)

Shanon goes on to show the limitations of the traditional representational–computational view of mind and concludes, among other things, that "representations" are the products of cognitive activity rather than either its process or its raw materials.

Similar arguments have been made by a number of writers in what appears to be a growing dissatisfaction with linear, serial, and reductionistic models of mind (cf. Fischer, 1987). Thus, Waltz and Pollack (1985) state that "computer scientists, like cognitive scientists, tend to be limited by the conceptual framework of serial processing, the 30-year-old framework of the 'von Neumann' machine, with its Central Processing Unit connected to its passive array of memory by a small bundle of wires" (p. 69). This movement away from discrete serial processing models has been encouraged, in part, by the development of what have been termed "distributed," "massively parallel," and "connectionist" models of cognition (Anderson, 1987; Feldman & Ballard, 1982; McClelland & Rumelhart, 1985; Waltz & Pollack, 1985; Winograd, 1980). Thus, for example, in his dramatic shift in conceptualizing language comprehension, Winograd (1980) joins Maturana and others in rejecting traditional representational views of cognition:

> In saying that a representation is "present in the nervous system," we are indulging in misplaced concreteness and can easily be led into fruitless quests for the corresponding mechanisms. (p. 227)
> Maturana proposes an understanding of the nervous system that is not built around the usual notions of input, output, memory, perception, etc. He adopts instead an orientation toward it as a system of components

whose activities trigger further activity within the system. The system is "structure determined" in that its activity at any moment is fully determined by the structure (or state) at that moment. It is "plastic" in that its structure can be changed by the activity, so that its structure at any moment is a product of the entire previous history of activity and changing structure. It is "closed," in the sense that the system can do only that which is determined by its own structure and activity—its action cannot be understood as a reflection of an external world it perceives. (pp. 222–223)

Applications of this approach from the perspective of neurobiology and short-term synaptic plasticity have rendered some of the most exciting recent developments in the dialogue between the cognitive and neurosciences (Bienenstock, 1985; Edelman, 1987; LeDoux & Hirst, 1986: Malsburg & Bienenstock, 1986; Schoner & Kelso, 1988).

In the interest of brevity, we here summarize some very basic assertions of constructive metatheory regarding the nature of mental representation:

1. The term *representation* is itself unfortunate and misleading when applied to either the contents or processes of mentation because it connotes concrete symbols that can "stand in for" their referents.

2. It is important to emphasize that the terms, concepts, and symbols used to describe mental activities are not themselves isomorphic with these activities.

3. The mental activities invoked by representational and computational models are neither iconic "copies" that correspond to (or approximate) their referents, nor are they formal symbolic propositions.

4. The traditionally acknowledged functions of memory "storage," "retrieval," and symbolic manipulation mistakenly imply a mental content to be acted upon rather than recognizing that the content—when it can be made explicit—is a product of ongoing self-organizing processes.

5. Mental "representation," to the limited extent it is currently understood, involves complex, dynamic, and abstract patterns of activity that create the mental contents traditionally studied.

These contentions obviously draw on the works of Hayek (1952, 1978), Maturana and Varela (1980, 1987), and Weimer (1977, 1982a, 1982b). In many ways, the problem of conceptualizing mental representation is similar to the problem of "correspondence" between scientific theories and the domains they purport to cover. As analyses of the correspondence problem in philosophy of science have shown, a theory inherently proposes a set of structured relations (Hanson,1970; Maxwell, 1970; Weimer, 1979). The correspondence of any theory to its domain of relevance does not entail a point-to-point mapping of particulars but, instead, a variably faithful reconstruction of patterns of relational structure.

Thus, from the perspective we have been discussing, humans do not *have* mental representations so much as they *are* interpretations of their worlds (internal and external). We are, in other words, embodied theories whose actions *are* the ongoing conjectural or construction processes that cognitive extremists have tried to localize in the head. It is in this sense that theories of embodied mentation and adaptation are decidedly more adequate than their cerebralized counterparts (Johnson, 1987; Lackoff, 1987).

CONCLUSION

All of which brings us toward some concluding remarks on the ongoing evolution within the cognitive sciences and the continuing debate over the nature and functions of mental activity. Our brief overview of three basic features of constructive metatheory has touched upon some fundamental assumptions and assertions in cognitive psychology. We concur with the writings of modern constructivists in their emphasis on the proactive, motoric aspects of all mentation and the functional inseparability of thought, feeling, and action. Likewise, we believe that the growing interest in parallel, distributed, and "connectionist" models of mind reflects a promising development in the area. With the help of conjectures emanating from the study of self-organizing systems, debates about the nature of mental representation are now being replaced with more fundamental epistemological problems about domains of reference (e.g., cognitive activity vs. its description) and the inescapable complexity of subject/object or observer/observed distinctions in analyses of knowing (Anderson, 1987; Kosslyn, 1980; Pattee, 1973, 1978; Pylyshlyn, 1984; Shanon, 1987). Although our analysis has not offered answers to the wave of new questions facing cognitive scientists, we hope that it has at least underscored the importance and potential promise of those questions.

Acknowledgment. The authors express their appreciation to Walter B. Weimer and Óscar F. Gonçalves for conversations that contributed to the present manuscript.

REFERENCES

Altman, I. (1987). Centripetal and centrifugal trends in psychology. *American Psychologist, 42,* 1058–1069.

Anderson, J. R. (1987). Methodologies for studying human knowledge. *Behavioral and Brain Sciences, 10,* 467–505.

Atlan, H. (1972). *L'organisation biologique et la theorie de l'information.* Paris: Hermann.

Bartlett, F. C. (1932). *Remembering.* Cambridge: Cambridge University Press.

Bartley, W. W. (1987). Philosophy of biology versus philosophy of physics. In G. Radnitzky & W. W. Bartley (Eds.), *Evolutionary epistemology, theory of rationality, and the sociology of knowledge* (pp. 7–45). LaSalle, IL: Open Court.

Berlin, I. (1976). *Vico and Herder: Two studies in the history of ideas.* New York: Viking.

Bever, T. G., Fodor, J. A., & Garrett, M. (1968). A formal limit of associationism. In T. R. Dixon & D. L. Horton (Eds.), *Verbal behavior and general behavior theory* (pp. 582–585). Englewood Cliffs, NJ: Prentice-Hall.

Bienenstock, E. (1985). Dynamics of the central nervous system. In J. P. Aubin, D. Saari, & K. Sigmund (Eds.), *Dynamics of macrosystems* (pp. 3–20). New York: Springer Verlag.

Bienenstock, E., Soulie, F. F., & Weisbuch, G. (Eds.) (1986). *Disordered systems and biological organization.* New York: Springer Verlag.

Blackmore, J. (1979). On the inverted use of the terms "realism" and "idealism" among scientists and historians of science. *British Journal for the Philosophy of Science, 30,* 125–134.

Bowlby, J. (1988). Developmental psychiatry comes of age. *American Journal of Psychiatry, 145,* 1–10.

Brent, S. B. (1978). Prigogine's model for self-organization in non-equilibrium systems: Its relevance for developmental psychology. *Human Development, 21,* 374–387.

Brent, S. B. (1984). *Psychological and social structures.* Hillsdale, NJ: Erlbaum.

Brentano, F. (1981). *Sensory and noetic consciousness.* New York: Routledge & Kegan Paul. (Original work published in 1929)

Butterworth, G., Rutkowska, J., & Scaife, M. (Eds.) (1985). *Evolution and developmental psychology.* Brighton, England: Harvester Press.

Callebaut, W., & Pinxten, R. (Eds.) (1986). *Evolutionary epistemology: A multiparadigm program.* Boston: Reidel.

Campbell, D. T. (1974). Evolutionary epistemology. In P. A. Schilpp (Ed.), *The philosophy of Karl Popper* (Vol. 14, Parts 1 & 2, pp. 413–463). LaSalle, IL: Open Court. (Reprinted in Radnitzky & Bartley, 1987)

Dell, P. F. (1982). Beyond homeostasis: Toward a concept of coherence. *Family Process, 21,* 21–41.

Depew, D. J., & Weber, B. H. (Eds.) (1985). *Evolution at a crossroads: The new biology and the new philosophy of science.* Cambridge, MA: MIT Press.

Eccles, J. C. (1977). *The understanding of the brain* (2nd ed.). New York: McGraw-Hill.

Edelman, G. M. (1987). *Neural Darwinism: The theory of neuronal group selection.* New York: Basic Books.

Eigen, M., & Schuster, P. (1979). *The hypercycle: A principle of natural self-organization.* New York: Springer Publishing Co.

Feldman, J. A., & Ballard, D. H. (1982). Connectionist models and their properties. *Cognitive Science, 6,* 205–254.

Fischer, R. (1987). On fact and fiction—the structure of stories that the brain tells itself about itself. *Journal of Social and Biological Structures, 10,* 343–351.

Fiske, D. W., & Schweder, R. A. (Eds.) (1986). *Metatheory in social science: Pluralisms and subjectivities.* Chicago: University of Chicago Press.

Gardner, H. (1985). *The mind's new science: A history of the cognitive revolution.* New York: Basic Books.

Goldberg, A. (Ed.) (1985). *Progress in self psychology.* New York: Guilford.

Granit, R. (1977). *The purposive brain.* Cambridge, MA: MIT Press.

Granit, R. (1982). Reflections on the evolution of the mind and its environment. In R. Q. Elvee (Ed.), *Mind in nature* (pp. 96–117). San Francisco: Harper & Row.

Guidano, V. F. (1984). A constructivist outline of cognitive processes. In M. A. Reda & M. J. Mahoney (Eds.), *Cognitive psychotherapies: Recent developments in theory, research, and practice* (pp. 31–45). Cambridge, MA: Ballinger.

Guidano, V. F. (1987). *Complexity of the self: A developmental approach to psychopathology and therapy.* New York: Guilford.

Guidano, V. F. (1991). *The self in process: Toward a post-rationalist cognitive therapy.* New York: Guilford.

Guidano, V. F., & Liotti, G. (1983). *Cognitive processes and emotional disorders.* New York: Guilford.

Hanson, N. R. (1970). A picture theory of theory meaning. In R. G. Colodny (Ed.), *The nature and function of scientific theories: Essays in contemporary science and philosophy* (pp. 233–274). Pittsburgh, PA: University of Pittsburgh Press.

Harland, R. (1987). *Superstructuralism: The philosophy of structuralism and post-structuralism.* London: Methuen.

Harter, S. (1983). Developmental perspectives on the self-system. In P. H. Mussen (Ed.), *Handbook of child psychology. Vol. 4: Socialization, personality, and social development* (pp. 275–385). New York: Wiley.

Hartman, L. M., & Blankenstein, K. R. (Eds.) (1986). *Perception of self in emotional disorder and psychotherapy.* New York: Plenum.

Hayek, F. A. (1952). *The sensory order.* Chicago: University of Chicago Press.

Hayek, F. A. (1978). *New studies in philosophy, politics, economics, and the history of ideas.* Chicago: University of Chicago Press.

Hilgard, E. R. (1977). *Divided consciousness: Multiple controls in human thought and action.* New York: Wiley.

Jantsch, E. (1980). *The self-organizing universe: Scientific and human implications of the emerging paradigm of evolution.* New York: Pergamon.

Jantsch, E. (Ed.) (1981). *The evolutionary vision: Toward a unifying paradigm of physical, biological, and sociocultural evolution.* Boulder, CO: Westview Press.

Johnson, M. (1987). *The body in the mind: The bodily basis of meaning, imagination, and reason.* Chicago: University of Chicago Press.

Kauffman, S. A. (1982). Filling some epistemological gaps: New patterns of inference in evolutionary theory. *Journal of the Philosophy of Science Association, 2,* 292–313.

Keeney, B. P. (1983). *Aesthetics of change.* New York: Guilford.

Kegan, R. (1982). *The evolving self: Problem and process in human development.* Cambridge, MA: Harvard University Press.

Kelly, G. A. (1955). *The psychology of personal constructs.* New York: Norton.

Kohn, D. (Ed.) (1985). *The Darwinian heritage.* Princeton, NJ: Princeton University Press.

Kosslyn, S. M. (1980). *Image and mind.* Cambridge, MA: Harvard University Press.

Kurtzman, H. S. (1987). Deconstruction and psychology: An introduction. *New Ideas in Psychology, 5,* 33–71.

Lackoff, G. (1987). *Women, fire, and dangerous things: What categories reveal about the mind.* Chicago: University of Chicago Press.

Leahy, R. L. (Ed.) (1985). *The development of the self.* New York: Academic Press.

LeDoux, J. E., & Hirst, W. (Eds.) (1986). *Mind and brain: Dialogues in cognitive neuroscience.* London: Cambridge University Press.

Liotti, G. (1987). The resistance to change of cognitive structures: A counter-proposal to psychoanalytic metapsychology. *Journal of Cognitive Psychotherapy: An International Quarterly, 1,* 87–104.

Maher, B. (Ed.) (1969). *Clinical psychology and personality: The selected papers of George Kelly.* New York: Wiley.

Mahoney, M. J. (1980). Psychotherapy and the structure of personal revolutions. In M. J. Mahoney (Ed.), *Psychotherapy process: Current issues and future directions* (pp. 157–180). New York: Plenum.

Mahoney, M. J. (1985a). Open exchange and epistemic progress. *American Psychologist, 40,* 29–39.

Mahoney, M. J. (1985b). Psychotherapy and human change processes. In M. J. Mahoney & A. Freeman (Eds.), *Cognition and psychotherapy* (pp. 3–48). New York: Plenum.

Mahoney, M. J. (1988). The cognitive sciences and psychotherapy: Patterns in a developing relationship. In K. S. Dobson (Ed.), *Handbook of cognitive–behavioral therapies* (pp. 357–386). New York: Guilford.

Mahoney, M. J. (1991). *Human change processes: The scientific foundations of psychotherapy.* New York: Basic Books.

Mahoney, M. J. (1995). *Constructive psychotherapy.* New York: Guilford.

Mahoney, M. J., & Gabriel, T. J. (1987). Psychotherapy and the cognitive sciences: An evolving alliance. *Journal of Cognitive Psychotherapy: An International Quarterly, 1,* 39–59.

Malsburg, C., & Bienenstock, E. (1986). Statistical coding and short-term synaptic plasticity: A scheme for knowledge representation in the brain. In E. Bienenstock, F. F. Soulie, & G. Weisbuch (Eds.), *Disordered systems and biological organization* (pp. 247–270). Berlin: Springer Verlag.

Manicas, P. T. (1987). *A history and philosophy of the social sciences.* New York: Basil Blackwell.

Marsella, A. J., Devos, G., & Hsu, F. L. K. (Eds.) (1985). *Culture and self: Asian and Western perspectives.* London: Tavistock.

Maturana, H. R., & Varela, F. J. (1980). *Autopoiesis and cognition: The realization of the living.* Boston: Reidel.

Maturana, H. R., & Varela, F. J. (1987). *The tree of knowledge: The biological roots of human understanding.* Boston: Shambhala.

Maxwell, G. (1970). Theories, perception, and structural realism. In R. G. Colodny (Ed.), *The nature and function of scientific theories: Essays in contemporary science and philosophy* (pp. 3–34). Pittsburgh, PA: University of Pittsburgh Press.

McClelland, J. L., & Rumelhart, D. E. (1985). Distributed memory and the representation of general and specific information. *Journal of Experimental Psychology: General, 114,* 159–188.

Pattee, H. H. (Ed.) (1973). *Hierarchy theory: The challenge of complex systems.* New York: George Braziller.

Pattee, H. H. (1978). The complementarity principle in biological and social structures. *Journal of Biological and Social Structures, 1,* 191–200.

Piaget, J. (1970). *Psychology and epistemology: Towards a theory of knowledge.* New York: Viking.

Pollard, J. W. (Ed.) (1984). *Evolutionary theory: Paths into the future.* New York: Wiley.

Pompa, L. (1975). *Vico: A study of the "New Science."* Cambridge: Cambridge University Press.

Popper, K. R. (1972). *Objective knowledge: An evolutionary approach.* London: Oxford University Press.

Pribram, K. R. (1971). *Languages of the brain.* Englewood Cliffs, NJ: Prentice-Hall.

Prigogine, I. (1980). *From being to becoming: Time and complexity in the physical sciences.* San Francisco: W. H. Freeman.

Prigogine, I., & Stengers, I. (1984). *Order out of chaos: Man's new dialogue with nature.* New York: Bantam.

Pylyshlyn, Z. W. (1984). *Computation and cognition: Toward a foundation for cognitive science.* Cambridge, MA: MIT Press.

Radnitzky, G., & Bartley, W. W. (Eds.) (1987). *Evolutionary epistemology, theory of rationality and the sociology of knowledge.* LaSalle, IL: Open Court.

Rosenberg, M. (1979). *Conceiving the self.* New York: Basic Books.

Roy, E. A. (1980). Cerebral substrates of action: Implications for models of motor behavior and rehabilitation. In P. Klavora & J. Flowers (Eds.), *Motor learning and biochemical factors in sport* (pp. 117–134). Toronto: University of Toronto.

Schoner, G., & Kelso, J. A. S. (1988). Dynamic pattern generation in behavioral and neural systems. *Science, 239,* 1513–1520.

Schore, A. N. (1994). *Affect regulation and the origin of the self.* Hillsdale, NJ: Erlbaum.

Shanon, B. (1987). On the place of representations in cognition. In D. N. Perkins, J. Lochhead, & J. Bishop (Eds.), *Thinking: The second international conference* (pp. 33–49). Hillsdale, NJ: Erlbaum.

Sheridan, A. (1980). *Michel Foucault: The will to truth.* London: Tavistock.

Vaihinger, H. (1924). *The philosophy of "as if."* London: Routledge & Kegan Paul.   (Original work published 1911)

Varela, F. J. (1979). *Principles of biological autonomy.* New York: Elsevier North Holland.

Verene, D. P. (1981). *Vico's science of imagination.* Ithaca, NY: Cornell University Press.

Vico, G. (1948). *The new science.* (Trans. T. G. Bergin & M. H. Fisch). Ithaca, NY: Cornell University Press. (Original work published 1725)

Von Foerster, H. (1984). On constructing a reality. In P. Watzlawick (Ed.), *The invented reality* (pp. 41–61). New York: W. W. Norton.

Von Glaserfeld, E. (1984). An introduction to radical constructivism. In P. Watzlawick (Ed.), *The invented reality* (pp. 18–40). New York: W.W. Norton.

Waltz, D. L., & Pollack, J. B. (1985). Massively parallel parsing: A strongly interactive model of natural language interpretation. *Cognitive Science, 9,* 51–74.

Watzlawick, P. (Ed.) (1984). *The invented reality: Contributions to constructivism.* New York: W. W. Norton.

Weimer, W. B. (1977). A conceptual framework for cognitive psychology: Motor theories of the mind. In R. Shaw & J. Bransford (Eds.), *Perceiving, acting, and knowing* (pp. 267–311). Hillsdale, NJ: Erlbaum.

Weimer, W. B. (1979). *Notes on the methodology of scientific research.* Hillsdale, NJ: Erlbaum.

Weimer, W. B. (1982a). Ambiguity and the future of psychology: Meditations Leibniziennes. In W. B. Weimer & D. S. Palermo (Eds.), *Cognition and the symbolic processes* (Vol. 2, pp. 331–360). Hillsdale, NJ: Erlbaum.

Weimer, W. B. (1982b). Hayek's approach to the problems of complex phenomena: An introduction to the theoretical psychology of *The Sensory Order.* In W. B. Weimer & D. S. Palermo (Eds.), *Cognition and the symbolic processes* (Vol. 2, pp. 267–311). Hillsdale, NJ: Erlbaum.

Weimer, W. B. (1987). Spontaneously ordered complex phenomena and the unity of the moral sciences. In G. Radnitzky (Ed.), *Centripetal forces in the sciences* (pp. 257–295). New York: Paragon House.

Wilber, K., Engler, J., & Brown, D. P. (1986). *Transformations of consciousness: Conventional and contemplative perspectives on development.* Boston: New Science Library.

Winograd, T. (1980). What does it mean to understand language? *Cognitive Science, 4,* 209–241.

Wuketits, F. M. (Ed.) (1984). *Concepts and approaches in evolutionary epistemology.* Boston: Reidl.

Wundt, W. (1912). *An introduction to psychology.* New York: MacMillan.

Zeleny, M. (Ed.) (1980). *Autopoiesis, dissipative structures, and spontaneous social orders.* Washington, DC: American Association for the Advancement of Science.

9

Personal Construct Therapy and the Relation Between Cognition and Affect

Kenneth W. Sewell

In 1955, George A. Kelly introduced his theory of personality with the publication of *The Psychology of Personal Constructs* in two substantive volumes. The theory, based on the philosophical position of constructive alternativism, is conveniently presented with a fundamental postulate and 11 corollaries (see Table 9.1). The theory and those who have written from its perspective have much to offer the psychotherapist.

This chapter focuses on how "affect" is viewed by personal construct theory and by the personal construct therapist, particularly in relation to the notion of "cognition." After briefly characterizing personal construct therapy, Kelly's (1955) theory of how humans mentally "construct" experience is summarized with a description of his theoretical views concerning the traditional distinction between cognition and affect. Other views of the role of affect within constructivist psychology will be described and compared to Kelly's notions. Extrapolations are made from research on "affective disorders" to the underpinnings of phenomena traditionally called affective (both functional and dysfunctional) and the therapeutic implications thereof. Finally, the argument is made that the adoption of Kelly's views regarding cognition and affect would be theoretically and therapeutically preferable to the other available alternatives. Case material is included to illustrate the application of these notions to the therapeutic relationship.

TABLE 9.1. Personal Construct Theory: Constructive Alternativism, Fundamental Postulate and Corollaries

---

Constructive Alternativism: There are always some alternative constructions (interpretations) to choose among in dealing with the world; therefore, it is assumed that all present interpretations of the world are subject to revision or replacement.

Fundamental Postulate: A person's mental processes are channelized by the ways in which she anticipates events.

Construction corollary: A person anticipates events by construing their replications.

Individuality corollary: Persons differ in their constructions of events.

Organization corollary: Each person characteristically evolves, to anticipate events, a construction system containing ordinal relations between constructs.

Dichotomy corollary: A person's construction system is composed of a finite number of dichotomous constructs.

Choice corollary: A person chooses for herself that alternative in a dichotomized construct through which the greater possibility for extension and definition of her system is anticipated.

Range corollary: A construct is convenient (applicable) for the anticipation of a finite range of events only.

Experience corollary: A person's construction system varies and changes as he successively construes the replications of events.

Modulation corollary: The variation in a person's construction system is limited by the permeability (changeability) of the constructs within whose ranges of applicability the variants lie.

Fragmentation corollary: A person can successively employ a variety of construction subsystems that are logically incompatible.

Commonality corollary: To the extent that one person employs a construction of experience that is similar to that employed by another, her psychologically processes are similar to those of the other person.

Sociality corollary: To the extent that one person construes the construction processes of another, he may play a role in a social process involving the other person.

PERSONAL CONSTRUCT THERAPY

Personal construct therapy (PCT) revolves around using the principle of sociality (see Table 9.1)—first to understand the client and then to intervene in the ways the client anticipates experience. These interventions are designed with the specific theory of personality provided by personal construct psychology as the guiding force. However, the techniques themselves vary widely in their content and modality. Interventions can be largely verbal, such as interchanges intended to introduce some superordinate construction onto a concretely understood experience. PCT techniques can also be highly experiential, such as fixed role assignments designed to have the client "try on" a new persona that will create a different range of experience and meet with novel social feedback. Between these two extremes, PCT most often balances the talk: experience ratio via techniques such as casual enactments of problematic or important situations designed to provide the client with a range of validational (or invalidational) experiences within the anticipated safety of the therapy room. Techniques specifically generated by personal construct psychology notwithstanding, PCT is a framework for understanding the client and then *creating* an intervention appropriate for that one human being. It is not a mere collection of techniques. Thus, *how* the personal construct therapist understands a client is more important than the existing technical armament. Because clients arrive at the therapist's door most often because they are "feeling bad" (rather than "thinking bad" or "behaving bad"), how the personal construct therapist understands feelings/emotions is of paramount importance.

OVERVIEW OF PERSONAL CONSTRUCT THEORY

Personal construct theory was founded on the assumption that human beings behave as "personal scientists." As such, they are continually creating conceptual templates (personal constructs) from their experiences. Kelly (1955) defined the term "construct"[1] as an aspect of elements (objects, people, etc. in one's environment) "on the basis of which some of the elements are similar to others and some are in contrast" (p. 61). Constructs then allow humans to interpret, predict, and appropriately respond to their subsequent experiences (Neimeyer, 1985). Personal construct theory was a drastic departure from the deterministic zeitgeist of the 1950s and before. On one hand was the environmental determinism of radical behaviorism; on the other hand, the intrapsychic determinism of classical psychoanalysis. Kelly's theory focused on the structure and function of the mental activity of construing. Of primary concern in personal construct theory is how an individual's personal constructs are organized and how they might change over time (Neimeyer, 1985). Although described here as crucial to PCT, this is exactly the concern of any constructivist psychotherapist (however reworded).

Psychotherapies, as well as individual psychotherapists, are often categorized by the extent to which they focus their attention (and consequently, the creative energies of themselves and their clientele) on "cognitive" versus "affective" content and processes.[2] This perceived dichotomy has prompted cognitive theorists to provide a coherent place for feeling states within their theories and therapies (e.g., Tomkins, 1992). The remainder of this chapter challenges this dichotomy and suggests that, from a personal construct perspective, psychotherapeutic work can be enhanced by an alternative construction.

DEVELOPMENT OF CONSTRUCT SYSTEMS

In order to consider "affect" in any comprehensive way, it is necessary to explore the early development of the construing person. Kelly died before he formally laid out his ideas on early construct system development (Bannister & Fransella, 1980). Much can and has been said, however, about the implications of the original theory for childhood development.

The theory of personal constructs views the child as a "form of motion" (Bannister & Fransella, 1980, p. 82) because each construction is contingent upon the individual who emerged from the previous construction. It can be said that it is not the same person who meets each constructive challenge. This fluidity of development carries the implication that dividing childhood into discrete "stages" might impede understanding the development of construct systems. Instead, development is seen as a branching network of experiments designed to know the world, the complexity increasing in both depth (e.g., how much do I know about X?) and breadth (how many X's do I know about and what do they have to do with each other?).

As described above, personal construct theory is based on discriminations between experienced events. Very small children do not have verbal labels for these distinctions. The lack of verbal labels, however, is not a cogent argument against the existence of personal constructs in small children. It is clear from the behavior of infants and small children that distinctions lie within their capabilities even though these mental acts cannot be connected to verbalization. Kelly (1955) recognized that a construct may continue to be employed to predict and construe experience on into adulthood, even though it has no consistent verbal label attached to it. He hypothesized that many such constructs are developed prior to the acquisition of language. Kelly referred to these as preverbal constructs even though some purely nonverbal constructs can arise after language is acquired (cf. Piaget, 1977).

A basic distinction needs to be noted in reference to viewing Kelly's theory from a developmental perspective—namely, the distinction between content and structure. It is clear that, relative to adults, children use different distinctions with which to predict their experience. Although examining the content of the differences could be enlightening, it is more central to understanding emotion to examine the changes in structure that a developing construct system undergoes. This distinction (i.e., content vs. structure) is important in many aspects of personal construct psychology.

Salmon (1970) has proposed that perhaps the major structural way in which a child's construct system develops over time is with increasing degrees of organization, especially in terms of superordination. Superordination within a construct system refers to the hierarchical nature of constructs such that some constructs subsume other constructs (e.g., "nice vs. mean" might be subsumed by "social vs. material"). Some research has been reported that offers limited support to this developmental aspect of construct systems (Bannister & Agnew, 1977; Bannister & Salmon, 1967; Brierly, 1967; Honess, 1979).

The area of construct system development that might bear most relevance to affect is "self-concept." In personal construct terms, self-concept refers to the construing of self. Self-concept development is particularly important in terms of distinguishing the self from other environmental or social elements. Bannister and Agnew (1977) have investigated this self-construction as it differs among various age groups. They found that 5-year-olds were not able to verbalize coherent answers to questions such as "How do we become different from others?" Children questioned at 7 years of age seemed to rely on a genetic, deterministic hypothesis, such as "We're all born different." The most drastic shift was with the 9-year-old children, who were beginning to generate the idea the persons are distinct because they have had different experiences. Additionally, when Bannister and Agnew asked adults to retrospectively identify when they first experienced themselves "as individuals," subjects often recounted situations in which they were lonely or feeling rejected by others. These studies offer support to Kelly's (1955) original notion that individuals begin construing the self via the bipolar construct of "self versus others." This self-construction may be the core of so-called affective experience. Kelly (1955) gave special significance to the constructs that "govern the client's maintenance processes" (p. 565) and are therefore highly self-relevant. He called such constructs "core constructs." "Self versus others" is a common core construct, which carries broad implications for (1) how the individual construes a wide range of experience and therefore (2) the affective tone and stability of the individual. this point is elaborated in a later section in the context of affective disorders.

KELLY'S VIEWS ON THE COGNITION – AFFECT DICHOTOMY

Kelly's (1955) original theoretical formulation dealt with affect mainly in terms of a direct connection between depression and anxiety. Depression, as a syndrome, was seen as a way to "constrict" the world to be construed. This constriction would reduce anxiety (defined as the inability to construe certain aspects of experience) by reducing the amount of incongruity between anticipation and experience. In outlining how his theory applies to guilt, anxiety, fear, and threat as "transitional diagnostic constructs," Kelly treated subjective emotional events as the awareness that one's construct system is in a state of transition. These conceptions of particular feeling states appear consistent with his overall theoretical formulation. However, Kelly also addressed affect in a more generic sense, assuming the radical position that the terms *affect* and *cognition* should be discarded by psychologists—briefly in a posthumously published chapter synopsizing his theory (1970), again briefly in a collection of posthumously published essays (e.g., Kelly, 1969a, 1969b), and more thoroughly in several personal documents that were never published. These latter papers have been made available to several personal construct psychologists for elaboration and debate. What follows is a description of sections of these personal documents relating to the distinction between cognition and affect.

In 1962, Kelly reviewed a constructivist manuscript for a former student of his that contained several references to "affective" responses. In his comments, Kelly (personal correspondence, to R. L. Cromwell, July 19, 1962) argued that the term *affect* should be abandoned. Not surprisingly, this generated a lengthy response from Cromwell (personal correspondence, R. L. Cromwell to Kelly, August 3, 1962). Cromwell argued that, although processes termed affective had been contrasted to processes that might be termed cognitive by other theories, personal construct theory could accept the terms for their descriptive value but deny their dichotomization. Cromwell concluded, "Rather than there being a psychology of personal constructs and a psychology of emotions, I am arguing that the psychology of personal constructs is at the same time a psychology of emotion (or affect)" (Cromwell's underlining).

Kelly's next correspondence (personal correspondence to Cromwell, August 23, 1962) elaborated on his own position, stating that the term *cognition* should be likewise abandoned on the same logical grounds. He wrote:

> If we take the view that the psychology of personal constructs—or any modern psychology for that matter—applies equally to phenomena that

we have formerly been calling "affective" as well as those we have been calling "cognitive" we are essentially denying the dichotomy, not just the half of it. This is to say, that if no useful distinction is to be made between cognition and affect, then neither term has served any useful purpose. It is the dichotomy that I think has outlived its usefulness, not the phenomena that we have formerly called affective any more that those phenomena that we have called cognitive.

In sum, Kelly's view was that the terms *affect* and *cognition* should be rejected for the sake of theoretical parsimony and purity. "The boundary between cognition and affect is obliterated, rendering the terms meaningless" (Kelly, 1970, p. 58). Moreover, "construing is a far cry from cognition" (Kelly, 1969a, p. 198), the former connoting the totality of processes involved in psychological differentiation, including "levels which have been called 'physiological' or 'emotional'" (Kelly, 1969b, p. 219). Kelly observed that the term *cognition* was most commonly invoked to denote only verbal knowing—an observation with considerable validity today as well.

Despite such strong dispersions from this influential theorist, constructivist writers continue to use the terms. The dichotomy between the two constructs has never been clearly rejected. Nonetheless, Kelly's views, at least as they exist in the cited personal correspondence and late writings, remain clear: affect does not exist as separate and apart from cognition, and vice versa. It is not even two different sides of the same coin; it is more like the same side of the same coin viewed through two different windows.

EMOTION IN PERSONAL CONSTRUCT PSYCHOLOGY

Miall (1989) has recently published a personal construct model of emotion that revives the issue addressed in the section above. Miall notes that most previous attempts by personal construct theorists to integrate emotion or affect into the general theoretical framework have adopted an "interruption" model of emotion (e.g., Mancuso, 1985; Mancuso & Hunter, 1983; cf. Mascolo & Mancuso, 1990). The interruption model assumes that affect disrupts, or interrupts, cognitive processes. It should be noted that although the interruption concept is relatively simple, these theoretical variations of the interruption model are by no means simple. For example, Mancuso and his colleagues have presented complex variations of a disequilibrium framework (Mancuso 1985; Mancuso & Hunter, 1983; Mascolo & Mancuso, 1990). Emotions are those states of activation created by discrepancies between construction and perceptual input, thus disrupting normal cognitive functioning. However complex it may become, such an interruption model acknowledges, by definition, a dichotomization of affect and cognition.

Bannister (1977) suggested that constructivists have dealt with emotion from a passive, "deterministic" viewpoint and have therefore failed "to develop the idea of feeling in its active sense as meaning exploration, grasp, understanding, as in feeling the surface of a material, feeling our way towards" (p. 24). Some theorists have begun to move in the direction suggested by Bannister. Miall's (1989) own model attempts to adopt Bannister's view in a way that would be more consistent with the whole of personal construct psychology. His model proposes that emotion can be viewed as an "anticipation of the self." Miall attributes constructive processes to the emotional anticipation of the future state of the self. These constructive processes are proposed as separate from the constructive processes involved in anticipation at the behavioral, or event, level. These latter processes are the cognitive aspects of Miall's model. Thus, according to Miall's model, cognition and emotion are still dichotomized, although the dichotomy is one of differing levels of operation, rather than one of opposing forces, as discussed above.

Although Miall's (1989) model is more consistent theoretically than the interruption models discussed earlier, it still seems to leave at least one major question unanswered: What does the addition of the second level of anticipation (i.e., emotional) add to the theory that is not encompassed by merely choosing not to dichotomize affect and cognition? The answer, in my opinion, is that it does not add additional explanatory value to the theory and therefore cannot be of heuristic value to a therapist operating within the theory. It does provide a way to separate affect from cognition without hypothesizing constructive differences (other than the notion that emotional anticipation is what occurs whenever the self-concept is involved). This distinction seems more in the service of preserving our terminology that advancing constructive understanding. Additionally, Miall's emotional construction appears to operate at a relatively verbal level. The other, nonverbal aspects of construction need to be incorporated in order to further Kelly's earlier views.

Another general way in which emotion has formally been incorporated into constructivist theory has been to consider emotional experiences as epiphenomena of various constructural states. Katz (1984) adopted an epiphenomenal view wherein emotions are simply the experience of the activation of certain primitive, "psychophysiological" constructs (cf. McCoy, 1977). Finally, Fisher (1990) extended Katz's (1984) model in a manner that seems maximally consistent with Kelly's various presentations. Fisher outlined a model of emotional functioning in which emotional experience is considered to be the utilization of "phylogenetically available, evaluative sensorimotor constructs" (p. 183). Fisher's model proposes that emotion is nothing other than construction at a primitive and nonverbal level (although the model outlines the various dimensions hypothesized to comprise the emotional realm). Thus, Fisher's model serves to functionally bridge the gap between what psychologists have typically dealt with as affective phenomena and Kelly's "construing" (the latter being often misunderstood as purely cognitive).

As stated above, Miall's (1989) model deals mainly with verbal construction. Conversely, Fisher's (1990) model deals mainly with nonverbal construction. Some combination or fusing of these two models might be beneficial, given that experiences termed emotional are neither exclusively verbal nor exclusively nonverbal. For example, sensorimotor constructs (à la Fisher) that are brought to bear on highly self-relevant anticipations (à la Miall) would most likely be elaborated by the construing person in a manner that makes at least portions of the construction verbally accessible. Such emotions would likely be the constructions of most relevance to the psychologist. Moreover, it is just such constructions that are implicated in mood disorders. Evidence for this latter assertion is presented below.

AFFECT AND THE CONSTRUCTION OF EXPERIENCE

Regardless of the theoretical or terminological position adopted, there still seems to be merit in investigating the constructive underpinnings of problems (and, conversely, adaptation) regarding emotion. It is consistent with any of the proposed models to be concerned with what have been called affective disorders, the most common of which is depression. Kelly's clinical notion of depression was described earlier. More recently, some investigations have taken place that suggest certain constructive differences between individuals who are clinically depressed and those who are not (Space & Cromwell, 1980; Sperlinger, 1971). The findings are consistent with Miall's (1989) general model in that depression (constructively) appears to be a maladaptation in the self-perception sphere, and at the same time, the depressive phenomenology likely necessitates the nonverbal orientation of Fisher (1990).

It has been well documented that depressed persons construe themselves more negatively than do others (Beck, 1967). Space and Cromwell (1980) found this to be empirically observable (i.e., depressed persons assigned the "self" more often and more extremely to the negative poles of their own constructs than did controls). However, this self-negative bias was not found to be the most salient dimension in relation to the depression. Two other constructive differences appeared to be important in depression: People who were depressed, as compared to normal and psychiatric controls, tended to (1) see themselves as "more different" from others in their social environment and (2) make more mixed valence attributions to themselves within construct clusters (via factor analysis). These results are worthy of further discussion.

The first difference seems self-explanatory. Depressed persons were more psychologically alienated than were nondepressed persons. It should be emphasized, however, that the "more different" attribution of depressed individuals applied to constructs on which the self was seen as positive as well as to constructs on which the self was seen as negative. Thus, the depressed client feels alone in the most complete sense. Reifying this position, "I am worthless at social relationships and others are better at them; I like the fact that I am friendlier than anyone I know."

The second difference (mixed self-valence attribution within clusters) warrants reflection. Assuming that factor analysis of a person's role-construct repertory grid (Fransella & Bannister, 1977) is tapping some organizational structure, constructs that factor together could be seen as serving, for that individual, some particular domain of life (i.e., range of convenience). Depressed individuals tend to rate themselves in a mixed fashion (i.e., positive on some constructs, negative on others) *within* factors. This belies an instability in the structure that could lead to greater equivocation regarding the self and to a propensity toward shifting the overall self-attribution within the factor to a negative one. Contrasting examples are provided to help in understanding this complex difference.

> John is coming in for occupational assessment and counseling. He is not depressed. He sees himself as caring, socially adept, and stable—all traits he values. For John, these constructs are highly correlated (i.e., they form a cluster). Another positive cluster contains the constructs of hardworking, trustworthy, and attentive. However, John thinks he is a lousy speaker in front of groups, can't remember prices for particular items, and gets nervous operating a computer. He does not like these aspects of himself, and together (as a cluster) these traits make John a poor pharmaceuticals salesperson. He is frustrated, at times anxious, and motivated for change—but he is not depressed. His clusters of self-relevant constructions are valence-consistent.
>
> Carla isn't sure why she is coming to therapy; she simply knows that she feels terrible. She sees herself as socially adept and stable—traits she values—yet uncaring. As for John, these constructs are highly correlated in Carla's construct system (i.e., they form a cluster). Another cluster

contains the constructs of hardworking, trustworthy, and attentive. Although hardworking, Carla sees herself as untrustworthy and inattentive. Carla says she is a good speaker in front of groups, but she can't remember prices for particular items and gets nervous operating a computer. Although her opinion of herself is mixed, these traits allow Carla to be a relatively successful pharmaceuticals salesperson. Carla feels alone and is depressed. A single ambiguous reaction from one of her clients during a presentation can make her feel like a terrible speaker (a trait on which she usually feels positive). Her clusters of self-relevant constructions are valence-inconsistent and therefore unstable. This instability, along with her general tendency to view herself as negative and different, makes Carla prone to frequent bouts of depression.

Thus, it seems that a consistent self-attribution within particular domains of life is more important for a person's emotional development than is a totally positive view of the self. When negative self-attributions are isolated or grouped together, the anticipatory functions of the construct system will continue to effectively predict experience. If, however, feedback is regularly confusing or inconsistent, clusters of constructs wherein the self has mixed valence attributions might develop. Then, because the whole of personal construct theory posits that subsequent experiences are anticipated and interpreted on the basis of existing construct organization, the individual would be prone to ineffective prediction, equivocal interpretation, and finally even more instability in the organization of the system. Sperlinger (1971; also cf. Space & Cromwell, 1980) suggested that people who are depressed tend to change their self-attributions in light of new (particularly negative) experience, rather than develop new constructs. This could be viewed as a manifestation of mixed self-valence attribution within clusters.

Thus far in this chapter, I have briefly discussed several interpretations of personal construct theory regarding the relation between affect and cognition in general and, specifically, the bearing of this relation on development of adaptive or maladaptive construction systems. Some of Kelly's own views regarding the affect–cognition dichotomy that challenge the theoretical utility of such a dichotomy were incorporated into the discussion. Other theorists have formally attempted to integrate affect into personal construct theory while preserving the dichotomy. It is my assertion, however, that their respective theoretical positions might be strengthened by abandoning the dichotomy. Such abandonment would bring the theoretical positions more in line with existing research findings. Finally, and most important, this position has potentially useful implications for the conduct of psychotherapy. The question remains as to whether or not constructivist theory (and, by implication, the constructivist therapist) could function practically and terminologically without the separation of affect and cognition.

PRACTICAL IMPLICATIONS FOR CONSTRUCTIVIST PSYCHOTHERAPY

As described above, Kelly argued that the dichotomy between affect and cognition should be abandoned to the point of rendering the terms useless. It is my contention that constructivist therapists could benefit greatly by following Kelly in abandoning this dichotomy. To appreciate these benefits, I begin with one of the foundations of PCT—sociality. One of many important therapeutic issues to which Kelly (1955) addressed his theory was the evaluation of the client's construction system. The evaluation assumes prime importance as the therapist determines the client's accessibility (i.e., by the particular therapist) and levels of communication to allow the client's construct system to be subsumed into that of the therapist. Kelly noted that analytic forms of therapy encourage "emotional insight" so that emotions can be verbalized rather than "acted out." As noted above, a personal construct therapist must be perfectly at ease with the knowledge that much of how a client understands and anticipates her experience will not be *word-bound.* The goal of therapy is not to impose verbiage where once was emotion (to parallel the psychoanalytic maxim, "Where id once was, there ego shall be"). Rather, the frequent goals of therapy can be stated roughly as follows: building structure where once was anxiety, building sociality where once was alienation, building courage for experimentation where once was constriction and hostile replication. None of these goals is likely to be met wholly within the verbal realm.

The problems of adjustment are almost always *known* by the client via verbal as well as nonverbal constructions (or unknown altogether). In fact, this can be said of most important experiences. A personal example I often use to explain this concept to my psychotherapy students involves the seemingly straightforward experience of smelling coffee. Were I an anatomy/physiology expert, I could perhaps explain the phenomenon of smelling coffee via some impressive sequence of sensory registers and selective neuronal firing rates. But such an explanation would miss the *meaning* of my experience. The smell of coffee, for me, invokes a configuration of feeling states that involves my very sense of maleness—an experience that resides somewhere just beneath the sternum. Having smelled coffee most vividly as a child on construction sites with my father more defines its aroma than the neuronal firing pattern. Smelling coffee is not a thought; it is not a feeling. Rather, it is a complex constellation of verbal and nonverbal constructions that, together, create the experience. If smelling coffee can be this complex, how much more so must be the psychological problems that bring our clients to therapy?

Given that important knowledge appears composed of admixtures of verbal and nonverbal understanding, several implications follow. First, the therapist—in order to adequately subsume the client's construction system—must come to anticipate the client in similar terms (i.e., both verbal and nonverbal). We (perhaps inadvertently) teach the skill of nonverbal empathic understanding to beginning therapists in their very first course on interviewing techniques. We teach them to track with the client's pace of interaction, postural attitude, paralinguistics (intonation, even accent), and so on. We do this with the rationale that we are enhancing rapport and *making the client feel heard and understood.* What is often ignored is the effect that this nonverbal tracking has on the interviewer. Via such low-level mimickry, the interviewer gains a knowledge of the client that is often quite apart from the content of the interview. I often parallel this process in clinical supervision by spontaneously thrusting one of my graduate trainees into the role of the client being discussed. The trainees often make the mistaken assumption that I am merely trying to grill them on their memory of their latest session. They soon find that I am pushing them to conceive their clients from the inside out. What they learn is seldom captured by words but usually appears useful in their subsequent sessions.

Second, acting out a problem is not only allowable but necessary and inevitable if change is to take place. Just as our clients anticipate their experience via verbal and nonverbal psychological elements, they also construe their worlds via actions. My former client who often "felt like an impostor" was surprised to find her conflicted self-concept undergoing change as a result of filling the most expensive prescription that I, as a nonmedical practitioner, have ever written—a T-shirt with the words "I'm a fake" across the back, as though it were her name. Wearing the shirt and fielding the litany of questions that the moniker generated redefined her experience in a positive way.

Third, as discussed somewhat within the first implication, the change that a client experiences is unlikely to be completely knowable via verbiage alone, and thus fourth, the adjusted goal-state of the client might be no more word-bound than the maladjusted state that brought the client to the therapist. Thus, the "new structure is stabilized by means of some portable symbols which are not necessarily verbal in nature" (Kelly, 1955, p. 804). My former impostor–client can no more articulate fully her reconstructed self-conception than I can tell you what coffee smells like.

There exist some dangers for the therapist who espouses the cognition–affect dichotomy in relation to working within the framework described above. If cognition and affect are conceived as different in some important way, the therapist will likely utilize this construct during the evaluation process, anticipating some of the client's constructs as *cognitive* and others as *affective*. Not only will sociality be impaired (if one adopts the theoretical assertions above), but several therapeutic roadblocks and pitfalls arise that would be irrelevant if the dichotomy were not used. First, and most ubiquitous, would be the helplessness and "stuckness" that would consume the therapeutic relationship when a problem is encountered that is almost entirely nonverbal and for which verbal elaborations are unsuccessful (i.e., unhelpful from the client's perspective). The therapist who integrates cognition and affect would be comfortable assisting the client in elaborating and structuring problematic anticipations fully via some "as if" format or acting out (e.g., casual enactments, role assumption, etc.). The client—and perhaps even the therapist—might not be able to verbalize changes thus attained.[3] This would likely be difficult for the cognition–affect-dichotomized therapist. PCT, as illustrated here, is certainly not "talking-heads" therapy (as can be said of many so-called *cognitive* therapies, however integrated *affect* might be).

Second, a pitfall to which the cognition–affect-dichotomized therapist is susceptible is that of assuming that emotions (as feeling states) are facts unto themselves. The existentialists have declared that "to have an emotion is one decision, and to act on it is another decision" (Maddi, 1985, p. 204). As theorized here, emotions are themselves constructions that are experienced in ways other than verbal symbolism. As constructions, they are subject to revision or rejection (as per constructive alternativism). Thus, within this framework the maxim would be "To have an emotion is one construction; to revise it is another construction." The frequently held goal of *accepting* or *identifying* one's feeling states for the mere sake of doing so would be rejected. Feeling states are not givens—pieces of facticity that must be worked around as an athlete learns to accept and compensate for some genetic malinheritance. Rather, feelings are attempts at understanding and anticipating experience that can be altered and improved, more like a skill developed for one sport that hinders performance in another—the athlete, finding herself in a different domain of experience, must alter her constitution to best anticipate performance. In this sense (and this is probably the only important sense), feeling states are no different from any other constructs.

Related to the notion described above, that feelings are as subject to reconstruction as any other construction, is the need to allow clients to repeatedly and ambiguously characterize their feeling states. "Interacting with my father evokes my *pain* all over again," a client has stated. By repeatedly encouraging him to elaborate the "pain" with nondefining queries—such as "What sense do you have of that pain now that you haven't seen your father in over a month?" and "How are you experiencing the pain given that today is your birthday?"—the pain was elaborated and understood in a fluid and complex manner. Such perseveration showed that the pain, first construed as guilt and later as anger, eventually came to be understood as extreme sadness. Assuming his feeling to be fixed once characterized would have missed this multilayered understanding of the client's experience and deprived him of the elaborative encouragement of the therapeutic encounter.

The therapist's creativity in applying personal construct theory to psychotherapy is thus considerably liberated by abandoning the cognition–affect dichotomy. Transformation of the client's construct system into some purely verbal domain need not be attempted. Detours around dysfunctional feeling states need not be undertaken. Instead, the constructivist psychotherapist can subsume the client's construct system *as it is*, communicate the sociality, and then work with the client, both verbally and otherwise, to improve the client's experience.

As a warning, it should be noted (if it is not obvious) that the therapist cannot emerge from PCT unscathed from the encounter. Subsuming another's construct system, according to the present interpretation of the theory, involves *knowing* the client's world in nonverbal as well as verbal ways and should never be undertaken lightly. If the therapist refuses to separate cognition from affect in the construction system of her client, she gives up the option to do so within her own psychological space as well. Creativity thus has a price: intimacy.

ONE STEP FURTHER: WORDS ABOUT NONWORDS

The terminological issue appears simple but merits explicit attention. The term *construction* in our current jargon refers generically to the psychological processes of interest. Thus, it could easily be adopted to subsume the now-irrelevant dichotomy of cognition–affect, rendering the latter disused. For more specific reference to phenomena historically called affective or cognitive, one can simply use a descriptive term that applies to the particular type of construction, such as "depression," "euphoria," "anxiety," "logical analysis," "curious exploration," and the like. To refer to all of these phenomena, collectively, as "construction" and to abandon "affect" and "cognition" truly rejects the dichotomy. Moreover, it places the relevant issues (development, psychopathology, psychotherapy, etc.) in a more theoretically and pragmatically useful perspective.

SUMMARY AND CONCLUSIONS

This chapter has focused on a reconstruction of the relation between affect and cognition in PCT. PCT and the theory from which it is derived were summarized with an emphasis on Kelly's theoretical views concerning the traditional distinction between cognition and affect. The various roles of affect within more recent applications of personal construct theory and research were reviewed and compared to Kelly's notions. Finally, I have argued that the adoption of Kelly's goal of abandoning the cognition–affect dichotomy would represent a theoretical and therapeutic step forward for PCT. This argument is made by pointing out the benefits such a posture would yield in the therapeutic endeavor. Like all constructions, these are subject to revision and reinterpretation. Their worth as therapeutic constructs must be measured by those willing to employ them in anticipating actual clients.

NOTES

1. Actually, this is only one of several ways that Kelly used to define the term. This definition is most operationalized and theoretically explicit. For other conceptual definitions, see Kelly (1955).
2. Note that this comprises only two-thirds of the time-honored tripartite view of psychology: cognition, emotion, and *behavior*. This is because it is assumed that behavior will *always*, in some form, be a component of the change process, even if the behavior of importance is internal, verbal, or otherwise divergent from the limits of obsolete behavioral materialism.
3. Regarding such inarticulable changes, Kelly (1955) noted that the client "may be able to talk *about* it, but still be inarticulate as to what it *was* (p. 804; italics in original)

REFERENCES

Bannister, D. (1977). The logic of passion. In D. Bannister (Ed.), *New perspectives in personal construct theory*. London: Academic Press.

Bannister, D., & Agnew, J. (1977). The child's construing of self. In A. W. Landfield (Ed.), *Nebraska Symposium on Motivation 1976*. Lincoln: Nebraska University Press.

Bannister, D., & Fransella, F. (1980). *Inquiring man: The psychology of personal constructs*. Malibar, FL: Robert E. Krieger Publishing Co.

Bannister, D., & Salmon, P. (1967). Measures of superordinacy. Unpublished study cited in Bannister, D., & Fransella, F. (1980). *Inquiring man: The psychology of personal constructs*. Malibar, FL: Robert E. Krieger Publishing Co.

Beck, A. T. (1967). *Depression: Clinical, experimental, and theoretical aspects.* New York: Harper & Row.

Brierly, D. W. (1967). The use of personality constructs by children of three different ages. Unpublished doctoral dissertation, University of London.

Fisher, D. D. V. (1990). Emotional construing: A psychobiological model. *International Journal of Personal Construct Psychology, 3,* 183–203.

Fransella, F., & Bannister, D. (1977). *A manual for repertory grid technique.* London: Academic Press.

Honess, T. (1979). Children's implicit theories of their peers: A developmental analysis. *British Journal of Psychology, 70,* 417–424.

Katz, J. O. (1984). Personal construct theory and the emotions: An interpretation in terms of primitive constructs. *British Journal of Psychology, 75,* 315–327.

Kelly, G. A. (1955). *The psychology of personal constructs,* 2 vols. New York: Norton.

Kelly, G. A. (1969a). In whom confide: On whom depend for what? In B. Maher (Ed.), *Clinical psychology and personality: The selected papers of George Kelly* (pp. 189–206). New York: John Wiley & Sons.

Kelly, G. A. (1969b). The psychotherapeutic relationship. In B. Maher (Ed.), *Clinical psychology and personality: The selected papers of George Kelly* (pp. 216–223). New York: John Wiley & Sons.

Kelly, G. A. (1970). A summary statement of a cognitively-oriented comprehensive theory of behavior. In J. C. Mancuso (Ed.), *Readings for a cognitive theory of personality* (pp. 27–58). New York: Holt, Rinehart and Winston.

Maddi, S. R. (1985). Existential psychotherapy. In S. J. Lynn & J. P. Garske (Eds.), *Contemporary psychotherapies: Models and methods* (pp. 191–219). Columbus, OH: Merrill.

Mancuso, J. C. (1985, August). *The fundamental postulate and emotions as self construction.* Paper presented at the Sixth International Congress for Personal Construct Psychology, Cambridge, MA.

Mancuso, J. C., & Hunter, K. V. (1983). Anticipation, motivation, or emotion: The fundamental postulate after twenty-five years. In J. R. Adams-Webber & J. C. Mancuso (Eds.), *The construing person.* New York: Praeger.

Mascolo, M. F., & Mancuso, J. C. (1990). Functioning of epigenetically evolved emotion systems: A constructive analysis. *International Journal of Personal Construct Psychology, 3,* 205–222.

McCoy, M. M. (1977). A reconstruction of emotion. In D. Bannister (Ed.), *New perspectives in personal construct theory* (pp. 93–124). London: Academic Press.

Miall, D. S. (1989). Anticipating the self: Toward a personal construct model of emotion. *International Journal of Personal Construct Psychology, 2,* 185–198.

Neimeyer, R. (1985). *The development of personal construct psychology.* Lincoln: University of Nebraska Press.

Piaget, J. (1977). *The grasp of consciousness: Action and concept in the young child* (S. Wedgwood, Trans.). London: Routledge and Kegan Paul.

Salmon, P. (1970). A psychology of personal growth. In D. Bannister (Ed.), *Perspectives in personal construct theory.* London: Academic Press.

Space, L. G., & Cromwell, R. L. (1980). Personal constructs among depressed patients. *Journal of Nervous and Mental Disease, 168,* 150–158.

Sperlinger, D. J. (1971). *A repertory grid and questionnaire study of individuals receiving treatment for depression from general practitioners.* Unpublished doctoral thesis, University of Birmingham, England.

Tomkins, S. S. (1992). *Affect, imagery, consciousness: Vol. 4. Cognition: Duplication and transformation of information.* New York: Springer Publishing Co.

10

Cognitive Narrative Psychotherapy: The Hermeneutic Construction of Alternative Meanings

Óscar F. Gonçalves

Cognitive therapies are undergoing important changes (cf. Gonçalves, 1989). Among several dimensions of change the following are worth noticing: (1) a shift from a rationalist toward a more constructivist philosophy (cf. Mahoney, 1991), (2) a shift from an information-processing model toward a narrative model of the knowing processes (cf. Gonçalves, in press; Russell, 1991), (3) a shift from an emphasis on conscious processes toward an emphasis on unconscious dimensions of experience (cf. Kihlstrom, 1987), (4) a shift from an emphasis on strict cognitive processes toward an acknowledgment of the emotional dimension of experience (cf. Safran & Greenberg, 1988), (5) a shift in therapeutic methodologies from personal and logical procedures to more analogic and interpersonal strategies (cf. Gonçalves & Craine, 1990; Guidano, 1991; Safran & Segal, 1990).

Central to all these changes is the core theme of cognitive theory—the problem of mental representation. That is, how do individuals come to mentally represent information about themselves and the world? Two conflicting positions are currently apparent regarding the nature of cognitive representations: the rationalist paradigm and the narrative paradigm (cf. Bruner, 1986, 1990; Lakoff, 1987; Mahoney, 1991; Polkinghorne, 1988; Russell, 1991).

The rationalist paradigm states that (a) humans are mostly rational beings, (b) thoughts are constituted by an algorithm computation of abstract symbols, (c) the manipulation of abstract symbols obeys the principles of a universal logic, and (d) reality is seen as a puzzle accessed only through reason and logic. The narrative paradigm, on the other hand, states that (a) humans are seen as storytellers, (b) thoughts are essentially metaphorical and imaginative, (c) the manipulation of thoughts is an intentional pursuit of meaning, and (d) reality is seen as a set of ill-structured problems that can be accessed through hermeneutic and narrative operations (Lakoff, 1987).

The narrative conception of mental representations advanced by recent cognitive theory (cf. Bruner, 1990) calls for the development of new therapeutic methodologies able to effect deep changes in the knowing processes. This chapter attempts to address these issues by presenting and illustrating a new therapeutic methodology, hereafter referred as to cognitive narrative psychotherapy. I begin with a clinical description of a client. Next, the main features of cognitive narrative psychotherapy are presented and illustrated.

THE CLIENT

Fernando[1] came to the University Counseling Services complaining of persistent academic underachievement and difficulties in concentration and memory.

Fernando is a 23-year-old single college student. His parents own a small business. His mother was described as an accepting person, very concerned with his school achievement, valuing the importance of an education that she was not able to get for herself. Fernando's father was presented as a cold and distant person, always very involved with his work and exclusively focused on assuring a stable financial situation for all the family. Fernando is the eldest of five children. He described a good relationship with his two sisters and two brothers. However, the relationship between him and his family has been mostly affectionless across his life history.

The client did not describe any significant problematic occurrences before college. Despite a personal appearance of physical weakness and absence of appropriate communication skills, he was always a satisfactory student, and his interests were directed toward research and technically oriented subjects. Unable to be admitted to astronomy (a very selective program at his university), he managed to be admitted to computer science (also a very selective program).

During his first year at the university he began to experience generalized underachievement, failing almost every course. He described this situation as a terrible shock and a major threat to his self-image. He began questioning his aptitudes for that program as well as doubting his general intellectual abilities. As a consequence he experienced long periods of frustration and depression during which he was absolutely unable to study, concentrate, or memorize. His life turned rapidly into a random wheel moving along with the wind, as he felt unable to set any kind of direction for his life. He described feelings of guilt and helplessness, along with an increasing sense of physical and psychological vulnerability and reduced self-esteem. Meanwhile, he got a job as a substitute teacher at a local high school, but he described the situation as a dissatisfying and frustrating one. He is unable both to enjoy and experience any teaching effectiveness. Reflecting upon his life, he recurrently experiences the following thought, "I am already 23 and absolutely unable to make any sense out of my life." In other words, as Markus and Nurius (1986) would put it, Fernando is typically struggling for the emergence of possible selves.

COGNITIVE NARRATIVE PSYCHOTHERAPY

Recent developments in cognitive therapy have acknowledged the central role of narrative in cognitive organization (e.g., Bamberg, 1991; Gonçalves, in press; Leahy, 1991; Russell, 1991; Van den Broek & Thurlow, 1991). Guidano (1987, 1991), for example, argues that tacit levels of cognitive representation have their origins in early moments of attachment–separation development. That is, our original constructions take place in a prelogic or even preverbal period and allows only the possibility of an analogical-narrative representation. Research on the development of narrative capacity has consistently shown that narratives are indeed the earliest and most used tools to describe life events, as well as to understand the present and predict the future (cf. Van den Broek & Thurlow, 1991). As was recently pointed out by Van den Broek and Thurlow (1991), "The narrative constitutes the person's life as he/she perceives it, and the person's sense of self-identity is dependent upon the content and cohesiveness of the life story" (p. 261).

The acknowledgment of the importance of narrative in cognitive representation led Howard (1991) to suggest that we should designate humans as *Homo fabulus* rather than *Homo scientus*, to emphasize that humans represent reality and themselves not with algorithms but with meaningful personal narratives.

If we assume that humans represent their most basic and tacit information about self and reality with narratives, a narrative approach to therapy is called for (cf. Mair, 1989; White & Epston, 1990). The cognitive narrative psychotherapy here presented is founded on three central assumptions:

1. Knowledge (epistemology) and existence (ontology) are inseparable, and they are organized in terms of narratives. Our knowing processes are concurrent with our existential tasks or, as Weimer (1977) puts it, living beings are theories of their environments, and these theories have a narrative nature.

2. The psychological understanding of the client implies the identification and analysis of her/his prototype narratives. In other words, individuals have idiosyncratic ways of organizing knowledge that are typified in certain types of narratives that assume the role of best examples, root metaphors, or prototypes (Haskell, 1987; Lakoff, 1987).

3. Psychotherapy can be seen as a scenario for the identification, construction and deconstruction of narratives. Clients are supposed to acquire a narrative attitude, not only by being able to identify their idiosyncratic ways of functioning through the understanding of their prototype narratives but also by constructing and projecting alternative metaphors (Crites, 1986; Gonçalves, in press; Gonçalves & Craine, 1990; Wurf & Markus, 1991).

In sum, and as it was appropriately remarked by Russell (1991), "The formulation, elaboration, clarification, transformation and enactment of these narrative trajectories are integral to the process of becoming" (pp. 253–254).

Based on these assumptions, a therapeutic approach was structured following a sequence of five stages: (1) recalling narratives, (2) objectifying narratives, (3) subjectifying narratives, (4) metaphorizing narratives, and (5) projecting narratives. The main objectives and therapeutic methodologies for each stage are summarized in Figure 10.1. At each stage two distinct, although complementary, types of work are carried out: synchronic and diachronic. At the synchronic level, client and therapist apply the narrative attitudes recently acquired in the context of their daily life experiences, thus enabling clients to deal with some of their immediate symptomatic concerns.

At the diachronic level, client and therapist apply the narrative attitudes learned from each stage to the central themes of clients' life experiences. That is, prototype narratives are elected as best examples of personal meaning making, to be worked through along the therapeutic process.

Several connections can be identified between the current proposal and models from other traditions also subscribing to the narrative metaphor (cf. Gergen & Kaye, 1992; Russell & Van den Broek, 1992; Schaffer, 1981; Siegelman, 1990; White & Epston, 1990). Despite the differences in therapeutic technology, the majority of these approaches share the idea that our knowing processes are essentially narrative and that the change of the narrative structure is the essential task for psychotherapy.

Recalling Narratives

The objective of this initial phase of the therapeutic process is twofold: (1) to develop a recalling attitude and (2) simultaneously to allow an opportunity to identify different meaningful narratives across the life span.

Central to the narrative approach is the capacity of the individual to recollect experiences. Those experiences are indeed the most important tools for the constructions of personal stories relevant for identity development. Identity can be understood as a personal effort to construct coherent and meaningful experiences across the life span. This phase of the therapeutic process attempts to make the client acquainted with memoing life narratives as well as identifying blind spots in her/his personal history.

The process usually begins with a warm-up exercise of guided imagery across life span. This is accomplished by inviting clients to go through the process of recalling meaningful personal narratives in a three-stage process: (1) induction of a relaxing attitude, (2) guided imagery with temporal regression, and (3) selecting specific narratives.

The induction of a relaxing attitude, whose technique may vary according to client and therapist preferences, has the objective of bringing the client into a sensorimotor level of experience that has been found to facilitate a more associative mode, particularly useful for the task of personal recall. Following the induction of a relaxing attitude, the client is invited to focus, using a process of guided imagery with temporal regression , on several meaningful personal narratives. The following instructions are illustrative of this phase:

> Focus now your attention on the images and thoughts that come to your mind and let them flow freely. . . . I'm now asking you to use the sound of my voice as a stimulus for recalling the past and recollect certain meaningful experiences of your life. We'll begin with yesterday and will attempt to go as far back as possible. Try now to recollect something that happened yesterday . . . last week . . . last month . . . last year . . . three years ago . . . when you were in high school . . . in elementary school . . . in kindergarten . . . before kindergarten . . .

After going through this process, clients share their experiences and discuss their reactions with the therapist.

Following the guided imagery work, clients are instructed to exercise and develop this recalling ability by identifying, for every day of the following week, a specific event that they think is worthy of memorizing and to make an entry in a notepad with a brief description of the event—memoing daily life narratives. The objective of this exercise is to make the client aware of the importance of daily events in story development.

As clients get involved with recalling, therapist and client move in the direction of exploring meaningful narratives across the life span. This is accomplished by using a variation of the life review project introduced by Mahoney (1991). Clients are instructed, as a homework assignment, to make a separate memo for each year of their existence, from 0 to their current age. On each separate memo they are supposed to identify a specific meaningful episode of that age.

Therapist and client schedule at least one session to review the life review project homework. Clients are invited to lay down their lives like a deck of cards, illustrating their life scripts through their episodic narratives.

After reviewing meaningful daily and life span narratives, clients are instructed to selected a narrative that functions as a prototype of their current meaning-making activities—electing a prototype narrative.

Clients should be told that the selected narrative is the one that is going to be worked through across all the therapeutic processes and as such is expected to be experienced as a prototype or best example of their narratives. The objective is that the narrative functions as a good perceptograph, a way of "symbolically expressing abstract perceptions under the guise of depicting actual historical events" (Bruhn, 1992, p. 4).

Most clients prefer to go through this process in a tentative way, first selecting three or four narratives and then moving progressively to the selection of one that represents a better illustration of their lives.

Fernando, our case example, went through all of the narrative recall sequence and came up with the following selection of a prototype narrative:

> In my first day at college there was a particular incident that has marked me definitely. The door of the classroom was open, and the professor was walking restlessly and silently for 10 minutes from one side to another. Everybody was wondering what was going to happen. Suddenly, the professor closed the door and began to query the students one by one about why they had chosen computer science as a major and what was their GPA, commenting simultaneously that if they didn't have this major as their first choice or had a low GPA they should quit right away.

Objectifying Narratives

Once the prototype narrative is identified, the therapist initiates the process of objectifying the narrative. Again, there are two central objectives of this phase of the therapeutic process: (1) the development of an objectifying attitude by the client and (2) objectifying the spectrum of sensorial dimensions of his/her prototype narrative.

The development of an objectifying narrative is central to narrative development. What brings the reader into the text is, to a certain extent, the capacity of the writer to construct the scenario for the narrative. This is accomplished by specifying the sensorial dimensions of the event being introduced. For example, the simple statement "Today I woke up 6:00 a.m." is easily transformed into a narrative process when enriched with the sensorial and behavioral dimensions of the experience, such as the following:

> At 6:00 a.m. the old round alarm clock went off with a strident and aggressive noise. There was some light coming through the window. In the air there was a paradoxical mixture of French perfume and sweat. I felt a dry taste in my mouth. My lazy body was revolting against the idea of moving. Slowly I began to stand up in tentative stretches of different parts of my body, realizing that I was finally waking up.

Objectifying an event does not make the narrative, but it certainly contributes to setting the context for narrative development. It is interesting how writers are able to spend significant portions of their writing time in objectifying their narrative and by this process bring the reader into the text.

As a warm-up for the development of this objectifying attitude, the client is confronted with the modeling of the objectifying attitude. That is, quotations from different writers illustrating the objectifying attitude are presented. Note, for instance, the following quotation by David Lodge (1991) as he sets the initial scene of *Paradise News*:

> Passengers are being closely questioned at the check-in desks about the provenance of their luggage this morning, and their persons and hand baggage are scrutinized with more than usual zeal by the security staff. Long, slow-moving lines stretch from the check-in desks nearly to the opposite wall of the concourse, crosshatched by two longer lines converging upon the narrow gate that leads to Passport Control, the Security Gates, and the Departure Lounge. The queuing passengers shift their weight from one foot to another, or lean on the handles of their heaped baggage trolleys, or squat on their suitcases. Their expressions are variously anxious, impatient, bored, stoical—but not yet weary. They are still relatively fresh: their bright casual clothes are clean and pressed, their cheeks smooth from recent application of razor or makeup, their hair groomed and glossy. (p. 3)

	Syncronic	Diachronic
Recalling		
Objectives	Development of recalling attitude	Identification of meaningful experiences across life span
Process	Guided imagery across life span memoing daily narratives	Life review project Electing a prototype narrative
Objectifying		
Objectives	Development of objectifying attitude	Objectifying the prototype narrative
Process	Modeling the objectifying attitude In session exercises with objectifying cues Objectifying daily narratives	In session exercises with objectifying cues for the prototype narrative Detailed objectifying of the prototype narrative
Subjectifying		
Objectives	Development of subjectifying attitude	Subjectifying the prototype narrative
Process	Modeling the subjectifying attitude In session exercises in emotional subjectifying Emotional subjectifying daily narratives In session exercises in cognitive subjectifying Cognitive subjectifying daily narratives	In session exercises with emotional subjectifying cues for the prototype narrative Detailed emotional subjectifying for the prototype narrative In session exercises with cognitive subjectifying cues for the prototype narrative Detailed cognitive subjectifying for the prototype narrative
Metaphorizing		
Objectives	Development of metaphorizing attitude	Metaphorizing the prototype narrative
Process	Modeling the metaphorizing attitude In session exercise of metaphorizing Metaphorizing daily narratives	Constructing the root metaphor for the prototype narrative Historical analysis of root metaphor
Projecting		
Objectives	Development of projecting attitude	Projecting alternative metaphors and scripts
Process	Modeling the projecting attitude In session exercises in the construction of alternative meanings Projecting daily life narratives	Construction of alternative root metaphors Historical analysis of alternative metaphors Projecting alternative narratives Evaluating alternative narratives

FIGURE 1. Structure of Cognitive Narrative Psychotherapy

Examples such as the above are discussed with the client, and she/he is asked to identify the different sensorial dimensions of the narrative (e.g., visual, auditory, gustatory, olfactory, tactile/ kinesthetic).

The second task—exercises with objectifying cues—consists of presenting the client with several stimulus situations and asking him/her to improvise the development of sensorial dimensions. For instance the therapist gives the stimulus situation:

"You arrive 30 minutes late, and your boss confronts you; what are you seeing?" (visual cue). After the client elaborates on the visual dimensions, the therapist progresses, introducing the remaining cues: "And now, what are you hearing?" (auditory cue), "And now what are you tasting?" (olfactory cue), "And smelling?" (gustatory cue), "And sensing?" (tactile/kinesthetic cue).

Finally, the homework of objectifying daily narratives is used to consolidate the development of this objectifying attitude. Similar to what happened with the development of the recalling attitude, the client is instructed to identify, for every day of the following week, a specific event and to develop an objectifying memo of this event, specifying the sensorial dimensions of the event (e.g., visual, auditory, gustatory, olfactory, tactile/kinesthetic).

After developing the objectifying attitude, the client is invited to apply this attitude and skills to the selected prototype narrative. The process is initiated in the consulting room—in-session exercises with objectifying cues—with the therapist presenting step by step the different cues for the different dimensions of the narrative. This is not an easy task, given that for most clients getting in touch with the objectifying dimensions initiates an overwhelming sequence of deep emotions. This often leads the client into a discussion of the internal dimensions of the experience. The client should be instructed to refocus continuoually on the objective dimensions and to hold the internal dimension of the narrative in abeyance for later work. The objective at this point is exclusively to develop the capacity to focus narratively on the different sensorial dimensions of the experience.

Following the work done in the session, a detailed objectifying of the prototype narrative takes place by inviting the client to elaborate, as a homework assignment, on the prototype narrative, bringing whatever documents will help in objectifying the different dimensions of the experience (e.g., pictures, music, letters, films). At the end of this phase the client should be able to develop this objectifying attitude toward different past and current life episodes and as a consequence construct a prototype narrative with abundant sensorial details.

Fernando went through this process of objectifying with detail his prototype narrative. Examples of the different dimensions explored are presented below:

Visual dimensions: The professor is standing on the stage with an aggressive attitude, with a dark outfit, walking from one side to the other looking as though the room was empty . . .

Auditory dimensions: There is a heavy silence in the room broken only by the sound of the heavy steps of the professor in his lonely march . . . speaking fast and confusing . . . voice shaking . . .

Gustatory dimensions: My mouth is completely dry . . .

Olfactory dimensions: A mixture of smells coming from different perfumes and groups of the students . . . the smell of recent paint on the walls . . . the smell of my own sweat . . .

Tactile/kinesthetic dimensions: heart beating fast . . . tension in my back and neck . . . hands humid . . . moving impatiently in my chair . . .

Subjectifying Narratives

After having completed the therapeutic work of objectifying narratives, the therapist shifts the attention to an equally important therapeutic phase—subjectifying narratives. Two central tasks are here presented: (1) developing a subjectifying attitude and (2) increasing the client's awareness of the subjective or internal dimensions of his/her prototype narrative.

The development of a subjectifying attitude is characterized by an increased capacity to identify the internal dimensions of experience, both cognitive and emotional. This is a central issue for every cognitive therapy, to gain awareness into the internal or subjective dimension of every experience. Our capacities to act upon our thoughts and emotions are strictly dependent on our capacity to construct the internal side of human experience. This internal side of experience is one of the core aspects of narrative grammar structure (Mandler, 1984) and represents one of the most important dramatic maneuvers responsible for the construction of meaning out of every narrative (Gergen & Gergen, 1986).

As a warm-up for the development of the subjectifying attitude the client is often confronted with models of subjectifying attitude illustrated by narratives from several writers exemplifying the shift to the internal side of experience. Let me illustrate again with David Lodge (1975) this time from his novel Changing Places:

Philip Swallow has, in fact, flown before; but so seldom, and at such long intervals, that on each occasion he suffers the same trauma, an alternating current of fear and reassurance that charges and relaxes his system in a persistent and exhausting rhythm. While he is on the ground, preparing for his journey, he thinks of flying with exhilaration—soaring up, up and away into the blue empyrean, cradled in the aircraft that seems, from a distance, effortlessly at home in that element, as though sculpted from the sky itself. This confidence begins to fade a little when he arrives at the airport and winces at the shrill screaming of jet engines. (p. 9)

This passage illustrates both the cognitive and emotional processes that allow an easy empathic movement into the character's experiencing.

Having illustrated the importance and operation of subjectifying narratives, the therapist introduces in-session exercises in emotional subjectifying. First, a set of stimulus situations relevant for the client are introduced by the therapist as cues for the construction of different emotions. For instance, the previous stimulus situation can now be introduced: "You arrive 30 minutes late and your boss confronts you." However, this time, to improvise and construct his/her emotional dimension of the narrative, the client goes through a process of emotional work similar to the one advanced by Greenberg and Safran (1987, 1989; Safran & Greenberg, 1988). First, the therapist asks the client to activate emotional schemes, using two types of cues:

1. Imagery cues (e.g., "Please go back to what we have done in the objectifying phase, and try to bring to the here and now all the sensorial dimensions of the experience, in present tense and in the here and now").
2. Motor cues (e.g., "Please notice, repeat and develop any gestures, movements of facial expressions as you are describing your images". The client is instructed to repeat and exaggerate the motor dimensions of experience that he or she is aware of.

Second, the therapist initiates the focusing process, using two types of cues:

1. Intensifying cues (e.g., "Now try to intensify your experience through more elaboration of the sensorial images and an increased expression of your motor reactions").
2. Refocusing cues (e.g., "Focus this time only on the inner side of your experience in the here and now. Don't worry at this moment about words to describe what you are experiencing; allow yourself to be aware only of what you are experiencing now").

The third and final phase of emotional construction is the symbolizing process, which is accomplished through two additional cues:

1. Symbolizing cues (e.g., "Stay with the experience and try now to identify a word or symbol that reflects more appropriately what you are experiencing at this point").
2. Resymbolyzing cues (e.g., "Try now to go back to the experience and match your symbol with what you are experiencing to see if this is a good symbol to make meaning out of your experience. Adjust the symbol to better fit your experience").

As in previous phases, homework assignments are used to consolidate the construction of emotional narratives—emotional subjectifying of daily narratives. The client is instructed to identify for every day of the following week a given event and to follow this three-stage process of activation, focusing, and symbolizing.

Another aspect of the subjectifying phase consists of the construction of cognitive narratives. Here the therapist attempts to make the client aware of the internal, but this time cognitive, side of his/her experience (i.e., thoughts, inner dialogue, cognitions). The cognitive work is introduced with exercises in cognitive subjectifying. Again, the same situations used in the emotional work are the cues for the construction of the client's cognitions. A sequence of two types of cues is used here by the therapist following what is traditionally done in cognitive psychotherapy (cf. Gonçalves, 1993):

1. Thought-listing cues (e.g., "As you go back to the situation and reexperience the situation, try to share all the thoughts and internal dialogues that come to your mind").
2. Peeling the onion or downward-arrowing cues (e.g., "Try now to pick one of your thoughts and uncover the thought that is behind it until you reach what it seems to be your most basic thought").

Again, the process is completed with homework assignments in cognitive subjectifying of daily narratives. The client is instructed to identify daily events and to follow the cues discussed above for the construction of the cognitive side of his/her narratives.

After completing the work on the development of a subjectifying attitude, both emotional and cognitive, the therapist directs the client in the use of these instruments for the emotional and cognitive construction of the selected prototype narrative. In the session, the therapist goes over each of the emotional and cognitive cues discussed above for every relevant event of the narrative. This is what I refer to as the in-session exercises with subjectifying cues for the prototype narrative (both emotional and cognitive).

As a follow-up for work done in the therapeutic session, the client is asked to elaborate, between sessions, on the internal side of narrative —detailed emotional and cognitive subjectifying for the prototype narrative).

Let us now illustrate briefly with examples from Fernando's process:

Emotional Construction

Activating emotions: As I see the professor coming to me, I am feeling high tension in my back . . . my shoulders are uptight and my hands freezing. . . . I feel my heart pumping in my throat . . .

Focusing: (Therapist: "Please try to elaborate more on those sensations") . . . My back . . . my back is becoming heavier and heavier, and I cannot move; my head is moving down due to the weight of my back. . . . As the shoulders get increasingly uptight . . . I feel shrinking. . . . My throat is blocked, and I can hardly speak . . .

Symbolizing: I am feeling scared . . . absolutely scared and panicked . . . yes, what I am feeling is terror and panic . . .

Cognitive Work

Thought listing and peeling the onion: I am going to freeze. . . . He's going to make fun of my freezing. . . . Everybody is going to see me freezing. . . . Everybody is going to see that I am absolutely ridiculous, childish and cowardly. . . . If everybody sees me as ridiculous, childish, and cowardly, I must be an absolute piece of shit. . . . Pieces of shit are useless and do not deserve to pollute the world. . . . As a piece of shit I do not deserve to live . . .

Metaphorizing Narratives

Once the client has accomplished all the prescribed tasks of the recalling, objectifying, and subjectifying narratives, the therapist introduces the work of the metaphorizing phase. Here, again, two objectives are considered central to the work of the therapist: (1) to help the client with the development of a metaphorizing attitude and (2) to identify the root metaphor of the selected prototype narrative.

Lakoff and Johnson (1980) have aptly reminded us that "our ordinary conceptual system, in terms of which we both think and act, is fundamentally metaphorical in nature" (p. 3). According to these authors, all knowledge processes imply an objectivation of the known and thus require the development of metaphors. Three groups of metaphors are prevalent in our constructions of self and reality: (1) structural metaphors, in which one concept is metaphorically structured in terms of another (e.g., conceptualizing "love relationships" as wars); (2) orientation metaphors: a whole system of concepts is organized in a spatial relationship to one another (e.g., happy is up; sad is down); (3) physical metaphors: understanding our experience in terms of physical objects (including our bodies) and substances (e.g., conceptualizing people as food) (Lakoff & Johnson, 1980).

The clients' narratives reveal the structural, orientation, and physical metaphors characteristic of their representational systems (Gonçalves & Craine, 1990). What we attempt to develop first in this phase of therapy is a metaphoric attitude, "a mode of communication where the form or structure of a message is isomorphic with the content of the message" (Haskell, 1987, p. 253)—a way of finding a symbolic structural representation of the client's construct system. In other words, the objective of this phase is to help the client in the construction of meanings out of her/his experience. This is accomplished by training the client in the development of structural, orientation, and physical metaphors of different narratives.

The process begins with modeling the metaphorizing attitude. The modeling process is accomplished through confrontation with different models exhibiting the attitude of metaphorizing. A good way of illustrating for the client what is meant by metaphorizing is the presentation of short tales or chronicles. After reading a given tale or chronicle, the client discusses the possible core meanings of the written material and how they are condensed in the metaphorical title chosen by the author. A similar process can take place with movies, theater, and even dance and music, depending on the specific interests of the client.

Next, the therapist conducts in-session exercises of metaphorizing. Instrumental in this process is the use of narratives that were developed by the client in the context of in-session and homework training for the development of an objectifying and subjectifying attitude. For instance, the therapist can go on reviewing with the client the objectifying and subjectifying narrative that the client developed for the stimulus situation, "You arrive 30 minutes late, and your boss confronts you." However, this time four new types of cues are used to promote the development of a metaphorizing attitude:

1. Structural cue (e.g., if you were to find a concept that symbolizes, in a metaphoric way, your experience in this situation, what would that be?)
2. Orientation cue (e.g., if you were to find a spatial relationship metaphor that symbolizes your experience in this situation, what would that be?)
3. Physical cue (e.g., if you were to find an object or substance that symbolizes, in a metaphoric way, your experience, what would that be?)

4. Summarizing cue (e.g., from all the metaphors that you have just developed, which one or which combination would best symbolize your experience?).

Similar to the process that has taken place in previous phases, the therapeutic work is consolidated with homework assignments that instruct the client to follow up with brainstorming of different metaphors of daily situations (metaphorizing daily narratives).

When the client has developed the capacity to metaphorize his/her experiences, the therapist instructs the client to go through this stage process to construct the root metaphor for the selected prototype narrative. The structural, orientation, physical, and summarizing cues are used to facilitate the client's construction of the most appropriate metaphors.

Finally, once the metaphor construction is appropriately tuned, a process of historical analysis of the root metaphor takes place. First, in session, the therapist instructs the client to trace similar situations of his/her current life in which this metaphor was operating. Second, the client is invited to go through several stages of his/her life (i.e., infancy, childhood, adolescence, adulthood)—a life review project (Mahoney, 1991)—identifying situations that illustrate the operation of the selected metaphor. This process is usually followed by intensive homework assignments in which the client finds for each life stage an illustrative narrative and develops this narrative according to the requirements of the objectifying and subjectifying work.

At this point in therapy, the client is supposed to have constructed a good awareness of the core symbolic constructs that have been ruling her/his life and to be able to apply this metaphorizing attitude to current and forthcoming life events.

Ideally, also at this point in therapy, a prototype narrative is constructed with the details of the sensorial objectivity and the richness of emotional and cognitive subjectivity. Additionally, a root metaphor is identified as the central meaning of the narrative. Finally, a network of additional narratives subsumed under the same metaphor provides the necessary historical and contextual background.

Again I will illustrate with the case of Fernando. Responding to the stimuli cues, Fernando came up with three central metaphors: (1) structural metaphor—"lousy actor"; (2) orientation metaphor—"outsider"; (3) physical metaphor—"snake." Responding to the summarizing cues, be came up with the following metaphor, according to him, "the ideal title for his narrative": "a creeping, avoiding actor." After the identification of the metaphor, the therapist introduces the following guided imagery process intended to confirm the construction of the root metaphor.

> *Therapist (instructions for guided imagery):* the professor is standing up on the stage with an aggressive attitude, with a dark outfit, walking from one side to the other, looking as the room was empty. . . . There is a heavy silence in the room, broken only by the sound of the heavy steps of the professor in his lonely march. . . . Your mouth is completely dry. . . . A mixture of smells coming from different perfumes and groups of students . . . the smell of recent paint on the walls . . . the smell of your own sweat. . . . Your heart beating fast . . . tension in your back and neck . . . hands humid. . . . As you see the professor coming to you, you are feeling high tension in your back. . . . Your shoulders are uptight and your hands freezing. . . . You're feeling your heart pumping in your throat. . . . Your back is becoming heavier and you cannot move; your head is moving down due to the weight of your back. . . . As your shoulders get increasingly uptight, you feel shrinking. . . . Your throat is blocked, and you can hardly speak. . . .

You are feeling scared. . . . You think, "I am going to freeze. . . . He is going to make fun of my freezing. . . . Everybody is going to see me freezing. . . . Everybody is going to see that I am absolutely ridiculous, childish, and cowardly. . . . If everybody sees me as ridiculous, childish, and cowardly, I must by an absolute piece of shit. . . . Pieces of shit are useless and do not deserve to pollute the world. . . . As a piece of shit I do not deserve to live. . . ." As you have these thoughts you get more and more scared, absolutely scared and panicked. . . . Yes, what you are feeling is terror and panic. . . .

> As you go through to narrative, bring back the image of a creeping, avoiding actor and try to match it with what you are experiencing right now . . . try to tune the metaphor as you feel appropriate. . . .
> *Client:* I don't need . . . That's exactly the image of a creeping, avoiding actor, a slippery grounded fake . . . an actor that exits the scene creeping and crawling . . . a creeping avoiding actor . . .
> *Therapist (introducing historical analysis):* Let's now move on and try to identify other life narratives where this metaphor seems prevalent.
> *Client:* Everything . . . this metaphor is the story of my life . . . my script . . .
> *Therapist:* O.K., but nevertheless, let's try to particularize with the construction of other narratives from your life.

Projecting Narratives

We come now to the closing phase of narrative cognitive psychotherapy. This final stage tries to accomplish two main objectives: (1) developing a projecting attitude and (2) applying the projecting attitude to the development of alternative metaphors and scripts.

The development of a projective attitude parallels what Hazel Markus has described as possible selves (Markus & Nurius, 1986). Possible selves represent alternative path developments for the client: 'how one thinks about one's potential and one's future . . . images of the individual as he would like to be, and fantasizes about or dreads being" (Wurf & Markus, 1991, p. 40).

A projective attitude is the capacity of the client to provide alternative meanings for his/her narratives by the construction of alternative metaphors and the validation of those metaphors by projecting new narratives.

The objective of every therapy should be to orient the client into new life narratives, bringing with it a sense of acting and authorship. That is, the client is invited through the projecting attitude to develop new alternative characters (i.e., alternative metaphors). These alternatives, in turn, contribute to the definition of a new author, bringing back to the client an alternative sense of identity and authorship (cf. Lehrer, 1988). As aptly noted by Crites (1986) (reminding us of Kierkegaard): while we understand backward, we always live forward; and it is the development of a more flexible dialectic between constructing and deconstructing the narrative toward which therapy should be aimed. The venture into the unknown, the world of possibility, is indeed the final objective of therapy.

The final stage of therapy is the modeling of the projecting attitude. This phase begins with inviting clients to inspect how change processes are introduced through the development of a projective attitude. Examples from literature, movies, theater, or known persons are used to illustrate and discuss with clients the different aspects involved in the projecting attitude. Likewise, a useful modeling strategy at this point in therapy is to use other change situations experienced by the client as a self-modeling process.

In-session exercises in the construction of alternative meanings initiate the client in the exploration and construction of alternative metaphors. Again, the therapist goes through the stimuli situations introduced at other therapeutic stages and assists clients in the development of alternative metaphors and scripts. This is accomplished by using a set of three strategies for a given stimulus situation (e.g., "You are 30 minutes late, and your boss confronts you"). These strategies consist of the application of what was previously learned but this time in the context of the development of alternative narratives.

1. Constructing the alternative metaphor: the client is instructed to construct new and alternative root metaphors following a process similar to the one used for constructing the root metaphor.

2. Objectifying the alternative metaphor: based on the alternative root metaphor, the client is invited to objectify an alternative narrative based on the new metaphor.
3. Subjectifying the alternative metaphor: finally, what was learned during the subjectifying phase is now used to project the subjective experience of the alternative metaphor. Again, this is done both for the emotional and the cognitive dimensions of the narrative.

The routine of homework assignments is again used to consolidate the therapeutic work through the process of projecting daily life narratives. Clients are instructed to select alternative metaphors for certain events of the following week. The following process is suggested:

1. Construction of an alternative metaphor for an anticipated life event. For example, the client decides that, in a dinner that he is going to have with his ex-wife, he is going to explore the metaphor of a master Buddhist.
2. Objectifying the alternative metaphor. The client is instructed to carefully objectify the scenario. The client writes the scenario for the dinner—how he is dressed, the details of the restaurant, the colors and flavors of food, the cologne he is going to wear, and so on.
3. Subjectifying the alternative metaphor. Likewise, the client anticipates the inner scenario by constructing proactively the emotional and cognitive processes of a master Buddhist.
4. Implementing the alternative metaphor. When all of the script is developed, the client is encouraged to implement the metaphor to the best of his ability, feeling free to improvise within the meaning role that he has decided to explore.
5. Evaluating the alternative metaphor. Once the scene is completed, the client is instructed to objectify and subjectify a narrative report of the situation.

Once clients are familiar with this process, the therapist introduces the process of constructing alternative root metaphors. The alternative root metaphor is a conceived as a set of new meaning lenses with which to explore and make sense of a reality contrasting with the first one.

Similarly to what took place in the metaphorizing phase, the therapist introduces metaphorizing cues to help the client with the construction of an alternative metaphor:

1. Structural cue. *Therapist*: If you were to find a concept that symbolizes an alternative metaphor to your current way of meaning making (root metaphor) what would that be?

2. Orientation cue. *Therapist*: If you were to find a spatial relationship metaphor that symbolizes an alternative metaphor to your current way of meaning making (root metaphor), what would that be?

3. Physical cue. *Therapist*: If you were to find an object or substance that symbolizes an alternative metaphor to your current way of meaning making (root metaphor), what would that be?

4. Summarizing cue. *Therapist*: From all the metaphors that you have just developed, which one or which combination would best symbolize an alternative metaphor to your current way of meaning making (root metaphor)?

Every alternative metaphor needs to be grounded in the client's experiences. No metaphor can be used without a historical foundation in the client's life experiences. In this way, clients are instructed to conduct a historical analysis of the alternative metaphor in order to find narrative episodes in which they were, at least in part, operating under this alternative metaphor.

First, in the clinical situation, the therapist asks clients to identify past situations across the life span (i.e., infancy, childhood, adolescence, adulthood) in which they were operating with this metaphor. Second, clients conduct intensive homework activities, using narratives of the alternative metaphor.

As clients come to own, through historical analysis, their alternative metaphors (i.e., possible self), the projecting of alternative narratives is introduced through several fixed-role experiences (Kelly, 1955). The following steps are followed in this process.

1. Selection of stimuli situations. Several stimuli situations are selected with clients. These are situation scenarios relevant for the clients' lives.

2. Objectifying and subjectifying the narrative. For these situations, clients are invited to construct a narrative based on the alternative root metaphor, with both the objectifying and subjectifying dimensions. This work is usually completed at home with additional details.

3. Rehearsing the narrative. The script developed is rehearsed in the context of the therapeutic situation. The therapist provides detailed feedback on behavioral, cognitive, and emotional dimensions of the client's performance. Both the script and the client's performance are adapted accordingly.

Finally, once the scripts are developed and rehearsed, the therapist initiates the process of evaluating alternative narratives by inviting clients to implement a test of the viability of these narratives with in vivo experiences. They are advised to follow, at this moment, the attitude of an actor and, for the planned situation, to implement the narrative that was constructed and rehearsed in therapy.

Additionally, clients are instructed to maintain an accurate monitoring of the implementation phase, following the same narrative procedures developed across therapy. That is, a detailed objectifying and subjectifying of the situation is brought for discussion with the therapist. Depending on the results of these evaluations, new scripts are planned based on the alternative metaphor or on new metaphors that may be constructed.

The process has no ending. Quite the contrary, the objective is for the client to be able to apply this narrative attitude to develop a continuous sense of actorship and authorship in his/her life. The client should allow opportunity for the construction and deconstruction of a never-ending set of narratives. When both therapist and client agree that this objective is in process, the scenario and experience of the therapeutic relationship themselves become history: "Becoming is a process that may never be completed; however, the process is not even started until the person attempts to validate the desired possible self, however tentatively" (Wurf & Markus, 1991, p. 54).

With Fernando, the final phase of therapy was a stimulating experience. It took some time before he familiarized himself with the challenges and possibilities of a projecting attitude. Feeling stuck across his history with the "creeping, avoiding actor" metaphor, it took a long effort to help him in the creative development of alternative metaphors. Step by step, he became excited about the idea of constructing new possibilities for himself in different and sometimes trivial situations. It was during this phase of therapy that he began spontaneously to introduce a considerable amount of change into his daily life. While we were doing the training of alternative metaphors, he came with a new haircut, a new style of dressing, and even an exercise program. Somehow, Fernando was tacitly assuming for himself the most central objective of narrative cognitive psychotherapy. When the time came for the construction of an alternative metaphor of his prototype narrative, he came up with an interesting structural metaphor—private investigator. In fact, his hypersensitivity to social cues had allowed him to construct good observing and decentering skills. Sherlock Holmes was indeed one of his favorite characters in his past reading. Needless to say, Fernando was invited to go back to his reading and to find points of contact between his and Holmes's narratives. We constructed and implemented several episodic narratives where he applied the distancing, observing, and creative skills of a PI.

As we were enjoying the progression of these micronarratives,

Fernando was drawing privately some implications at the macro level. Close to the end of the therapy process, he arrived at the decision of shifting his major to psychology. When I asked what meaning he made out of this decision, he answered with the arrogant attitude of Sherlock Holmes: "Elementary, my dear Watson. It does not take much to go from a private investigator to an investigator of the private!"

CONCLUSION

Cognitive psychotherapies are experiencing dramatic conceptual changes. An increasing constructivist orientation, along with a narrative model of the knowing processes, is apparent in the most recent developments in cognitive theory. These changes demonstrate the need to develop new therapeutic methodologies able to effect deep changes in the knowing processes. This chapter has tried to address these issues by presenting an illustration of a new therapeutic methodology—cognitive narrative psychotherapy. Let me summarize some of the core ideas presented.

First, it was argued that cognitive psychology has found increasing evidence that humans can be seen as storytellers and that their basic cognitive representations are structured in terms of narratives (Polkinghorne, 1988). Second, cognitive therapists should approach clients' representational systems more as narratives and metaphorical processes than as propositional logical algorithms (Gonçalves, in press). Finally, the therapeutic process of recalling, objectifying, subjectifying, metaphorizing, and projecting narratives may contribute to the development of a cognitive therapy that overcomes the mechanist conception of correcting information processing in favor of the core human experience of meaning construction (Bruner, 1986, 1990).

In sum, narrative cognitive therapy is part of a constructivist effort that attempts, by constructing new root metaphors of human knowledge (i.e., narrative), to provide alternative and creative paths for cognitive therapy (cf. Guidano, 1991; Joyce-Moniz, 1989). The viability of these methodologies should be tested in the realm of the therapeutic scenario requiring the creative use of new hermeneutic methodologies currently being developed (cf. Angus & Hardtke, 1992; Angus & Rennie, 1989).

We are still a long way from an acceptable understanding of the effective ingredients of our clinical practices. I believe though, as remarked by Donald Polkinghorne (1988), that there is some promising ground in the exploration of the common ventures of psychotherapy and narrative:

Psychotherapy and narrative have in common the construction of a meaningful human existence. When they come to the therapeutic situation, clients already have life narratives, of which they are both the protagonist and author. The life narrative is open-ended: future actions and occurrences will have to be incorporated into the present plot. (p. 182)

Acknowledgments. The author is indebted to E. Thomas Dowd and two anonymous reviewers for their comments and suggestions on a previous version of this manuscript. Thanks are also due to Dowan Jones, who typed the final draft of the manuscript.

The preparation of this paper was partially funded by the Grant PCHS/C/PSI/267/91 from JNICT (Portuguese Council for Scientific and Technological Research).

All correspondence regarding this paper should be sent to Óscar F. Gonçalves, Departamento de Psicologia, Universidade do Minho, Campus de Gualtar, 4700 Braga, Portugal.

NOTE

1. To avoid possible identification of the client, the following clinical description combines features of various therapeutic processes that have been used in our clinic for the past 2 years.

REFERENCES

Angus, L. E., & Hardtke, K. (1992). *Narrative processes in psychotherapy.* Unpublished manuscript, York University, Toronto.

Angus, L. E., & Rennie, D. L. (1989). Envisioning the representational world: The client's experience of metaphoric expression in psychotherapy. *Psychotherapy, 26,* 372–379.

Bamberg, M. (1991). Narrative activity as perspective taking: The role of emotionals, negations, and voice in the construction of the story realm. *Journal of Cognitive Psychotherapy, 5,* 275–290.

Bruhn, A. R. (1992). The early memory procedures: A projective test fo autobiographical memory: Part 1. *Journal of Personality Assessment, 58,* 1–15.

Bruner, J. (1986). *Actual minds, possible worlds.* Cambridge, MA: Harvard University Press.

Bruner, J. (1990). *Acts of meaning.* Cambridge, MA: Harvard University Press.

Crites, S. (1986). Storytime: Recollecting the past and projecting the future. In T. R. Sarbin (Ed.), *Narrative psychology: The storied nature of human conduct* (pp. 152–173). New York: Praeger.

Gergen, K. J., & Gergen, M. M. (1986). Narrative form and the construction of psychological science. In T. R. Sarbin (Ed.), *Narrative psychology: The storied nature of human conduct* (pp. 22–44). New York: Praeger.

Gergen, K., & Kaye, J. (1992). Beyond the narrative and the negotiation of therapeutic meaning. In S. McNamee & K. J. Gergen (Eds)., *Therapy as social construction.* London: Sage.

Gonçalves, O. F. (Ed.) (1989). *Advances in the cognitive therapies.* Porto, Portugal: APPORT.

Gonçalves, O. F. (1993). *Terapias cognitivas: Teoria e prática* [Cognitive therapies: Theory and practice]. Porto, Portugal: Afrontamento.

Gonçalves, O. F. (in press). Hermeneutics, constructivism and cognitive-behavioral therapies: From the object to the project. In R. A. Neimeyer & M. J. Mahoney (Eds.), *Constructivism in psychotherapy.* Washington, DC: American Psychological Associatic.

Gonçalves, O. F., & Craine, M. (1990). The use of metaphors in cognitive therapy. *Journal of Cognitive Therapy, 4,* 135–150.

Greenberg, L. S., & Safran, J. D. (1987). *Emotion in psychotherapy.* New York: Guilford.

Greenberg, L. S., & Safran, J. D. (1989). Emotions in psychotherapy. *American Psychologist, 44,* 19–29.

Guidano, V. F. (1987). *Complexity of the self: A developmental approach to psychopathology and therapy.* New York: Guilford.

Guidano, V. F. (1991). *The self in process: Toward a post-rationalist cognitive therapy.* New York: Guilford.

Haskell, R. E. (1987). Structural metaphor and cognition. In R. E. Haskell (Ed.), *Cognition and symbolic structures: The psychology of metaphoric transformation* (pp. 241–256). Norwood, NJ: Ablex.

Howard, G. (1991). Cultural tales: A narrative approach to thinking, cross-cultural psychology, and psychotherapy. *American Psychologist, 46,* 187–197.

Joyce-Moniz, L. (1989). Structures, dialectics and regulation of applied constructivism: From developmental psychopathology to individual drama therapy. In O. F. Gonçalves (Ed.), *Advances in the cognitive therapies: The constructive-developmental approach.* Porto, Portugal: APPORT.

Kelly, G. A. (1955). *The psychology of personal constructs* (Vols. 1 & 2). New York: Norton.

Kihlstrom, J. F. (1987). The cognitive unconscious. *Science, 237,* 1445–1452.

Lakoff, G. (1987). *Women, fire and dangerous things: What categories reveal about the mind.* Chicago: University of Chicago Press.

Lakoff, G., & Johnson, M. (1980). *Metaphors we live by.* Chicago: University of Chicago Press.

Leahy, R. L. (1991). Scripts in cognitive therapy: The systemic perspective. *Journal of cognitive Psychotherapy, 5,* 291–304.

van den Broek, P., & Thurlow, R. (1991). The role and structure of personal narratives. *Journal of Cognitive Psychotherapy, 5,* 257–276.

Lehrer, R. (1988). Characters in search of an author: The self as a narrative structure. In J. C. Mancuso & M. L. Shaw (Eds.), *Cognition and personal structure: Computer access and analysis* (pp. 195–228). New York: Praeger.

Lodge, D. (1975). *Changing places.* Middlesex, England: Penguin.

Lodge, D. (1991). *Paradise news.* London: Secker & Warburg.

Mahoney, M. J. (1991). *Human change processes: The scientific foundations of psychotherapy*. New York: Basic Books.

Mair, M. (1989). *Between psychology and psychotherapy: A poetics of experience*. London: Rutledge.

Mandler, J. (1984). *Scripts, stories and scenes: Aspects of schema theory*. Hillsdale, NJ: Erlbaum.

Markus, H., & Nurius, P. (1986). Possible selves. *American Psychologist, 41*, 954–969.

Polkinghorne, D. E. (1988). *Narrative knowing and the human sciences*. Albany: State University of New York Press.

Russell, R. L. (1991). Narrative, cognitive representations, and change: New directions in cognitive theory and therapy. *Journal of Cognitive Psychotherapy, 5,* 241–256.

Russell, R. L., & Van den Broek, P. (1992). Changing narrative schemas in psychotherapy. *Psychotherapy, 29,* 344–354.

Safran, J. D., & Greenberg, L. S. (1988). Feeling, thinking and acting: A cognitive framework for psychotherapy integration. *Journal of Cognitive Psychotherapy, 2,* 109–132.

Safran, J. D., & Segal, Z. V. (1990). *Interpersonal processes in cognitive therapy*. New York: Basic Books.

Schaffer, R. (1981). *Narrative actions in psychoanalysis*. Worcester, WA: Clark University Press.

Siegleman, E. Y. (1990). *Metaphor and meaning in psychotherapy*. New York: Guilford.

Weimer, W. B. (1977). A conceptual framework for cognitive psychology: Motor theories of the mind. In R. Shaw & J. Bransford (Eds.), *Perceiving, acting and knowing* (pp. 276–311). Hillsdale, NJ: Erlbaum.

White, M., & Epston, D. (1990). *Narrative means to therapeutic ends*. New York: W. W. Norton.

Wurf, E., & Markus, H. (1991). Possible selves and the psychology of personal growth. *Perpectives in Personality, 3,* 39–62.

11

An Appraisal of Constructivist Psychotherapies

Robert A. Neimeyer

> Constructivist therapy is not so much a technique as a philosophical context within which therapy is done, and more a product of the *zeitgeist* than the brainchild of any single theorist. These approaches work with a part of the human psyche that is surprisingly neglected in many schools of therapy—the form-giving, meaning-making part, the narrator who at every waking moment of our lives spins out its account of who we are and what we are doing and why we are doing it. (Anderson, 1990, p. 137)

Just as models of psychotherapy have continued to evolve in recent decades, so too have the metatheoretical frameworks that inform and constrain clinical practice and research. One such philosophic framework is *constructivism*, a metatheory that emphasizes the self-organizing and proactive features of human knowing and their implications for human change (Mahoney, 1988a, 1991; R. A. Neimeyer & Harter, 1988). My goal in this chapter is to describe the distinguishing features of various constructivist approaches to psychotherapy, in terms of both their epistemological commitments and their potential contributions to psychological assessment and intervention. Because constructivism also presents unique challenges (and resources) for psychological research, I will move on to discuss some of the prominent themes and models in the growing empirical literature associated with various schools of constructivist therapy. Finally, I will close by considering a few of the problems and prospects associated with the constructivist trend and sketching some of the diverse horizons of application toward which contemporary constructivists are moving.

CONSTRUCTIVISM IN THE POSTMODERN WORLD

All products of human thought are products of their place and time, and theories of psychotherapy are no exception. Typically, preferred clinical frameworks are presented as self-contained packages, with at most an allusion or two to their philosophical assumptions. But it could be more revealing to present them in the context of the broader cultural trends that they express and on which they (often unconsciously) draw. In the case of constructivist models of therapy, this cultural context is distinctively postmodern, reflecting recurrent themes in intellectual, social, and political life that have gained prominence chiefly in the 20th century. As O'Hara and Anderson (1991, p. 20) noted:

> Without quite noticing it, we have moved into a new world, one created by the cumulative effect of pluralism, democracy, religious freedom, consumerism, mobility, and increasing access to news and entertainment. This is the world described as "postmodern" to denote its difference from the modern world most of us were born into. A new social consciousness is emerging in this new world and touching the lives of all kinds of people who are not in the least bit interested in having a new kind of social consciousness. We are all being forced to see that there are many beliefs, multiple realities, an exhilarating but daunting profusion of worldviews to suit every taste. We can choose among these, but we cannot choose not to make choices.

Perhaps the core of postmodern consciousness is the increasingly widespread awareness that the belief systems and apparent "realities" one indwells are socially constituted rather than "given," and hence can be constituted very differently in various cultures (or subcultures), times, and circumstances, although they might appear to carry the force of necessity to those who inhabit them (Berger & Luckmann, 1976). Unfortunately, the "trendiness" of this assertion within the social sciences disguises its radical import for ongoing debates in areas as diverse as legal studies (Levinson, 1989), anthropology (Mead, 1939), literary criticism (Derrida, 1981), and philosophy of science (Woolgar, 1989). Across these seemingly unrelated domains, constructivist critics have begun to undermine people's traditional faith in their quest for the "timeless truths" embodied in social charters, cultural mores, masterworks of literature, educational curricula, and even science itself (Anderson, 1990; R. A. Neimeyer, 1992). Thus, several divergent scholarly disciplines are converging on a distinctively postmodern conclusion: "What we think we know is anchored only in our assumptions, not in the bed rock of truth itself, and that world we seek to understand remains always on the horizons of our thoughts" (Kelly, 1977, p. 6).

TRUTH OR CONSEQUENCES

Nowhere has this postmodern perspective had more profound ramifications than in the field of psychology. From such "basic science" domains as cognitive science (Agnew & Brown, 1989; Ford & Chang, 1989) and neuropsychology (Sacks, 1985) to the study of emotion (Mascolo & Mancuso, 1991) and lifespan development (Carlsen, 1991), a constructivist view of human beings as meaning-making agents has challenged traditional depictions of people in more mechanistic terms (cf. Mahoney, 1991). Of particular relevance in the present context is the challenge posed by a postmodern constructivism for psychotherapy, especially for therapies having a broadly cognitive orientation.

Placed in historical context, traditional cognitive therapies express the ambitions of a modern, early-20th-century philosophy of science founded on the principles of logical empiricism (cf. Radnitzky, 1973). Like the idealized image of the scientist espoused by Vienna Circle philosophers, the well-adjusted human being envisioned by theorists such as Beck (Beck, Rush, Shaw, & Emer (1979) and Ellis (1973) is viewed as a paragon of rationality, avoiding illogical inferences and objectively testing hypotheses against publicly observable outcomes. However, whether as a result of environmental conditioning (Jaremko, 1987) or a biological tendency to think crookedly and childishly (Ellis, 1973), human beings in this view frequently deviate from the principles of rationality and scientific method to form conclusions about themselves, others, and the future that are absolutistic, overgeneralized, and illogical (cf. Beck et al., 1979; Burns, 1980). It follows that psychological adjustment requires active disputation and "reality testing" of negative and irrational self-statements, so that the individual becomes able to process information in a more accurate and mature fashion (Beck et al., 1979; Merluzzi, Rudy, & Glass, 1981). In this respect, cognitive therapists are the inheritors of a long tradition of realism in the mental health field, in which "the perception of reality is called mentally healthy when what the individual sees corresponds to what is actually there" (Jahoda, 1958. p. 6). This implies a correspondence theory of truth, which holds that the validity of one's belief systems is determined by their degree of "match" with the real world, or at least with the "facts" as provided by one's senses.

Unfortunately, the postmodern era has been hard on this quaintly objectivist philosophy of science and its clinical derivatives. Late-20th-century philosophers of science have redefined the concept of rationality to give greater priority to the preservation of central theoretical concepts than to their immediate rejection when they fail to square with the facts (Lakatos, 1974; Laudan, 1977). More radical philosophers (e.g., Feyerabend, 1975) and sociologists (e.g., Woolgar, 1989) have even questioned the fundamental ideals of objectivity and scientific method that are central to the cognitivist's image of "the person as scientist." Perhaps more important, the very pluralism of beliefs in the postmodern world challenges the credibility of any psychological system that equates adjustment with accuracy of reality contact. As Anderson (1990, p. 46) noted, "It is very hard, in a world with many realities, to maintain the position that satisfactory adjustment to one reality is equivalent to mental health, and that unsatisfactory adjustment is a form of illness."

In addition to such cultural and intellectual trends, psychological science has begun to produce growing evidence that systematically inaccurate and self-serving "illusions" are both widespread and functional (see Taylor & Brown, 1988, for a review). Even apparently irrational beliefs could be functional in many circumstances. For example, Rich and Dahlheimer (1989) manipulated success and failure feedback on a word-construction task given to two sets of subjects, one high and one low in endorsement of irrational beliefs. As predicted on the basis of the self-handicapping literature, high-irrational subjects receiving failure feedback dramatically decreased their performance expectations across trials, but actually increased their output. In comparison, failure feedback had a much more deleterious effect on the output of low-irrational subjects. Such a pattern of findings would be difficult to accommodate within a traditional cognitive therapy framework. In a broader view, research within the cognitive–behavioral tradition now suggests that negative thinking might not be negative in its consequences, and that a precise balance of negative to positive thinking could facilitate coping and attention to potentially threatening information (Schwartz, 1992; Schwartz & Michelson, 1987). In summary, mounting evidence has begun to call into question the objectivist equation of mental health with the accuracy, rationality, or positivity of one's cognitions. This, in turn, has challenged the assumptive base of traditional cognitive therapies, prompting the further evolution of these approaches as outlined in Mahoney's opening chapter in this volume.

As an outgrowth of these philosophical, cultural, and scientific developments, new forms of psychotherapy have begun to evolve in the postmodern era. These constructivist therapies are united in their rejection of a correspondence theory of truth and its corollary assumption that any beliefs that fail to correspond to objective reality are, by definition, dysfunctional. Instead, they hold that the viability of any given construction is a function of its consequences for the individual or group that provisionally adopts it (cf. von Glasersfeld, 1984), as well as its overall coherence with the larger system of personally or socially held beliefs into which it is incorporated (R. A. Neimeyer & Harter, 1988).

At the core of constructivist theory is a view of human beings as active agents who, individually and collectively, co-constitute the meaning of their experiential world. Although the origins of constructivism as a systematic metatheory can be traced to the writings of the philosophers Vico, Kant, and Vaihinger (Mahoney, 1988a), its emergence as a fully developed "participatory epistemology" had to await the decline of logical empiricism, classical rationalism, and linear determinism in 20th century philosophies of science (Mahoney, 1989). From this perspective, human knowledge is ultimately (inter)personal (cf. Polanyi, 1958) and evolutionary (Campbell, Heyes, & Callebaut, 1987), with no simple prospect of validation against an objective reality beyond people's constructions. Corresponding with this epistemological position is a psychological one, which emphasizes that human cognition is proactive (Mahoney, 1988a) or anticipatory (Kelly, 1955; R. A. Neimeyer, 1987) rather than merely passive or determined. Moreover, the constructivist position stresses the structure of psychological space, which is viewed as morphogenic and nuclear, with superordinate or core processes constraining or modulating the development of more peripheral ones (Kelly, 1955; Mahoney, 1991). To a greater extent than traditional cognitive therapies, constructivist approaches to clinical practice also situate the self firmly in social context. As Guidano (1991, p. 10) noted, in the case of humans as well as higher primates, "a highly complex social world has been superimposed on the mere physical environment, bringing about an intersubjective reality in which knowing oneself and the world is always in relation to others." Finally, constructivists assert that human systems are characterized by self-organizing development, evolving in such a way as to protect their internal coherence and integrity (Maturana & Varela, 1987). A summary of the contrasts between constructivist and objectivist epistemologies is presented in Table 11.1 More extended treatments of these metatheoretical issues have been provided by Mahoney (1991) and R. A. Neimeyer and Feixas (1990).

The differences between constructivist and objectivist epistemologies imply equally fundamental practical differences between traditions of psychological assessment and therapy that subscribe to these two philosophical positions. For orthodox cognitive therapists, the target of

TABLE 11.1. Philosophical Constrasts between Objectivist and Constructivist Epistemologies

Objectivism	Constructism
Nature of knowledge	
Knowledge as a direct representation or copy of the real world	Knowledge as construction of the subject's experience and action
Knowledge as discovery of the existing facts	Knowledge as invention of new interpretive frameworks
Knowledge is shaped by successive approximations to an absolute truth, progress through accumulation of facts	Knowledge as evolutionary (i.e., shaped by the invalidation resulting from selection processes and adaptation); evolution through more comprehensive
Criteria for validation of knowledge	
Validation of knowledge provided by the real world through the senses	Validation of knowledge through internal consistency with existing knowledge structures and social consensus among observers
Identical matching or correspondence of representation with reality	Fitting and viability (i.e., accuracy of predictions according to that interpretive framework)
Only one true meaning (i.e., the truth)	Diversity of possible meanings and alternative interpretations
Structural traits of knowledge	
Knowledge as concept formation (i.e., abstraction of the qualities inherent to the real objects in the world)	Knowledge as grasping of differences
Knowledge consists of classification, categorization, and cumulative storing	Knowledge is structured in hierarchical, self-organized systems
Human beings	
Reactive organism	Proactive, goal-directed, and purposive organism
Human interaction	
Instructive (i.e., the transmission of information from one organism to another)	Structural coupling (i.e., the fitting together of structures and the coordinations of behaviors of various self-organized systems)

Notes. Adapted from "Constructivist Constributions to Psychotherapy Integration" R. A. Neimeyer and G. Feixas, 1990, *Journal of Integrative and Eclectic Psychotherapy, 9,* p. 7. Copyright 1990 by International Academy of Eclectic Psychotherapists. Adapted by permission.

measurement and intervention is a series of relatively isolated self-statements, in the form of automatic thoughts (Beck et al., 1979) or irrational beliefs (Dryden & Ellis, 1987) experienced under stressful circumstances. Therapy is characteristically present-oriented and problem-focused, with the goal being the "correction" of faulty, unrealistic cognitions that generate emotional distress. Therapy is therefore highly directive (Beck et al., 1979) or psychoeducational (Lewinsohn, Steinmetz, Antonuccio, & Teri, 1984), and typically focused on the individual client, whether in a one-on-one or group therapy context. Because the goal of cognitive therapy is usually modification of the client's current beliefs rather than the creation of a radically different worldview, such therapies have been described as fostering "first order change" in beliefs, a legitimate aim in some therapy contexts (Lyddon, 1990a). As such, these therapies are quintessentially modern in Anderson's (1990) sense, promoting the systematic revision of one's beliefs to make them more realistic and data-driven.

In contrast, constructivist psychotherapists tend to assess and facilitate changes in broader systems of personal constructs (Kelly, 1955; G. J. Neimeyer & R. A. Neimeyer, 1981) or personal narratives (Howard, 1990; White & Epston, 1990), rather than the more circumscribed thought units disputed by traditional cognitive therapists. Because these belief systems and personal accounts are seen as having substantial continuity over time, therapy is more likely to examine the developmental dimensions of the client's psychopathology (Keating & Rosen, 1991; Mahoney, 1988b), paying particular attention to the primary attachment relationships that shaped the client's most fundamental assumptions about self and world (Guidano & Liotti, 1993; Lorenzini & Sassaroli, 1987). The goal of constructivist therapies is ultimately more creative than corrective, insofar as they attempt to foster the broader development of the client's constructions rather than eliminate or revise cognitive distortions (R. A. Neimeyer & Harter, 1988). Accordingly, therapy is likely to be more exploratory than directive and tends to target the family and systemic processes that validate an individual client's constructions (Feixas, 1992). Because these therapies attempt to foster profound changes in the client's core ordering processes, they have been described as seeking "second-order change" in belief systems, a goal that might be especially relevant to the treatment of more severe forms of disruption of self-knowledge (Lyddon, 1990a), such as psychotic or borderline conditions (cf. Leitner, 1987, 1988). As such, constructivist approaches are quintessentially postmodern, promoting the collaboration of the client's narrative without the convenience of simple criteria for determining what constitutes an acceptable story.

Traditional cognitive and constructivist therapies also differ in the clinical heuristics that guide a therapist's interventions. For the orthodox cognitive therapist, the meanings of the client's verbalizations are typically treated as unproblematic and literal, permitting fairly efficient logical analysis, empirical assessment of their validity, and the generation of rational responses (Weishaar & Beck, 1987). Emotions are understood in equally straightforward fashion, as the result of one's cognitive appraisal of situations. Negative emotions predicated on distorted appraisals therefore become problems to be controlled or eliminated in treatment (Burns, 1980). Finally, client resistance to the therapist's technical efforts, when encountered, is typically viewed as a lack of motivation or as a pernicious form of recalcitrance that requires "vigorous attack and disputation" (Ellis, 1973, p. 309).

Not surprisingly, constructivist therapists tend to diverge from their cognitive colleagues in most of these technical and stylistic respects. Influenced by a hermeneutic, phenomenologic perspective, constructivists characteristically inquire closely into the personal meanings that form the subtext of the client's explicit statements (Kelly, 1955), making extensive use of metaphor (Siegelman, 1990) and idiosyncratic imagery (Mair, 1989a). Emotion is construed as informative, suggesting the adequacy of clients' current attempts to construct meaning out of their experiences (McCoy, 1981). It follows that therapist interventions are more likely to be reflective, elaborative, and intensely personal, rather than persuasive, analytical, and technically instructive (R. A. Neimeyer, 1985a). Resistance, in this context, takes on a different meaning, emerging as an understandable form of self-protection at points when therapy threatens a client's core ordering processes (Mahoney, 1991; R. A. Neimeyer, 1987). Table 11.2 summarizes these practical points of departure between traditional cognitive and constructivist psychotherapies; fuller treatments of these issues can be found in G. J. Neimeyer (1992a), R. A. Neimeyer (1985a, 1987), and Mahoney (1988b, 1991).

VARIETIES OF CONSTRUCTIVIST EXPERIENCE

Although the foregoing discussion has tended to highlight common philosophical and applied features of constructivist approaches that distinguish them from traditional cognitive therapies, it would be misleading to present them as a single coherent school of psychotherapy. Instead, constructivist psychotherapy is better viewed as a "fuzzy set" with indistinct boundaries, whose members manifest considerable diversity and even occasional contradiction (cf. the "Concluding

Table 11.2. Practical Contrasts between Traditional Cognitive and Constructivist Approaches to Psychotherapy

Feature	Traditional cognitive therapies	Constructivist therapies
Diagnostic emphasis	Disorder-specific	Comprehensive, general
Target of intervention and assessment	Isolated automatic thoughts or irrational beliefts	Construct systems personal narratives
Temporal focus	Present	Present, but more developmental emphasis
Goal of treatment	Corrective; eliminate dysfunction	Creative; facilitate development
Style of therapy	Highly directive and psychoeducational	Less structured and more exploratory
Context of therapy	Individualistic	Individualistic to systemic
Therapist role	Persuasive, analytical, technically instructive	Reflective, elaborative, intensely personal
Tests for adequacv of client beliefs	Logic, objective validity	Internal consistency, consensus, personal viability
Interpretation of client's meanings	Literal, universal	Metaphoric, idiosyncratic
Interpretation of emotions	Negative emotion results from distorted thinking, represents problem to be controlled	Negative emotion as informative signal of challenge to existing constructions, to be respected
Understanding of client "resistance"	Lack of motivation, dysfunctional pattern	Attempt to protect core ordering processes

Thoughts" section of this article). To provide a more balanced portrayal of this family of approaches, I will selectively highlight a few of the interacting "lineages" that constitute the genealogy of this clinical tradition and suggest some of the distinctive contributions that each makes to this emerging perspective.

Personal Construct Theory

The first systematic attempt to articulate a constructivist theory of clinical practice was made by George Kelly, an experimental psychologist-turned-clinician originally working at a rural college in Kansas during the Great Depression (R. A. Neimeyer, 1985c). Encountering immense human need (particularly in the school systems) with minimal institutional resources, he quickly confronted the limitations of a psychodynamic model of practice predicated on the gradual development of client insight through judicious therapist interpretation (Kelly, 1969). In the absence of sufficiently well-developed alternative models of therapy, he set out to devise his own, integrating features of Korzybski's (1933) general semantics, with its emphasis on the reality-defining role of language, with procedures inspired by Moreno's (1937) psychodrama (Stewart & Barry, 1991). As a result, he began experimenting with role therapies in the late 1930s, which attempted to develop with clients plausible alternative identities, complete with implications for their personality, pastimes, and social interactions. Clients would then secretly enact these hypothetical characters in their daily lives for a limited period of time, during which they would rehearse the character and discuss the results of their ongoing experiments with the therapist. At the end of the enactment period, the client would be encouraged to "derole," but to consider what he or she had learned from this brief but novel immersion in a clearly hypothetical but possible world (Kelly 1973). The results of such brief therapies were often impressive, and they led Kelly and his students to refine related techniques throughout the 1940s and early 1950s.

In spite of the successes of these technical innovations—indeed, because of them—Kelly became increasingly dissatisfied with a purely pragmatic approach to fostering psychotherapeutic change. As he later recounted in the foreword to his magnum opus:

> It was no good, this business of trying to tell the reader merely how to deal with clinical problems: the *why* kept insistently rearing its puzzling head. So we started to write about the *whys*. . . . Yet no sooner had we started than something strange began to happen; or rather, we discovered that something unexpected had already happened. It turned out to be this; in the years of relatively isolated clinical practice we had wandered far off the beaten paths of psychology, much farther than we had ever suspected.
>
> And how far afield were we? Or, what was more important, could our readers ever find us? Obviously, we had been making many basic assumptions implicitly—taking for granted our somewhat unusual convictions. Unless we were now able to become explicit about such matters could we ever hope to say sensible things to anybody about the whys of clinical practice? It seemed not.
>
> We backed off and started writing again, this time at the level of system building. It was a half-and-half job; half invention of coherent assumptions which would sustain a broad field of inquiry, and half articulation of convictions we had already taken for granted. (Kelly, 1955, pp. ix–x)

The result of Kelly's system-building efforts was *The Psychology of Personal Constructs* (1955), an unusually comprehensive theory of personality and clinical practice. Working as a contemporary of Piaget (1937/1971) and Bartlett (1932), Kelly shared their concern with the human "effort after meaning," which progressed through the individual's construction of recurrent themes encountered in the flux of living. But unlike these other theorists, Kelly focused primarily on methods for conceptualizing, eliciting, and modifying the content and structure of the idiographic construct systems devised by his clients, paying relatively less attention to the developmental or experimental implications of his personality theory. As he had hoped, the resulting theory has sustained a broad field of inquiry, generating a largely empirical literature of nearly 2,000 publications, in areas as diverse as education (Novak, 1990), career development (G. J. Neimeyer, 1992b), artificial intelligence (Agnew & Brown, 1989: Bringmann, 1992), communication (Applegate, 1990), thanatology (R. A. Neimeyer & Epting, 1992), psychopathology (Button, 1985; Gara, Rosenberg, & Mueller, 1989), and industrial organizational psychology (Jankowicz, 1990).

In the present context, the most distinctive conceptual contributions of personal construct theory include its original metaphor of the person as scientist and its sophisticated and testable model of the process of construing, the structure of personal knowledge, and the social embeddedness of people's construing efforts (R. A. Neimeyer, 1987). The aspect of construct theory that is perhaps best known is its emphasis on the bipolar or dichotomous nature of construing, which suggests that every assertion is simultaneously an implied negation (e.g., to describe myself as laid back is also to imply that I am definitely not anxious, emotional, or socially forceful, whatever represents for me an informative contrast). This hypothesis, that people's constructions ultimately frame distinctions that operate as binary tools for subjectively categorizing experience, making choices, and channeling behavior, has received support in a number of studies using procedures developed within cognitive science (Millis & Neimeyer, 1990; Rychlak, 1992; Slife, Stoneman, & Rychlak, 1991).

Construct theorists have also devised the most frequently used constructivist method for eliciting a subject's or client's belief system, the role construct repertory grid (or repgrid); (Bell, 1990; Landfield & Epting, 1987). In recent years, the administration and scoring of grids has benefited greatly from innovations in computer hardware and software (Sewell, Adams-Webber, Mitterer, & Cromwell, 1992), as well as novel attempts to explicate the structure of personal construct systems in terms amenable to symbolic and mathematical operationalization (Chiari, Mancini, Nicolo, & Nuzzo, 1990; Ford & Adams-Webber, 1991). But perhaps most important, construct theory has contributed an approach to psychotherapy that is coherent with an overarching theory of personality and social relationships. As a consequence, it has generated clinical applications that are surprisingly varied, in such areas as marital therapy (Kremsdorf, 1985; G. J. Neimeyer, 1985), family therapy (Feixas, 1990; Procter, 1987), group therapy (Llewelyn & Dunnett, 1987; R. A. Neimeyer, 1988), and psychotherapy for the severely disturbed or borderline client (Leitner, 1988: Soldz, 1987). Thus, Kelly's original theory and its contemporary adherents continue to contribute to the present and future of constructivist psychotherapy.

Structural–Developmental Cognitive Therapy

Like personal construct theorists, psychotherapists working within the structural–developmental tradition are primarily concerned with the relationship between different aspects and levels of cognition within the client's system, some of which are more central and others of which are more peripheral (Guidano & Liotti, 1983; Liotti, 1987; Mahoney, 1991). However, these theorists place relatively greater emphasis on the unique developmental trajectory that shapes each individual's personal knowledge of self and world. For example, Guidano and Liotti (1983) extended Lakatos's (1974) model of scientific research programs to describe the "metaphysical hard core" of assumptions about themselves that people elaborate as a result of childhood experience and that is, in some measure, protected from refutation by subsequent events. This tacit attitude toward oneself operates as the main control structure of one's entire knowledge organization, generating the "rules" that govern the assimilation of further experience and the procedures by which one attempts to solve problems in daily life. In this way, people's core ordering processes define the emotional valence they attribute to events, provide them with a stable psychological reality, govern their sense of self-identity, and influence the sense of control or power they have to direct their lives (Mahoney, 1991).

Among the distinctive contributions of the structural–developmental approach to constructivist therapy is its study of the relation between problematic patterns of childhood attachment and restrictive "self-theories" later in life (Liotti, 1987). For example, the agoraphobic is hypothesized to have experienced a pattern of anxious attachment (Bowlby, 1973) to a caregiver who was overprotective or overcontrolling but was, nonetheless, largely unavailable to meet the child's requests for companionship or help. As a result, the "hard core" of the patient's knowledge is likely to include the tacit assumption that companionship and protection can only be paid for by a sharp reduction in autonomous exploration of the environment and lead to the development of an overcontrolling attitude toward the self and intimate others (Guidano & Liotti, 1983). Similar models have been developed to assist in conceptualizing a range of phobic and anxiety states and other disorders (Lorenzini & Sassaroli, 1987; Mancini & Semerari, 1990).

Although the structural–developmental approach makes a sophisticated theoretical contribution to the constructivist literature, especially in the area of selfhood processes (Guidano, 1991), it also carries strong practical implications for psychotherapy. To a greater extent than most schools of cognitive therapy, it legitimizes developmental exploration of a client's attachment relationships, and in this respect converges with psychodynamic therapies (Mahoney, 1988b). Similarly, it heightens awareness of the working relationship between client and therapist, insofar as this can suggest the sorts of disrupted attachment patterns that undergird a patient's disturbance (Liotti, 1991). Finally, it has begun to generate some novel therapeutic techniques (e.g., life review and mirror time) that help clients confront and integrate aspects of their identities that they experience as painful or conflictual (Mahoney, 1991). Along with personal construct theory, structural approaches are beginning to have an impact on other cognitive models of assessment and therapy, suggesting the relevance of both horizontal and vertical exploration of clients' problematic interpersonal schemata (Safran, Vallis, Segal, & Shaw, 1986).

Narrative Reconstruction

Although Kelly (1955) provided a prototypic model of psychotherapy as narrative reconstruction in his work with clients' self-characterizations (cf. Fransella, 1981; R. A. Neimeyer, 1992), fuller development of this perspective is a relatively recent phenomenon, one with expressions in several areas of psychology. For example, within social psychology, Harvey and his colleagues (1989) have studied the function of interpersonal account making in restoring a sense of meaning and self-esteem for individuals whose lives have been disrupted by relationship loss or the death of significant others. From a more cognitive psychological vantage point, script theory (Abelson, 1989; Carlson & Carlson, 1984) offers a conceptual framework for understanding how prototypical affect-laden nuclear scenes are organized and sequenced to preserve an aura of consistency and predictability in ongoing experience. Finally, Bruner (1990) argued for a program of "cultural psychology," the ultimate goal of which is to interpret (rather than explain) the linguistic and discursive means by which people construct lives and "selves" that take meaning from their unique social and historical circumstances.

The common assumption of these "literary" approaches to psychological phenomena is that the structure of human lives is inherently narrative in form; people constitute and are constituted by the stories that they live and the stories that they tell. As Mair (1988, p. 127) argued:

> I want to claim much more than the comfortable platitude that stories are a good thing and should be attended to.
>
> Stories are habitations. We live in and through stories. They conjure worlds. We do not know the world other than as story world. Stories inform life. They hold us together and keep us apart .
>
> We inhabit the great stories of our culture. We live through stories. We are lived by the stories of our race and place. It is this enveloping and constituting function of stories that is especially important to sense more fully.

To analogize lives to stories or texts that are coauthored by their protagonists and the culture in which they live does not imply that such narratives always have the quality of good literature: coherence, clarity, poignancy, and impact. Indeed, people can be construed as seeking therapy at points when their life stories become ineffective, necessitating editing, elaboration, or major "rebiographing" (Howard, 1990). Often, psychotherapeutic reconstruction becomes necessary when people become identified with their problems and subjected to a "dominant narrative" that disqualifies, limits, denies, or constrains their personhood (White & Epston, 1990). Developing the clinical implications of Foucault's (1970) writings on knowledge and power, White and Epston (1990) attempted to help clients "perform alternative stories" that liberate them from the "unitary knowledges" that tend to dominate their lives. The first crucial step in this process is the externalization of the problem, in which the therapeutic team works with the individual or family to define and even anthropomorphize the dysfunctional symptom or pattern as something external to the person of the identified patient. For example, an enuretic child might be implicitly and even explicitly encouraged to view "Sneaky Wee" as a trickster who fools the child into going to bed before pottying, only to "run out on the child" in the middle of the night. This enables exploration of effects of the problem on the patient (and family), as well as a consideration of the requirements for the problem's survival. Through this metaphoric distancing from the problem, the patient, family, and treatment team are able to join forces and find ways to "put Sneaky Wee in his place."

Among the novel contributions of the narrative approach to therapy are an objectification of the problem by viewing it as a self-defeating script, text, or metaphoric opponent that can be challenged by the client. White and Epston (1990), in particular, made explicit use of narrative means to therapeutic ends, by sharing with patients progress notes in the form of inquiries about how they were able to begin to refuse to conform to the requirements of the problem. Similarly, they made creative use of other forms of written documentation, such as "declarations of independence" from the problem or "certificates of special knowledge" gained as a result of clients' grappling with and surmounting their difficulties. In this sense, written "texts" serve as more than a (powerful) metaphor for the client's life, becoming active therapeutic procedures used by the therapist.

Several other practical contributions have derived from a view of psychotherapy as narrative reconstruction. These include the creative use of personal journal work to broaden and deepen a client's self-exploration and self-expression (Mahoney, 1991; Rainer, 1978) and strategies for the transformation of conflictual personal mythologies, Campbellian "inner myths" that guide people's actions and choices (Feinstein & Krippner, 1988). As is characteristic of constructivist therapists in general, practitioners working within this narrative tradition are typically highly reflexive. They view the explication and reconstruction of their own therapeutic stories over the course of treatment in the same terms as the narrative revisions made by their clients (Viney, 1990).

Constructivist Family Therapy

Of the various areas in which constructivist epistemology has been promulgated in recent years, the field of family therapy has been most thoroughly revolutionized (Efran, Lukens, & Lukens, 1990; R. A. Neimeyer & Feixas, 1990). Hoffman (1985), the leading chronicler of this trend, has described the pendulum swing of early family therapy away from an excessive focus on intrapsychic processes that characterized most individual therapies through the 1960s. Now, however, she maintains that the pendulum is swinging the other way, as "ideas, beliefs, attitudes, feelings, premises, values, and myths have been declared central again" (Hoffman, 1985, p. 390). Furthermore, Hoffman considers "a shift from behaviors to ideas" to be one of the commonalities of a "general style of systemic therapy . . . influenced by a constructivist approach," which assumes that "problems do exist, but only in the realm of meanings'' (1988, p. 124). Thus, whereas earlier systemic therapists focused on pathological behavior sequences that would explain the function of a symptom, constructivist family therapists have shifted their attention to the processes by which families negotiate a common reality.

Inspired by the work of von Glasersfeld (1984), von Foerster (1981), and Maturana and Varela (1987), systemic therapists have begun to conceptualize family systems as informationally closed to direct interventions by the therapist, just as they cannot be directly shaped by external realities. From this perspective, family construct systems (Feixas, 1990; Procter, 1987), family paradigms (Reiss, 1981), or family premises (Penn, 1985) are essentially language–determined, and the role of the therapist is to explicate and subtly challenge those "contractual agreements, maintained in language," that solidify the family members' (sometimes dysfunctional) relationship with one another (Efran et al., 1990).

One of the distinctive techniques used in this conversational construction of meaning in family therapy (Loos & Epstein, 1989) is circular questioning. Since its introduction by Selvini–Palazzoli, Boscolo, Cecchin, and Prata (1980), this method has undergone many further elaborations (e.g., Tomm, 1987). Circular questions are those that reveal relationships among family members and differences among relationships. They often involve triadic questions in which a family member is invited to describe how two members present in the therapy room relate or how they react to some family event. This "gossiping in the presence of others," however, is not the only type of circular questioning. In fact, this form of clinical interview can involve any procedure that elicits the meanings of family members, their interdependence, and their relationship with behavior. The potential of this technique to provoke change has led some authors (e.g., Tomm, 1987) to consider it a powerful therapeutic tool that obviates further intervention.

A number of other novel interventions have been contributed by constructivist family therapists. One example is the prescription of therapeutic rituals to prompt reconstruing of a family problem. As used by the later Milan associates (Boscolo, Cecchin, Hoffman, & Penn, 1987), a symbolic ritual prescription might be employed when two differing interpretations of a symptomatic behavior prevail within the family (e.g., when family members are divided over whether the mother's depression is biological or psychological in origin). Instead of taking a definite position for one of them, the therapists might suggest that the family act according to Interpretation A on Mondays, Wednesdays, and Fridays and according to Interpretation B on Tuesdays, Thursdays, and Saturdays. Sundays might be left free for each family member to construe the problem as he or she pleases. The procedure conveys the idea that more than one interpretation of a difficulty could be viable, and that each carries distinctive implications for behavior. As with the fixed role therapy used by personal construct theorists (Epting & Nazario, 1987; Kelly, 1973; R. A. Neimeyer, 1992), this can prompt the family to accept the epistemological responsibility for the existence of multiple meanings and become more open to loosening its system of construing and behavior.

CONSTRUCTIVISM IN PSYCHOTHERAPY RESEARCH

Having described some of the major schools or approaches to contemporary constructivism and suggested a few of their distinctive contributions to clinical practice, I will attempt to outline some of their representative applications to psychotherapy research. This effort will be limited, however, by both the recent emergence of constructivism as a clinical and empirical paradigm and the unique methodological requirements placed on constructivist researchers by their epistemological commitments.

Perhaps because of its longer history, its greater academic institutionalization, and its development of quantitative techniques, personal construct theory has provided much of the conceptual and methodological impetus for constructivist research in clinical psychology (R. A. Neimeyer, 1985c). Beginning with the pioneering work of Bannister (1960, 1963), experimental psychopathologists with a constructivist orientation have used the repertory grid technique to study distinctive structural features of the construct systems of such patient populations as schizophrenics (Gara et al., 1989; Pierce, Sewell, & Cromwell, 1992; van den Bergh, de Boeck, & Claeys, 1985), anorexics (Button, 1992; Fransella & Crisp, 1970), depressives (R. A. Neimeyer, 1984, 1985b; Space, Dingemans, & Cromwell, 1983), and neurotics in general (Winter, 1985). As a logical extension, investigators have used several of these same structural measures to assess changes in target groups over the course of treatment (e.g., Bannister, Adams-Webber, Penn, & Radley, 1975; Fransella, 1972; Landfield, 1971; Lorenzini & Sassaroli, 1987; R. A. Neimeyer, Heath, & Strauss, 1985; Ryle, 1980).

But in spite of the relatively extensive clinical literature deriving from personal construct theory, the usual comparative outcome study that characterizes much of psychotherapy research is conspicuous by its rarity. For example, empirical "horse races" between constructivist therapies and their rationalist alternatives (e.g., Karst & Trexler, 1970) have seldom been conducted. Instead, constructivists who perform psychotherapy research are more likely to study specific change processes that occur across a range of therapies at an individual rather than normative level. Studies by Caine, Wijesinghe, and Winter (1981), Ryle

(1980), and Koch (1983) illustrate this orientation, demonstrating superior confirmation of idiographic (patient-specific) hypotheses regarding changes in construing over treatment, as compared with the usual nomothetic (group-oriented) predictions.

The focus of construct theorists on individuality also has led to the study of client factors that predict favorable response to treatment, both within and across different formats of therapy. Exemplifying the first of these emphases, R. A. Neimeyer, Harter, and Alexander (1991) used repertory grids to study the relationship between perceptions of group process and outcome for several groups of women receiving group therapy for childhood sexual abuse. They found that clients who viewed other group members as similar to their ideal selves, and who were able to identify with their therapists, responded more favorably to treatment. However, the specific sets of predictor variables shifted across sessions, suggesting that a sense of cohesion with other group members faded in importance relative to the working alliance with the therapists over the course of treatment.

The second emphasis, on differential predictors of outcome in alternative treatments, is represented by the work of Winter (1990). Administering pretreatment repertory grids to clients assigned to either interpersonal group therapy or individual behavior therapy, he discovered that contrasting grid responses characterized improvers in the two conditions. Clients who responded to behavior therapy displayed more tightly organized, logically consistent construct systems, in which constructs pertaining to symptoms carried more implications; the reverse was true for responders to group therapy. Moreover, improvers in group therapy viewed their problems in less medical terms, construing themselves as less "ill" and their therapist as less like their general practitioner. Studies of this kind converge with the research of Beutler and his colleagues (Beutler, Mohr, Grawe, Engle, & MacDonald, 1991), who have begun to identify individual difference variables that permit systematic treatment selection tailored to the needs of specific patients.

In spite of the historical head start enjoyed by personal construct theorists, researchers from other schools of constructivist psychotherapy are also beginning to contribute to the empirical literature on psychotherapy process and outcome. One promising example is the emerging research on developmental therapy conducted by Ivey and his colleagues. Their approach, based on Piagetian constructivism, assumes that (a) it is possible to identify cognitive–developmental levels in the processes clients use to construct their knowledge of self and world, (b) counseling strategies can be matched to a client's or family's developmental level, and (c) therapy can facilitate movement within and between the several levels of development (Ivey & Gonçalves, 1988). Specifically, these authors hypothesize that adults repeat analogues of Piagetian stages—ranging from sensorimotor, through concrete operational and formal operational, to dialectical stages—in their experience and report of problems throughout life. Thus, in response to the "same" clinical syndrome (e.g., depression), the predominantly sensorimotor client might focus primarily on somatic symptoms, the concrete client might report problematic family interactions in great detail, and the formal or dialectical client might identify personal or larger systemic patterns that contribute to his or her distress. Using a standard interview procedure (Ivey, 1991), Rigazio-DiGilio and Ivey (1990) have begun to provide evidence for key tenets of this developmental therapy framework. In particular, they were able to demonstrate that session transcripts could be coded for depressed clients' developmental levels with impressive reliability, and that appropriate counselor inquiries could be used to prompt clients' processing of their problem in terms of these four distinctive epistemic styles. Extensions of this work to broader individual and family therapy contexts are now under way (e.g., Rigazio-DiGilio & Ivey, 1991).

A second example of innovative research compatible with a broader constructivist perspective derives from the work of Greenberg and his colleagues on the task analysis of change events in psychotherapy (e.g., Greenberg & Safran, 1987; Rice & Greenberg, 1984). Such research typically proceeds from a theoretical or intuitive model of a significant therapy process (e.g., resolution of a problematic reaction or taking responsibility for an emotion), which is then used to guide the study of numerous such therapeutic events, both within and across clients. The result of this progressive iteration of model building and validation against relevant transcript material is a revised and elaborated model that encompasses the sequence of client and therapist subprocesses that must occur for the task to be achieved.

This paradigm is nicely illustrated by the work of Clarke (1991), who investigated the "creation of meaning" of an experienced emotion in psychotherapy. She first posited a theoretical model of this change event, which is initiated when a client reports an experience that is highly discrepant with a cherished belief or expectation. She hypothesized that the commencement of meaning creation is marked by emotional arousal triggered by the perceived discrepancy, which then requires careful client and therapist attention, attempted "meaning symbolization" (which moves toward greater adequacy), eventual accommodation of the challenged belief, and, finally, emotional relief. This model was then used to identify a large set of relevant occurrences of this event in therapy transcripts, which then were systematically compared with the model, leading to its repeated revision. The resulting validated model proved more comprehensive, including distinct specification, exploration, and revision phases, each of which entailed specific cognitive and affective processing. In addition, model revision led to new discoveries about the requisites of meaning creation, such as the importance of entertaining some hypothesis as to the origin of the cherished belief during the exploration phase, a factor that had been neglected in the initial theoretical model. Qualitative, process-oriented research of this kind is likely to prove attractive to constructivist psychotherapy researchers.

Although constructivist contributions to the study of psychotherapy are growing in number and diversity, this emerging literature does not match the quantity or focus of studies that have been conducted from traditional cognitive perspectives. This pattern stems from more than the recency of constructivist psychotherapies; it also reflects the general ambivalence of many constructivist theorists toward the data collection methods and analytic procedures that characterize most social science research. At the analytic level, constructivist researchers are uncomfortable with the assumption of linear relationships among variables that are presumed by the most commonly used statistical procedures (Steenbarger, 1991). However, constructivist reservations about extant research methods at this statistical level are, at least in principle, surmountable, as more complex means of analyzing the multidirectional and cyclical influences that typify psychotherapy gain wider currency. For example, procedures such as stochastic modeling and time-series analyses are gaining greater recognition and might be more useful for detecting the nonlinear processes implied in constructivist ontologies (Steenbarger, 1991).

As daunting as the development of these new methodological competencies might be, a still more crucial question is the appropriateness of the paradigms for data collection currently in use. Viney (1988), for one, has described the experimenter orientation model that dominates psychological research, which allows the experimenter to function as a reflective knower but implicitly denies this capacity to the data contributor. As she has noted, the asymmetry of this relationship is at some odds with the constructivist view of people as proactive, hypothesis testing, "incipient scientists." In contrast, Viney proposes a mutual orientation model, in which both the data collector and data contributor give something to, and gain something from, the experimental process. To fully satisfy the requirements of this model, a study would have to include five stages, beginning with an experimenter "request," followed by the response of the data contributor, a reflection by the experimenter on the data contributed, the revelation of the results of this reflection to the contributor, and, finally, confirmation or disconfirmation of the experimenter's reflection on the basis of the feedback received. Viney (1988, p. 195) pointed out that "the assumption of total, accurate recall does not have to be made before [data contributors] can be considered worthy of consultation."

Unfortunately, even constructivist research in psychotherapy fails to meet these five criteria, at most satisfying the first three stages of the mutual orientation model. It is also ironic that part of the appeal of the repertory grid is the ease with which it can be used to derive abstract quantitative measurements of construct systems, which might actually obstruct the communication between data contributor and experimenter rather than promote it, as Kelly intended (Yorke, 1989). Thus, overreliance on a single method leaves constructivist psychotherapy researchers confronting a "crisis of methodology" that will only be overcome through greater methodological diversification (R. A. Neimeyer, 1985c).

At still deeper levels, however, a constructivist critique of existing methods might entail a fundamental reappraisal of one's approach to psychological inquiry, whether in its psychotherapeutic or scientific application. Arguing for an essentially "poetic" or "conversational" approach to human understanding, Mair (1989a, p. 197) wrote:

> Any approach to psychological understanding has to develop its own ways of working and these will make their own demands on those who seek to undertake them. The approach I am concerned with is *narrative* rather than *computational*. It involves speaking together and telling of what we know. In this it is of importance that we try to speak the "full word" from a position of imaginative participation, as well as speaking from more distant positions of reflective afterthought.

The resulting mode of inquiry might bear little resemblance to the apparently objective, nomothetic orientation of most psychotherapy research. Instead, its goal would be the articulation of deeply personal meanings and the construction of possible worlds through imaginative participation in conversation with the client. Ultimately, such a discipline of discourse would blur the line between basic research and clinical application altogether, suggesting a form of encounter between therapist and client that is simultaneously interrogative and therapeutic.

Given the variety of research paradigms (broadly defined) that characterize constructivist psychotherapies at this point in their development, perhaps the only safe prediction is that they are likely to increase in their diversity. Although this state of affairs might prove frustrating for psychotherapy researchers looking for a clearly defined alternative paradigm, it also represents a healthy, if preliminary, response to the calls for methodological reappraisal echoed throughout the literature on counseling and psychotherapy (Herman & Heesacker, 1991; Polkinghorne, 1991).

CLOSING THOUGHTS

Like the broader postmodern zeitgeist from which it derives, constructivist psychotherapy is founded on a conceptual critique of objectivist epistemology. In particular, it offers an alternative conception of psychotherapy as the quest for a more viable personal knowledge, in a world that lacks the fixed referents provided by a directly knowable external reality. From this perspective, human change processes can be facilitated but not directed, because neither therapist nor client can lay claim to a privileged vantage point that is justified by its greater authority or empirical validity. Instead, constructivist clinicians and counselors view their work in collaborative terms, as coinvestigators helping clients construct more coherent and comprehensive self theories or as coauthors assisting clients in the identification and revision of central themes in their personal narratives. The applied as well as theoretical contributions of this orientation to psychotherapy research and practice are already substantial and are likely to continue to grow in the coming years.

In spite of these prospects, the problems that characterize constructivist psychotherapy also deserve acknowledgment. The most obvious of these concerns the conceptual demands of constructivism as a philosophical outlook. As Steenbarger (1991, p. 193) observed, "conceptual frameworks in science are adopted not only for their predictive and explanatory value, but for their aesthetic appeal as well." Almost inevitably, constructivist epistemology lacks the straightforward elegance of more linear cognitive models, making an immersion in the perspective daunting for traditionally trained students and psychologists. Similarly, it is generally appreciated by sociologists of science that knowledge decays in the process of standardization. As Mulkay (1979, pp. 58–59) explained:

> Meaning is lost by translation in science as well as literature. Points of obscurity and conceptual difficulties are overlooked. The limitations of underlying assumptions are forgotten. And the balance and emphasis of the original formulation are altered to meet the needs of new areas of application. In addition, because the knowledge, technical skills and standards of adequacy of the various audiences involved are likely to be quite diverse, the standardized version must be considerably simplified.

For this reason, a certain loss of subtlety and meaning must be expected if constructivist formulations are to have a broader impact on the field of psychotherapy. But this simplification could be both unfair and unfortunate if constructivism were assimilated into more polarized positions that are easier to grasp (such as philosophical idealism or solipsism) and then discounted on this basis.

Although this external problem is worth acknowledging, internal difficulties also require the attention of constructivist theorists. For example, a constructivist model of the evolution of personal knowledge would benefit from a more detailed formulation of the role of the (social and physical) environment in the construction of meaning. Even if one grants that the world cannot directly confirm the validity of one's constructions, can it at least disconfirm them in some fashion, as suggested by Popper's (1963) falsificationist methodology (cf. Mancini & Semerari, 1988)? Accommodating the possibility that the world can say no to one's less viable constructions could pose less of a problem for orientations such as personal construct theory which ultimately accepts ontological realism (Kelly, 1955), than for radical constructivist approaches like Maturana and Varela's (1987), which consider reality entirely a function of linguistic distinctions.

Finally, the vitality of contemporary constructivism might itself be considered a problem, with many indigenous species of this general approach arising in the diverse environments in which psychotherapy is practiced. Although these variants are characterized by common commitments at an epistemological level, important theoretical, empirical, and applied differences exist between Piagetian and Kellian perspectives (Soffer, in press), radical and critical constructivists (Mahoney, 1988a), endogenous and exogenous approaches (Moshman, 1982), and mediational and predicational models (Rychlak, 1990). If these variations on a constructivist theme are to benefit from continued cross-fertilization, more attention needs to be paid to their possible integration, or at least to the establishment of boundary conditions that define when the various competing models are most applicable.

The currents of constructivist thought identifiable in contemporary clinical practice are both broad and fast moving, even if it is impossible to determine at this point where they might eventually lead. But however this inchoate tradition develops, it seems clear that it will continue to offer fresh glimpses into one of the possible futures of psychotherapy.

REFERENCES

Abelson, R. P. (1989). Psychological status of the script concept. *American Psychologist, 36,* 715–729.

Agnew, N. M., & Brown, J. L. (1989). Foundations for a model of knowing: I. Constructing reality. *Canadian Psychology, 30*, 152–167.

Anderson, W. T. (1990). *Reality isn't what it used to be.* New York: Harper & Row.

Applegate, J. L. (1990). Constructs and communication: A pragmatic integration. In G. J. Neimeyer & R. A. Neimeyer (Eds.), *Advances in personal construct psychology* (Vol. 1, pp. 203–230). Greenwich, CT: JAI Press.

Bannister, D. (1960). Conceptual structure in thought disordered schizophrenics. *Journal of Mental Science, 106*, 1230–1249.

Bannister, D. (1963). The genesis of schizophrenic thought disorder: A serial invalidation hypothesis. *British Journal of Psychiatry, 109*, 680–686

Bannister, D., Adams-Webber, J. R., Penn, W. I., & Radley, A. R. (1975). Reversing the process of thought disorder: A serial validation experiment. *British Journal of Social and Clinical Psychology, 14*, 169–180.

Bartlett, F. C. (1932). *Remembering.* Cambridge: Cambridge University Press.

Beck, A. T., Rush, J., Shaw, B., & Emery, G. (1979). *Cognitive therapy of depression.* New York: Guilford Press.

Bell, R. C. (1990). Analytic issues in the use of repertory grid technique. In G. J. Neimeyer & R. A. Neimeyer (Eds.), *Advances in personal construct psychology* (Vol. 1, pp. 25–48). Greenwich, CT: JAI Press.

Berger, P. L., & Luckmann, T. (1976). *The social construction of reality.* Harmonsworth, England: Penguin Books.

Beutler, L. E., Mohr, D. C., Grawe, K., Engle, D., & MacDonald, R. (1991). Looking for differential treatment effects: Cross-cultural predictors of differential psychotherapy efficacy. *Journal of Psychotherapy Integration, 1*, 121–141 .

Boscolo, L., Cecchin, G., Hoffman, L., & Penn, P. (1987). *Milan systemic family therapy.* New York: Basic Books.

Bowlby, J. (1973). *Attachment and loss.* London: Hogarth Press.

Bringmann, M. W. (1997). Computer-based methods for the analysis and interpretation of personal construct systems. In R. A. Neimeyer & G. J. Neimeyer (Eds.), *Advances in personal construct psychology* (Vol. 2, pp. 57–90). Greenwich, CT: JAI Press.

Bruner, J. (1990). *Acts of meaning.* Cambridge, MA: Harvard University Press.

Burns, D. (1980). *Feeling good.* New York: Signet.

Bulton, E. (Ed.). (1985). *Personal construct theory and mental health.* London: Croom Helm.

Button, E. (1990). Eating disorders and personal constructs. In R. A. Neimeyer & G. J. Neimeyer (Eds.), *Advances in personal construct psychology* (Vol. 2, pp. 187–213). Greenwich, CT: JAI Press.

Caine, T. M., Wijesinghe, O. A. B., & Winter, D. A. (1981). *Personal styles in neurosis: Implications for small group psychotherapy and behaviour therapy.* London: Routledge & Kegan Paul.

Camphell, D. T., Heyes, C., & Callebaut, W. (1987). Evolutionary epistemology. In W. Callehaut & R. Pinxter (Eds.), *Evolutionary epistemology* (pp. 139–158). Dordrecht, The Netherlands: Reidel.

Carlsen, M. B. (1991). *Creative aging.* New York: Norton.

Carlson, L., & Carlson, R. (1984). Affect and psychological magnification:

Derivations from Tompkins' script theory. *Journal of Personality, 52,* 36–45.

Chiari, G., Mancini, F., Nicolo, F., & Nuzzo, M. L. (1990). Hierarehical organization of personal construct systems in terms of the range of convenience. *International Journal of Personal Construct Psychology, 3,* 281–312.

Clarke, K . M. (1991). A performance model of the creation of meaning event. *Psychotherapy, 28,* 395–401.

Derrida, J. (1981). *Dissemination.* Chicago: University of Chicago Press.

Dryden, W., & Ellis, A. (1987). Rational emotive therapy (RET). In W. Dryden & W. Golden (Eds.), *Cognitive-behavioral approaches to psychotherapy* (pp. 129–168). New York: Hemisphere.

Efran, J. S., Lukens, M. D., & Lukens, R. J. (1990). *Language structure and change.* New York: Norton.

Ellis, A. (1973). Rational-emotive therapy. In R. Jurjevich (Ed.), *Direct psychotherapy* (pp. 295–331). Coral Gables. FL: University of Miami Press.

Epting, F. R., & Nazario, A. (1987). Designing a fixed role therapy: Issues, techniques, and modifications. In R. A. Neimeyer & G. J. Neimeyer (Eds.), *Personal construct therapy casebook* (pp. 277–289). New York: Springer.

Feinstein, D., & Krippner, S. (1988). *Personal mythology.* Los Angeles: Tarcher.

Feixas, G. (1990). Personal construct theory and the systemic therapies: Parallel or convergent trends? *Journal of Marital and Family Therapy, 16,* 1–20.

Feixas, G. (1992). Personal construct approaches to family therapy. In R. A. Neimeyer & G. J. Neimeyer (Eds.), *Advances in personal construct psychology* (Vol. 2, pp. 217–255). Greenwich, CT: JAI Press.

Feyerabend, P. (1975). *Against method.* London: Verso.

Ford, K . M., & Adams-Webber, J. R. (1991). Structure of personal construct systems and the logic of confirmation. *International Journal of Personal Construct Psychology, 4,* 15–42.

Ford, K. M., & Chang, P. (1989). An approach to automated knowledge acquisition founded on personal construct theory. In M. Fishman (Ed.), *Artificial intelligence research* (pp. 83–131). Greenwich, CT: JAI Press.

Foucault, M. (1970). *The order of things.* New York: Pantheon Books.

Fransella, F. (1972). *Personal change and reconstruction.* San Diego, CA: Academic Press.

Fransella, F. (1981). Nature babbling to herself: The self characterisation as a therapeutic tool. In H. Bonarius, R. Holland, & S. Rosenberg (Eds.), *Personal control psychology* (pp. 219–230). London: Macmillan.

Fransella, F., & Crisp, A. H. (1970). Conceptual organization and weight change. *Psychosomatics and Psychotherapy, 18,* 176–185.

Gara, A., Rosenberg, S., & Mueller, D. R. (1989). Perception of self and other in schizophrenia. *International Journal of Personal Construct Psychology, 2,* 253–270.

Greenberg, L., & Safran, J. (1987). *Emotion in psychotherapy.* NewYork: Guilford.

Guidano, V. F. (1991). *The self in process.* New York: Guilford Press.

Guidano, V., & Liotti, G. (1983). *Cognitive processes and emotional disorders.* New York: Guilford Press.

Harvey, J. H. (1989). People's naive understandings of their close relationships: Attributional and personal construct perspectives. *International Journal of*

Personal Construct Psychology, 2, 37–48.

Herman, R. A., & Heesacker, M. (1991). A developing model of exploratory psychotherapeutic research: The process within the process. *International Journal of Personal Construct Psychology, 4,* 409–425.

Hoffman, L. (1985). Beyond power and control: Toward a "second-order" family systems therapy. *Family Systems Medicine, 3,* 381–396.

Hoffman, L. (1988). A constructivism position for family therapy. *Irish Journal of Psychology, 9,* 110–129.

Howard, G. S. (1990). Narrative psychotherapy. In J. K. Zeig & W. M. Munion (Eds.), *What is psychotherapy?* (pp. 199–201). San Francisco: Jossey-Bass.

Ivey, A. E. (1991) *Developmental strategies.* Pacific Grove, CA: Brooks/Cole.

Ivey, A. E., & Gonçalves, O. F. (1988). Developmental therapy: Integrating developmental processes into the clinical practice. *Journal of Counseling and Development, 66,* 406–412.

Jahoda, M. (1958). *Current concepts of positive mental health.* New York: Basic Books.

Jankowicz, A. D. (1990). Applications of personal construct psychologs in business practice. In G. J. Neimeyer & R. A. Neimeyer (Eds.), *Advances in personal construct psychology* (Vol. 1, pp. 257–287). Greenwich, CT: JAI Press.

Jaremko, M. (1987). Cognitive-behavior modification. In W. Dryden & W. Golden (Eds.), *Cognitive-behavioral approaches to psychotherapy* (pp. 31–60). New York: Hemisphere.

Karst, T. O., & Trexler, L. D. (1970). Initial study using fixed role and rational-emotive therapy in treating public speaking anxiety. *Journal of Consulting and Clinical Psychology, 34,* 360–366.

Keating, D. P., & Rosen, H. (1991). *Constructivist perspectives on developlmental psychopathology and atypical development.* Hillsdale, NJ: Erlbaum .

Kelly, G. A. (1955). *The psychology of personal constructs.* New York: Norton .

Kelly, G. A. (1969). The autobiography of a theory. In B. Maher (Ed.), *Clinical psychology and personality* (pp. 36–45). New York: Wiley.

Kelly, G. A. (1973). Fixed role therapy. In R. M. Jurjevich (Ed.), *Direct psychotherapy: 28 American originals* (pp. 394–422). Coral Gables, FL: University of Miami Press.

Kelly, G. A. (1977). The psychology of the unknown. In D. Bannister (Ed.), *New perspectives in personal construct theory* (pp. 1–19). San Diego, CA: Academic Press.

Koch, H. C. H. (1983). Changes in personal construing in three psychotherapy groups and a control group. *British Journal of Medical Psychology, 56,* 245–254.

Korzybski, A. (1933). *Science and sanity.* New York: International Non-Aristotelian Library.

Kremsdorf, R. (1985). An extension of fixed-role therapy with a couple. In F. Epting & A. Landfield (Eds.), *Anticipating personal constructs psychology* (pp. 216–224). Lincoln: University of Nebraska Press.

Lakatos, I. (1974). Falsification and the methodology of scientific research programmes. In I. Lakatos & A. Musgrave (Eds.), *Criticism and the growth of knowledge* (pp. 91–196). Cambridge: Cambridge University Press.

Landfield, A. W. (1971). *Personal constructs systems in psychotherapy.* Chicago: Rand McNally.

Landfield, A. W., & Epting, F. R. (1987). *Personal construct psychology.* New York: Human Sciences Library.

Laudan, I., (1977). *Progress and its problems: Towards a theroy of scientific growth.* Berkeley: University of California Press.

Leitner, L. M. (1987). Crisis of thc self: The terror of personal evolution. In R. A. Neimeyer & G. J. Neimeyer (Eds.), *Personal construct therapy casebook* (pp. 39–56). New York: Springer.

Leitner, L. M. (1987). Terror, risk and reverence: Experiential personal construct therapy. *International Journal of Personal Construct Psychology, 1,* 251–261.

Levinson, S. (1989). *Constitutional faith.* Princeton, NJ: Princeton University Press.

Levinsohn, P. M., Steinmetz, J., Antonuccio, D., & Teri, L. (1984). Group therapy for depression. *International Journal of Mental Health, 13,* 8–33.

Liotti, G. (1987). Structural cognitive therapy. In W. Dryden & W. Golden (Eds.), *Cognitive–behavioral approaches to psychotherapy* (pp. 92–128). New York: Hemisphere.

Liotti, G. (1991). Patterns of attachment and the assessment of interpersonal schemata: Understanding and changing difficult patient–therapist relationships in cognitive psychotherapy. *Journal of Cognitive Psychotherapy, 5,* 105–114.

Llewelyn, S., & Dunnett, G. (1987). The use of personal construct theory in groups. In R. A. Neimeyer & G. J. Neimeyer (Eds.), *Personal construct therapy casebook* (pp. 245–258). New York: Springer.

Loos, V., & Epstein, E. S. (1989). Conversational construction of meaning in family therapy. *International Journal of Personal Construct Psychology, 2,* 149–167.

Lorenzini, R., & Sassaroli, S. (1987). *La paura della paura* [The fear of fear]. Rome: La Nuova Italia Scientifica.

Lyddon, W. J. (1990a). First- and second-order change: Implications for rationalist and constructivist cognitive therapies. *Journal of Counseling and Development, 69,* 121–127.

Lyddon, W. J. (1990b, May). *Forms and facets of constructivist psychology.* Paper presented at the First International Conference on Constructivism in Psychotherapy, Memphis, TN.

Mahoney, M. J. (1988a). Constructive metatheory: 1. Basic features and historical foundations. *International Journal of Personal Construct Psychology, 1,* 299–315.

Mahoney, M. J. (1988b). Constructive metatheory: 2. Implications for psychotherapy. *International Journal of Personal Construct Psychology, 1,* 299–315.

Mahoney, M. J. (1989). Participatory epistemology and the psychology of science. In B. Gholson, W. Shadish, R. Neimeyer, & A. Houts (Eds.), *The psychology of science* (pp. 138–164). Cambridge: Cambridge University Press.

Mahoney, M. J. (1991). *Human change processes.* New York: Basic Books.

Mair, M. (1988). Psychology as storytelling. *International Journal of Personal Construct Psychology, 1,* 125–138.

Mair, M. (1989a). *Between psychology and psycholherapy.* London: Routledge.

Mair, M. (1989b). Kelly, Bannister, and a storytelling psychology. *International Journal of Personal Construct Psychology, 2,* 1–14.

Mancini, F., & Semerari, A. (1988). Kelly and Popper: A constructivist view of knowledge. In F. Fransella & L. Thomas (Eds.), *Experimenting with personal construct psychology* (pp. 69–79). London: Routledge & Kegan Paul.

Mancini, F., & Semerari, A. (1990). Emozioni e sistemi cognitivi: Le teorie cognitive della sofferenza emotiva [Emotions and cognitive systems: Cognitive theories of emotional distress]. In F. Mancini & A. Semerari (Eds.), *Le teorie cognitive dei disturbi emotivi* [Cognitive theories of emotional disorders] (pp. 37–53). Rome: La Nuova Italia Scientifica.

Mascolo, M. F., & Mancuso, J. C. (1991). Functioning of epigenetically evolved emotion systems: A constructive analysis. *International Journal of Personal Construct Psychology, 3,* 205–222.

Maturana, H., & Varela, F. (1987). *The tree of knowledge.* Boston: New Science Library.

McCoy, M. (1981). Positive and negative emotion. In H. Bonarius, R. Holland, & S. Rosenberg (Eds.), *Personal construct psychology* (pp. 95–104). London: Macmillan.

Mead, M. (1939). *From the south seas.* New York: William Morras.

Merluzzi, T., Rudy, T., & Glass, C. (1981). The information-processing paradigm. In T. Merluzzi, C. Glass, & R. Genest (Eds.), *Cognitive assessment* (pp. 77–124). New York: Guilford Press.

Millis, K. K., & Neimeyer, R. A. (1990). A test of the dichotomy corollary: Propositions verus constructs as basic cognitive units. *International Journal of Personal Construct Psychology, 3,* 167–181.

Moreno, J. L. (1937). Interpersonal therapy and the psychopathology of interpersonal relationships. *Sociometry, 1,* 9–76.

Moshman, D. (1982). Exogenous, endogenous, and dialectical constructivism. *Developmental Review, 2,* 371–384.

Mulkay, M. J. (1979). *Science and the sociology of knowledge.* Winchester MA: Allen & Unwin.

Neimeyer, G. J. (1985). Personal constructs in the counseling of couples. In F. Epting & A. Landfield (Eds.), *Anticipating personal construct psychology* (pp. 201–215). Lincoln: University of Nebraska Press.

Neimeyer, G. J. (Ed.). (1992a). *Handbook of constructivist assessment.* Newbury Park, CA: Sage.

Neimeyer, G. J. (Ed.). (1992b). Thematic issue on personal constructs in career counseling and development. *Journal of Career Development, 3,* 188–232.

Neimeyer, G. J., & Neimeyer, R. A. (1981). Personal construct perspectives on cognitive assessment. In T. Merluzzi, C. Glass, & M. Genest (Eds.), *Cognitive assessment* (pp. 188–232). New York: Guilford Press.

Neimeyer, R. A. (1984). Toward a personal construct conceptualization of depression and suicide. In F. R. Epting & R. A. Neimeyer (Eds.), *Personal meanings of death: Applications of personal construct theory to clinical practice* (pp. 127–173). New York: Hemisphere.

Neimeyer, R. A. (1985a). Personal constructs in clinical practice. In P. C. Kendall (Ed.), *Advances in cognitive–behavioral research and therapy* (Vol. 4, pp. 275–329). San Diego, CA: Academic Press.

Neimeyer, R. A. (1985b). Personal constructs in depression: Research and clinical implications. In E. Button (Ed.), *Personal construct theory and mental health* (pp. 82–102). London: Croom Helm.

Neimeyer, R. A. (1985c). *The development of personal construct psychology,* Lincoln: University of Nebraska Press.

Neimeyer, R. A. (1987). An orientation to personal construct therapy. In R. A. Neimeyer & G. J. Neimeyer (Eds.), *Personal construct therapy casebook* (pp. 3–19). New York: Springer.

Neimeyer, R. A. (1988). Integrative directions in personal construct therapy *International Journal of Personal Construct Psychology, 1,* 283–297.

Neimeyer, R. A. (1992). Constructivist approaches to the measurement of meaning. In G. J. Neimeyer (Ed.), *Casebook of constructivist assesssment* (pp. 58–103). Newbury Park, CA: Sage.

Neimeyer, R. A., & Epting, F. R. (1992). Measuring personal meanings of death: 20 years of research using the Threat Index. In R. A. Neimeyer & G. J. Neimeyer (Eds.), *Advanccs in personal construct psychology* (Vol. 2, pp. 121–147). Greenwich. CT: JAI Press.

Neimeyer, R. A., & Feixas, G. (1990). Constructivist contributions to psychotherapy integration. *Journal of Integrative and Eclectic Psychotherapy, 9,* 4–20.

Neimeyer, R. A., & Harter, S. (1988). Facilitating individual change in personal construct therapy. In G. Dunnett (Ed.), *Working with people* (pp. 174–185). London: Routledge & Kegan Paul.

Neimeyer, R. A., Harter, S., & Alexander, P. C. (1991). Group perceptions as predictors of outcome in the treatment of incest survivors. *Psychotherapy Research, 1,* 149–158.

Neimeyer, R. A., Heath, A. E., & Strauss, J. (1985). Personal reconstruction during group cognitive therapy for depression. In F. R. Epting & A. W. Landfeld (Eds.), *Anticipating personal construct theory* (pp. 180–197). Lincoln: University of Nebraska Press.

Novak, J. M. (1990). Advancing constructive education: A framework for teacher education. In G. J. Neimeyer & R. A. Neimeyer (Eds.), *Advances in personal construct psychology* (Vol. 1, pp. 233–255). Greenwich, CT: JAI Press.

O'Hara, M., & Anderson, W. T. (1991, September/October). Welcome to the postmodern world. *Family Therapy Networker,* pp. 19–25.

Penn, P. (1985). Feed-forward: Future questions, future maps. *Family Process, 24,* 299–310.

Piaget, J. (1971). *The construction of reality in the child.* New York: Ballantine Books. (Original work published 1937).

Pierce, D., Sewell, K., & Cromwell, R. (1992). Schizophrenia and depression: Construing and constructing empirical research. In R. A. Neimeyer & G. J. Neimeyer (Eds.), *Advances in personal construct psychology* (Vol. 2, pp. 151–

184). Greenwich, CT: JAI Press.

Polanyi, M. (1958). *Personal knowledge.* New York: Harper.

Polkinghorne, D. E. (1991). Two conflicting calls for methodological reform. *The Consulting Psychologist, 19,* 103–114.

Popper, K. R. (1963). *Conjectures and refutations.* London: Routledge & Kegan Paul.

Procter, H. G. (1987). Change in the family construct system. In R. A. Neimeyer & G. J. Neimeyer (Eds.), *Personal construct therapy casebook* (pp. 153–171). New York: Springer.

Rainer, T. (1978). *The new diary.* Los Angeles: Tarcher.

Radnitzky, G. (1973). *Contemporary schools of metascience.* Chicago: Regency.

Reiss, D. (1981). *The family's construction of reality.* Cambridge, MA: Harvard University Press.

Rice, L. N., & Greenberg, L. S. (1984). The new research paradigm. In L. N. Rice & L. S. Greenberg (Eds.), *Patterns of change* (pp. 7–25). New York: Guilford Press.

Rich, A. R., & Dahlheimer, D. D. (1989). The power of negative thinking: A new perspective on "irrational" cognitions. *Journal of Cognitive Psychotherapy, 3,* 15–30.

Rigazio-DiGilio, S. A., & Ivey, A. E. (1990). Developmental therapy and depressive disorders: Measuring cognitive levels through patient natural language. *Professional Psychology: Research and Practice, 21,* 470–475.

Rigazio-DiGilio, S. A., & Ivey, A. E. (1991). Developmental counseling and therapy: A framework for individual and family treatment. *Counseling and Human Development, 24,* 1–20.

Rychlak, J. F. (1990). George Kelly and the concept of construction. *International Journal of Personal Construct Psychology, 3,* 7–19.

Rychlak, J. (1992). Oppositionality and the psychology of personal constructs. In R. A. Neimeyer & G. J. Neimeyer (Eds.), *Advances in personal construct psychology* (Vol. 2, pp. 3–25). Greenwich, CT: JAI Press.

Ryle, A. (1980). Some measures of goal attainment in focused integrated active psychotherapy: A study of 15 cases. *British Journal of Psychiatry, 137,* 475–486.

Sacks, O. (1985). *The man who mistook his wife for a hat.* New York: Summit.

Safran, J. D., Vallis, T. M., Segal, Z. V., & Shaw, B. F. (1986). Assessment of core cognitive processes in cognitive therapy. *Cognitive Therapy and Research, 10,* 509–526.

Schwartz, R. M. (1992). States of mind model and personal construct theory: Implications for psychopathology. *International Journal of Personal Construct Psychology, 5,* 123–143.

Schwartz, R. M., & Michelson, L. (1987). States of mind model: Cognitive balance in the treatment of agoraphobia. *Journal of Consulting and Clinical Psychology, 55,* 557–565.

Selvini-Palazzoli, M., Boscolo, L., Cecchin, G., & Prata, G. (1980). Hypothesizing-circularity-neutrality. *Family Process, 19,* 3–12.

Sewell, K., Adams-Webber, J., Mitterer, J., & Cromwell, R. (1992). Computerized repertory grids: Review of the literature. *International Journal of Per-*

sonal Construct Psychology, 5, 1–24.

Siegelman, E. (1990). *Metaphor and meaning in psychology.* New York: Guilford Press.

Slife, B. D., Stoneman, J., & Rychlak, J. F. (1991). The heuristic power of oppositionality in an incidental memory task: In support of the construing process. *International Journal of Personal Construct Psychology, 4*, 333–346.

Soffer, J. (in press). Jean Piaget and George Kelly: Toward a "stronger" constructivism. *International Journal of Personal Construct Psychology.*

Soldz, S. (1987). The flight from relationship. In R. A. Neimeyer & G. J. Neimeyer (Eds.), *Personal construct therapy casebook* (pp. 76–89). New York: Springer.

Space, L. G., Dingemans, P., & Cromwell, R. L. (1983). Self-construing and alienation in depressives, schizophrenics and normals. In J. Adams-Webber & J. Mancuso (Eds.), *Applications of personal construct theory* (pp. 365–377). New York: Wiley.

Steenbarger, B. N. (1991). All the world is not a stage: Emerging contextualist themes in counseling and development. *Journal of Counseling and Development, 70*, 288–296.

Stewart. A. E., & Barry, J. R. (1991). Origins of George Kelly's constructivism in the works of Korzybski and Moreno. *International Journal of Personal Construct Psychology, 4*, 121–136.

Taylor, S. E., & Brown, J. D. (1988). Illusion and well-being. *Psychological Bulletin, 103*, 193–210.

Tomm, K. (1987). Interventive interviewing: Part 2. *Family Process, 26*, 167–183.

van den Bergh, O., de Boeck, P., & Claeys. W. (1985). Schizophrenia: What is loose in schizophrenic construing? In E. Button (Ed.), *Personal construct theory and mental health* (pp. 59–81). London: Croom Helm.

Viney, L. (1988). Which data-collection methods are appropriate for a constructivist psychology? *International Journal of Personal Construct Psychology, 1*, 191–203.

Viney, L. (1990). Psychotherapy as shared reconstruction. *International Journal of Personal Construct Psychology, 3*, 437–456.

von Foerster, H. (1981). *Observing systems.* Seaside, CA: Intersystems Publications.

von Glasersfeld, E. (1984). An introduction to radical constructivism. In P. Watzlawick (Ed.), *The invented reality* (pp. 17–40). New York: Norton.

Weishaar, M. E., & Beck, A. T. (1987). Cognitive therapy. In W. Dryden & W. Golden (Eds.), *Cognitive-behavioral approaches to psychotherapy* (pp. 61–91). New York: Hemisphere.

White, M., & Epston, D. (1990). *Narrative means to therapeutic ends.* New York: Norton.

Winter, D. (1985). Neurotic disorders: The curse of certainty In E. Button (Ed.), *Personal construct theory and mental health* (pp. 103–131). London: Croom Helm.

Winter, D. (1990). Therapeutic alternatives for psychological disorder. In G. J. Neimeyer & R. A. Neimeyer (Eds.), *Advances in personal construct psychology* (Vol. 1, pp. 89–116). Greenwich. CT: JAI Press.

Woolgar, S. (1989). Representation, cognition and self. In S. Fuller, M. DeMey, T. Shinn, & S. Woolgar (Eds.), *The cognitive turn* (pp. 201–223). Dordrecht, The Netherlands: Kluwer.

Yorke, M. (1989). The intolerable wrestle: Words, numbers, and meanings. *International Journal of Personal Construct Psychology, 2,* 65–76.

12

The Cognitive and Constructive Psychotherapies: Contexts and Challenges

Michael J. Mahoney

The cognitive and constructive psychotherapies have become phenomena of interest in the second half of the 20th century. To understand their development, their contributions, and their prospects, they must be viewed from the broader perspective of developments around them in philosophy, general psychology, and psychotherapy. What follows is a reflection of ongoing reflections, if you will, and I shall use this first play on words as a transition to the related realms of semiotics, semantics, and hermeneutics.

SEMIOTICS, SEMANTICS, AND HERMENEUTICS

One of the first things that struck me in reviewing this collection of writings was the diversity of labels and apparent meanings employed by the different contributors. To the reader unfamiliar with the subtle nuances in this field, it may be perplexing to understand the commonalities and differences assumed by the diversity of approaches. Does the term cognition imply the same meaning when it is used by the various contributors to this volume? Indeed, does this term have a singular meaning *within* the writings of any of these individuals (let alone *across* them)? Is the distinction between cognitive and constructive therapies a viable or valuable one? (Since it is central to the title of this volume and to its organization, my personal response to this last question may be apparent.)

What is at issue here is meaning, and it has become an increasingly encountered issue in the cognitive sciences, general psychology, and philosophy:

> There is only one problem that has ever existed in psychology, and everything the field has investigated is merely a manifestation of that problem, a different aspect of the same elephant, an elephant we have grasped at since the dawn of reflective thought without ever reaching it at all. . . . No matter where one goes in psychology there comes a point at which one runs into an insurmountable wall that is, conceptually speaking, infinitely high and wide. All we can do is look up and see that written on that wall are the problems of the manifestations of meaning. (Weimer, 1974, pp. 427–429)

The problem of meaning has inspired and perplexed workers in the specializations of semiotics (theory of signs), semantics (theories of meaning), and hermeneutics (theories of interpretation), all of which are fundamental to our efforts in epistemology (theories of knowing) and phenomenology (theories of experience)[1] (Korzybski, 1924; Madison, 1988; Merleau-Ponty, 1962; Messer, Sass, & Woolfolk, 1988; Wachterhauser, 1986).

Although they often acknowledge issues of meaning, writers in the cognitive and constructive psychotherapies have not been immune to the problems of meaning within their own inquiries. For example, in this volume, is Meichenbaum's use of the term "cognitive behavior modification" similar or equivalent to other authors' use of "cognitive–behavioral therapy?" Likewise, Beck notes that "cognitive therapy has co-opted (or been co-opted by) a large sector of the behavior therapy approaches to psychopathology," and Ellis equates "general RET" with cognitive–behavior therapy. What, then, is the relation between cognitive and behavior therapies? It must clearly be more complex than one of super- and subordination, and one gets the sense that neatly overlapping Venn diagrams are also an inadequate depiction. Moreover, since Beck, Ellis, and Meichenbaum are now explicitly describing their approaches as "constructivist," what is the relation between the categories "cognitive" and "constructivist"? Are all cognitive psychotherapies subtypes of constructivism? (Until recently, the reverse relation was more widely assumed.) And given the relations between constructivist perspectives and ethology, evolutionary epistemology, hermeneutics, and humanist–existential–transpersonal approaches (Gonçalves, Guidano, and Neimeyer, *this volume*; Mahoney, 1995a, 1995b, 1995c), where does one draw a line between constructivist and nonconstructivist approaches?

What is conceptually challenging here is that there are simultaneous signs of differentiation and integration within and beyond cognitive and constructive perspectives. In my opinion, a more adequate (albeit still imperfect) understanding of these perspectives can be rendered only in the context of a view that incorporates broader developments in philosophy, psychology, and psychotherapy.

A BROADER CONTEXT: DEVELOPMENTS IN 20TH-CENTURY PHILOSOPHY, PSYCHOLOGY, AND PSYCHOTHERAPY

I have elsewhere ventured some reflections and conjectures on more general developments in the fields of philosophy, psychology, and psychotherapy during the past century (Mahoney, 1991). A brief synopsis of these developments may be worthwhile, however, in offering a tentative scaffolding for the present attempt to review the contexts and challenges presented by the cognitive and constructive psychotherapies. For the sake of brevity, these developments (more accurately, my constructions of them) are here compressed into a simplifying list. With the cognitive revolution and developments in the cognitive and constructive therapies being dealt with elsewhere in this volume and chapter, I have not included them in the enumeration below. The inter-relatedness of many of these developments will be apparent in the arbitrariness of what is clustered within any given item.

1. *There has been a progressive decline in the dominance of authoritarian epistemologies.* Whereas positivism and logical positivism went almost unchallenged in the first half of this century, they have come under increasing attack since midcentury (Bartley, 1984; Weimer, 1977). Justifications—those bedrock guarantees of validity and correct methods—have been recognized as illusions of human construction. Among other things, this development has resulted in sweeping shifts in strategies of "legitimation" in philosophy, psychology, and the social sciences (Kvale, 1992; Lyotard, 1984; Tarnas, 1991).

2. *There has been a significant change in the range of acceptable methodologies for inquiry, with a shift toward greater balance between "objective" and "subjective" methods.* In the 19th-century differentiation of psychology from philosophy and in the efforts of early psychologists to gain respectability as a science, the tradition of objectivism came to dominate.

Among other things, this tradition emphasized an absolute and necessary separation between the object of study and the "subject" carrying out the investigation. (Note that the meanings of these terms have been reversed in their currently accepted scientific use: the "subject" has become the "object" of study, and the researcher—formerly the subject—has become a paragon of objectivity.) Noteworthy in the past few decades are the beginnings of a relaxation of mathematical "quantophilia" and an increasing openness to the so-called qualitative methodologies characterized by narrative, phenomenological, and otherwise subjective expressions of human experience (Bernstein, 1983; Messer et al., 1988).

3. *There has been a recession of "prime mover" (first cause) arguments about the determinants of human experience in favor of more complex and dynamic models.* Much of 20th-century debate in psychology has focused on whether affect, behavior, or cognition is the most important or powerful determinant. Experiential and psychodynamic therapists emphasized affect, behaviorists championed behavior, and cognitivists argued for cognition as the most important realm for understanding and changing human experience. In the last quarter of the century, however, there has been a discernible move toward conceptualizations of human experience that are decidedly more holistic, complex, and coalitional, with models of multiple and reciprocal determination gaining ascendance (Bandura, 1986; Mahoney, 1991).

4. *The mind has become embodied.* The separation of mind and body has been a perennial problem for philosophy, psychology, and psychotherapy. Rationalists ranging from Pythagoras and Plato to Descartes and Minsky have argued the superiority of the mind over the body. This dualism continues in some extreme expressions of cognitivism, where futurists predict a welcome scenario of soon being able to download the brain into computers with less vulnerable bodies. (This scenario is a welcome one only to those for whom embodiment is more of an obstacle than a vehicle for knowing [Mahoney, in press].) With the noteworthy exception of the phenomenologists (e.g., Heidegger, Husserl, Merleau-Ponty), there were few challenges to the conceptual hegemony of dualism until the past two or three decades. It has been during this period that the specialization of health psychology has developed and the era of popularized physical fitness—what I like to call "the movement movement"—has begun to mature. It was also during these years that we witnessed what have come to be called "embodied mind" theories in the cognitive sciences, linguistics, and philosophy (Johnson, 1987). The latter are theories of knowledge development and representation that move beyond traditional notions of symbols stored in the head. According to embodied mind theories, all human knowledge,

including abstract thought and language, is based on protocols, prototypes, and differentiations of bodily experience (Leder, 1990; Zaner, 1971).

5. *Human rights have become a legitimized concern of psychologists and psychotherapists.* Human rights, which are inseparable from issues of ethics and values (see below), were once considered the exclusive domain of philosophers. This is no longer the case. Owing in part to the human rights movements on several continents as well as to the related maturation of feminist perspectives, psychology and psychotherapy have become disciplines wherein human dignity, issues of diversity, and basic rights and responsibilities have moved to the forefront of contemporary concerns. This development has been reflected in multifaceted maturations of ethical consciousness (e.g., social movements to prevent and address child and elder abuse, to protect the rights of homosexuals, to promote responsible care of animals and ecosystems, to reduce violence of any form, to protect the rights of handicapped individuals, and to foster respect for cultural, ethnic, and individual diversity). In the process of many of these developments, we have come to recognize that the history of so-called Western civilization has been a history of the politics of power that have maintained and protected a predominantly male, Caucasian, Western European–North American view of psychological life. This hegemony (dominating leadership) of "first world" male Anglo-American thinking is a major challenge facing the development of 21st-century psychology (see below and Fisher, 1989).

6. *Psychotherapy integration has become a major interest and forum of dialogue.* One of the major developments of 20th-century psychotherapy has been the emergence of a phenomenon variously termed eclectic psychotherapy, convergence, and psychotherapy integration. The seeds of this movement can be traced to diverse influences, and it is generally characterized by a strong interest in the exploration of similarities and common factors across the different approaches to psychotherapy (Mahoney, *this volume*; Neimeyer, *this volume*). For many observers, these developments are an exciting indication that the entire field of psychological services is moving through a developmental tranformation of significant proportions (Altman, 1987). Psychology may or may not approach a unification attributed to other sciences and professions (Bower, 1993; Koch, 1993), but open dialogue regarding its diversity is likely to be one of its saving graces in the centuries to come.

7. *Issues of value, including (but not limited to) aspects of religion and spirituality, have come to be recognized as inevitable in psychology in general and psychotherapy in particular.* As was mentioned in the earlier discussion of human rights, late-20th-century psychology has become much more conscious of value issues. An important, albeit still controversial, aspect

of this consciousness has been the softening of mainstream psychology's aversion to the relevance of religious and spiritual issues in human development and psychological services. The signs of this development are increasingly evident in general psychology (Campbell, 1975; Sperry, 1988), and they are even more apparent in the literatures of counseling, psychotherapy, and their increasing interfaces with the humanities (Allman, de La Rocha, Elkins, & Weathers, 1992; Bergin, 1991; Cushman, 1993; Kelly & Strupp, 1992; Kovel, 1991; London, 1964; McNamee & Gergen, 1992; Payne, Bergin, & Loftus, 1992; Vaughan, 1991). Recent surveys of psychotherapists have consistently found them to be rarely "religious" (i.e., a member of an organized church community) but commonly self-described as "spiritual."

8. *The phenomenon of globalization has created unprecedented challenges for both individual and social system development.* Although there is no single and accepted definition of globalization, its existence and exponential growth are now widely acknowledged. There are different ways of saying it: "the global village," "the shrinking of the planet," the postmodern movement toward "transnational" and "transcultural" identities, and so on (Balibar & Wallerstein, 1991; Fisher, 1989; Mato, 1993; Maturana & Verden-Zöller, 1993; Montero, 1991). The signs of it are everwhere: in telecommunications, the arts, worldwide organizations, the world peace and ecology movements, economic markets with unprecedented permeability and reciprocity, the technologies of travel and information transfer, and the saturation and complexity of the postmodern self (Gergen, 1991; Guidano, 1987, 1991). Globalization necessarily challenges old boundaries—boundaries among nations, races, cultures, religions, traditions, life-styles, and languages. In these most Protean times, how are we to understand and optimally counsel the individual, family, or community that is struggling with boundaries of experience and issues of identity, coherence, and the "larger self" of a global community? How does a child born in these times—and especially in nations or communities that are in the throes of revolutionary transitions—negotiate his or her identity and value? Such questions reflect and invoke the two remaining developments to be enumerated, namely, the self as situated in the social system and the priorities of children.

9. *The psychology of self has reemerged as a central concern, and it has been situated in the complex dynamics of social systems and interpersonal relationships.* With the important exceptions of some personality theorists and the object relations and ego psychologies of psychoanalysis, the problems of personal identity—what Guidano (1987, 1991) terms "selfhood"—were dropped by mainstream psychology soon after the ascent of radical behaviorism in the early part of this century. In the second half of the century, issues of self have returned to center stage

(Gergen, 1991; Sampson, 1993; Stolorow & Atwood, 1992). Importantly, this return has been marked by a recognition of the culture-bounded aspects of personal identity and the limitations of Anglo–North American ideologies of individualism. The self has come to be recognized as a "project" (Gonçalves, *this volume*) that always and necessarily develops within social systems. The practical relevance of this recognition is nowhere more apparent than in the contemporary expansion of concerns surrounding the welfare and well-being of children.

10. *Children have become increasingly central to the focus and future of psychology and psychotherapy.* With increasing frequency and proportion, the postmodern world has come to realize the priorities of child care, family life, and present responsibilities for the quality of future life. These realizations are being expressed in various ways—educational values, sensitivites to child abuse, debates over abortion, genetic engineering, the impact of the media on children's development, and so on. Moreover, the emotionally "secure base" required by all socialized mammals (Bowlby, 1988) is being recognized as an important priority in all human life-span development. Likewise, the power of early life experiences has become more widely acknowledged, with the result that psychologists and psychotherapists, among many others, have become increasingly vocal with parents, educators, and policymakers regarding the importance of such experiences in the development of socially responsible and self-respecting planetary citizens.

APPRAISAL IN THE LARGER CONTEXT

If we now return to our reflections on the cognitive and constructive psychotherapies in light of these larger contextual developments, some interesting observations are prompted. Beginning, for example, with the decline of authoritarian epistemologies, it can be seen that this has been a pivotal issue in the proposed distinction between cognitive and constructive approaches. The latter have generally faulted the former for being authoritarian. In other words, constructivists (including myself) have challenged the importance of formal rationality as the cornerstone of theories of psychopathology and psychotherapy. Rationalists like Albert Ellis (*this volume*) have responded by clarifying and elaborating their intended meanings of "rational," as well as by explicitly aligning themselves with the less justificational epistemologies embraced by constructivists.

Another interesting point emerges from a consideration of the ongoing shift toward more balance between traditionally "objective" and "subjective" research methodologies. The vast majority of objectified research has been generated by (or in relation to) Aaron Beck's cognitive therapy and the diverse hybrids of cognitive–behavioral treatments. Although the constructivists cite case illustrations and clinical vignettes, their research basis and "legitimation" has been decidedly more conceptual and qualitative and idiographic than quantitative and nomothetic (Neimeyer & Mahoney, 1995). This raises an important issue regarding future trajectories of development, and it sheds some light on the enduring attachment to the hyphen in "cognitive–behavioral" therapies. Some of that attachment, of course, is historical and ideological: some cognitive treatments emerged out of earlier behavioral conceptualizations, and many cognitivists remain respectful of the role of active behavioral performance in facilitating psychological change. But I believe there is more to the hyphen than that. At least part of the attachment stems from a desire to remain associated with the scientific respectability established by behavior therapists.

My conjecture about developmental trajectories runs as follows. For the most part, cognitive and cognitive–behavioral therapies have fueled their bids for respect as therapeutic systems by means of mainstream research efforts. They have employed the methodologies of traditionally objectivist inquiry, and their initial focus has been more on outcome than on process. Increasingly, however, cognitive researchers have moved in the direction of examining "mechanisms of change" (an interesting choice of metaphors because of its implicit appeal to a mechanistic model of change). This shift is apparent in many of the chapters in this volume, and it suggests an increasing interest in the *process* (as well as the *outcome*) of cognitivist psychotherapy.

Constructivists, on the other hand, have emphasized process almost exclusively, and they cannot as yet point to any major outcome studies addressed to the effectiveness of their approaches (Neimeyer, *this volume*; Neimeyer & Mahoney, 1995). The latter is, no doubt, related to their skepticism about the meaningfulness of traditional methodologies and instruments for measuring psychological impact. Nevertheless, the absence of outcome research in the constructivist tradition is likely to be an influence in its evaluation by mainstream scholars. To the extent that constructivists seek to popularize and propagate their views of psychotherapy, they will be forced to address this issue. Noteworthy here is the fact that constructivists have traditionally seemed much less interested in proselytization than many of their colleagues. The followers of George Kelly, for example, have never formed an official organization (replete with by-laws, officers, and publicists) like those that have flourished in other therapeutic traditions. Likewise, the international conferences on constructivism in psychotherapy—held in Memphis

(USA) in 1990, Barcelona (Spain) in 1991, Braga (Portugal) in 1992, and Buenos Aires (Argentina) in 1994—have only recently generated such an organization. At least among some of the participants, there appears to be a certain pride in the inchoateness and informality of this movement.

Will future constructivists become more formally organized, develop treatment manuals, and pursue collaborative outcome studies similar to those developed in cognitive and cognitive–behavioral therapies? Although this is not an inevitable scenario, I believe it is a likely one. Moreover, despite the potential pitfalls of such developments, I believe that they would ultimately lead to valuable clarifications and contributions. The pitfalls, in my opinion, involve the bureaucratic sequelae of institutionalization, as well as possible compromises to some basic aspects of constructivist metatheory. These vulnerable aspects of constructivism include the emphasis of idiographic over nomothetic issues, the appeal to guiding principles rather than routine prescriptions, and the epistemic challenge to many of the assumptions made by popular inferential statistics. I do not view these pitfalls as inevitable, however, and I think there would be much to be gained in the dialectics that would result from constructivists' increased participation in mainstream psychotherapy research. With Robert Neimeyer (*this volume*), I agree that preliminary investigations amply illustrate the potential merits of such participation.

With regard to the recession of prime mover arguments in psychology and the trend toward the embodiment of mind, I believe that constructivists have made relatively more progress and contributions than have their cognitivist colleagues. Issues of complexity and nonlinear dynamics are paramount here (Jantsch, 1980; Kauffman, 1993; Pattee, 1973; Salthe, 1985; Waldrop, 1992; Weimer, 1987). These are issues that are more frequently addressed in constructivist writings, some of which contend that these are central aspects of their epistemologies. To a lesser degree, the same may be said regarding the issue of human rights. Perhaps because of their interface with postmodern philosophy, constructivists have tended to be more attuned to developments in feminist theory, cultural diversity, and nonpathologizing accounts of human differences (Gergen, 1991; Kvale, 1992; McNamee & Gergen, 1992).

With regard to participation in the psychotherapy integration movement, both cognitivists and constructivists can claim considerable activity. (Constructivists might also note with pride that the 1994 meetings of the Society for Psychotherapy Integration and the International Conference on Constructivism in Psychotherapy were held in tandem in Buenos Aires.) Representatives of both groups have made claims about their respective relevance for psychotherapy integration, and more important, they have both participated in productive dialogues with representatives of other therapeutic traditions.

Value issues have been more extensively addressed by constructivists than by cognitivists, and this is also the case with the phenomenon and challenges of globalization. This may again be a corollary of the parallels between aspects of constructivism and postmodernism. In the realm of religiosity and spiritual issues in psychotherapy, however, neither the cognitivists nor the constructivists can claim to have been either liberal or contributory. Indeed, to the extent that Albert Ellis's remarks about the correlation between religiosity and psychopathology are attributed to cognitivists in general, the cognitive psychotherapies do not emerge with a tolerant image in this domain.

Both cognitivists and constructivists have contributed to the reemergence of self psychology. Their contributions have taken very different forms, however. Cognitivists have tended to emphasize the importance of "schemata," a term whose meanings appear to range from template-like mental representations to abstract ordering processes. Constructivists have emphasized the latter over the former, and they have also been decidedly more developmental in their conceptualizations of personal identity. These differences are particularly apparent in approaches to the treatment of children (Meichenbaum, *this volume*). Cognitivists have emphasized the importance of identifying and correcting "deficiencies" and "distortions" in children's thinking, and they have generated a substantial literature on the outcome of their interventions. With rare exceptions, constructivists have emphasized the importance of early life experiences in personal development but they have not made major contributions to either theory or practice in children's issues.[2]

CONCLUSION

So where does this leave us? In this final chapter I have ventured some observations and evaluations that may seem more critical than might be expected in a volume devoted to the cognitive and constructive psychotherapies. Were it not for some of its excess connotations, one might even say that I have assumed the role of the devil's advocate.[3] Although I am a strong advocate for these psychotherapies, I am also a believer in the role of criticism and dialectical exchange in epistemology (Bartley, 1984; Weimer, 1977). What I have shared here have been my personal reflections on 25 years of participation in those psychotherapies and almost 3 years of work in preparing this volume. As an avowed constructivist, I am well aware that my awareness is limited and necessarily evaluative. I do not claim it to be otherwise. My remarks are written representations of my own attempts to understand and facilitate the development of cognitive and constructive psychotherapies.

I shall close this chapter and the volume with a reminder that might well have warmed the cockles of George Kelly's Celtic heart. This is the reminder that we humans are contrast-dependent creatures and that the majority of our most important contrasts take the form of either/or dichotomies. My favorite illustration of this fact is the contention that there are two kinds of people in the world: (1) those who believe that there are two kinds of people in the world and (2) those who do not. This pithy little maxim is more than a play on words. It is a reminder that we are always engaged in efforts after meaning and that we use contrasts to create the dimensions that allow us to dialogue. The dialogue between and about cognitive and constructive psychotherapies is an extremely valuble one, in my opinion, and I am grateful for having had this opportunity to again participate in it.

NOTES

1. Phenomenologists might well cringe at this equation because phenomenology emphasizes the experience of being over theoretical abstractions about experience.
2. A noteworthy exception here is the work of Tammie Ronen of Tel Aviv University in Israel, the bulk of which is available only in Hebrew. There may be other important contributions to constructive therapies for children, but I confess ignorance about them.
3. In the Roman Catholic church, the devil's advocate is a person whose role it is to protect the purity of the faith by critically examining any information potentially unfavorable to candidates for canonization. I know of no such candidates in either cognitive or constructive quarters, and I am hardly an aspirant to the role of protector of the faith.

REFERENCES

Allman, L. S., de La Rocha, O., Elkins, D. N., & Weathers, R. S. (1992). Psychotherapists' attitudes toward clients reporting mystical experiences. *Psychotherapy, 29,* 564–569.

Altman, I. (1987). Centripetal and centrifugal trends in psychology. *American Psychologist, 42,* 1058–1069.

Balibar, E., & Wallerstein, I. (1991). *Race, nation, class: Ambiguous identities.* London: Verso.

Bandura, A. (1986). Social foundations of thought and action. Englewood Cliffs, NJ: Prentice-Hall.

Bartley, W. W. (1984). The retreat to commitment. LaSalle, IL: Open Court. (Original work published 1962)

Bergin, A. E. (1991). Values and religious issues in psychotherapy and mental health. American Psychologist, 46, 394–403.

Bernstein, R. J. (1983). Beyond objectivism and relativism: Science, hermeneutics, and praxis. Philadelphia: University of Pennsylvania Press.

Bower, G. H. (1993). The fragmentation of psychology? American Psychologist, 48, 905–907.

Bowlby, J. (1988). A secure base. New York: Basic Books.

Campbell, D. T. (1975). On the conflicts between biological and social evolution and between psychology and moral tradition. American Psychologist, 30, 1103–1126.

Cushman, P. (1993). Psychotherapy as moral discourse. Journal of Theoretical and Philosophical Psychology, 13, 103–113.

Fisher, D. (1989). Boundary work: A model of the relation between power and knowledge. Knowledge: Creation, Diffusion, Utilization, 10, 156–176.

Gergen, K. J. (1991). The saturated self: Dilemmas of identity in contemporary life. New York: Basic Books.

Guidano, V. F. (1987). Complexity of the self: A developmental approach to psychopathology and therapy. New York: Guilford.

Guidano, V. F. (1991). The self in process: Toward a post-rationalist cognitive therapy. New York; Guilford.

Jantsch, E. (1980). The self-organizing universe: Scientific and human implications of the emerging paradigm of evolution. New York: Pergamon.

Johnson, M. (1987). The body in the mind: The bodily basis of meaning, imagination, and reason. Chicago: University of Chicago Press.

Kauffman, S. A. (1993). The origins of order: Self-organization and selection in evolution. Oxford: Oxford University Press.

Kelly, T. A., & Strupp, H. H. (1992). Patient and therapist values in psychotherapy: Perceived changes, assimilation, similarity, and outcome. Journal of Consulting and Clinical Psychology, 60, 34–40.

Koch, S. (1993). "Psychology" or "the psychological studies"? American Psychologist, 48, 902–904.

Korzybski, A. (1924). Time-binding: The general theory. Lakeville, CT: Institute of General Semantics.

Kovel, J. (1991). History and spirit. Boston: Beacon Press.

Kvale, S. (Ed.). (1992). Psychology and postmodernism. London: Sage.

Leder, D. (1990). The absent body. Chicago: University of Chicago Press.

London, P. (1964). The modes and morals of psychotherapy. New York: Holt, Rinehart & Winston.

Lyotard, J. F. (1984). The postmodern condition. Minneapolis: University of Minnesota Press.

Madison, G. B. (1988). The hermeneutics of postmodernity. Bloomington: Indiana University Press.

Mahoney, M. J. (1991). Human change processes: The scientific foundations of psycho-

therapy. New York: Basic Books.

Mahoney, M. J. (1995a). The continuing evolution of the cognitive sciences and psychotherapies. In R. A. Neimeyer & M. J. Mahoney (Eds.), *Constructivism in psychotherapy.* Washington, DC: American Psychological Association.

Mahoney, M. J. (1995b). The psychological demands of being a constructive psychotherapist. In R. A. Neimeyer & M. J. Mahoney (Eds.), *Constructivism in psychotherapy.* Washington, DC: American Psychological Association.

Mahoney, M. J. (1995c). *Constructive psychotherapy.* New York: Guilford.

Mahoney, M. J. (in press). *The bodily self in psychotherapy.* New York: Guilford.

Mato, D. (Ed.). (1993). *Diversidad cultural y construcción de identidades.* Caracas: Fondo Editorial Tropykos.

Maturana, H., & Verden-Zöller, G. (1993). *Amor y juego: Fundamentos olvidados de lo humano.* Santiago, Chile: Instituto de Terapia Cognitiva.

McNamee, S., & Gergen, K. J. (Eds.). (1992). *Therapy as social construction.* London: Sage.

Merleau-Ponty, M. (1962). *Phenomenology of perception* (C. Smith, Trans.). London: Routledge & Kegan Paul.

Messer, S. B., Sass, L. A., & Woolfolk, R. L. (Eds.). (1988). *Hermeneutics and psychological theory: Interpretive perspectives on personality, psychotherapy, and psychopathology.* New Brunswick, NJ: Rutgers University Press.

Montero, M. (1991). *Ideología, alienación e identidad nacional.* Caracas: Universidad Central de Venezuela.

Neimeyer, R. A., & Mahoney, M. J. (Eds.). (1994). *Constructivism in psychotherapy.* Washington, DC: American Psychological Association.

Park, C. L., & Cohen, L. H. (1993). Religious and non-religious coping with the death of a friend. *Cognitive Therapy and Research, 17,* 561–577.

Pattee, H. H. (1973). *Hierarchy theory: The challenge of complex systems.* New York: George Braziller.

Payne, I. R., Bergin, A. E., & Loftus, P. E. (1992). A review of attempts to integrate spiritual and standard psychotherapy techniques. *Journal of Psychotherapy Integration, 2,* 171–192.

Salthe, S. N. (1985). *Evolving hierarchical systems.* New York: Columbia University Press.

Sampson, E. E. (1993). *Celebrating the other: A dialogic account of human nature.* New York: Harvester Wheatsheaf.

Sperry, R. W. (1988). Psychology's mentalist paradigm and the religion/science tension. *American Psychologist, 43,* 607–613.

Stolorow, R. D., & Atwood, G. E. (1992). *Contexts of being: The intersubjective foundations of psychological life.* Hillsdale, NJ: Analytic Press.

Tarnas, R. (1991). *The passion of the Western mind.* New York: Ballantine.

Vaughan, F. (1991). Spiritual issues in psychotherapy. *Journal of Transpersonal Psychology, 23,* 105–119.

Wachterhauser, B. R. (Ed.). (1986). *Hermeneutics and modern philosophy.* Albany: State University of New York Press.

Waldrop, M. M. (1992). *Complexity: The emerging science at the edge of order and chaos.* New York: Simon & Schuster.

Weimer, W. B. (1974). Overview of a cognitive conspiracy. In W. B. Weimer &

D. S. Palermo (Eds.), *Cognition and the symbolic processes* (Vol. 1, pp. 415–442). Hillsdale, NJ: Erlbaum.

Weimer, W. B. (1977). *Notes on the methodology of scientific research.* Hillsdale, NJ: Erlbaum.

Weimer, W. B. (1987). Spontaneously ordered complex phenomena and the unity of the moral sciences. In G. Radnitzky (Ed.), *Centripetal forces in the sciences* (pp. 257–296). New York: Paragon House.

Zaner, R. M. (1971). *The problem of embodiment.* The Hague: Martinus Nijhoff.

Index